From a faith perspec[illegible]
God is to love your [illegible]
mother of five youn[illegible]
She realized that while she had been diligently focused on the [illegible] ds of her family and her community, it was time to offer what she could to her global neighbours.

On her 37th birthday, she left her young family for two-weeks and, together with a handful of health care colleagues, went to offer her services in Northern Ghana. That first mission expanded to become an international collaboration spanning fifteen years and transforming thousands of lives. Detailing the health challenges in one of Africa's most impoverished regions, this book illuminates grinding global inequalities while offering hope that each of us can play a role in transforming our world.

Grant Us Tomorrow is both a thoroughly enjoyable and heart-wrenching read. The experiences in Ghana that Dr. Wilson chronicles, bring to life a journey of commitment, passion, faith, hope, and love. This memoir will force readers to challenge their assumptions and beliefs, and examine the value of the human connection. My perspective has been forever changed after reading this book

~ **JO-ANNE MARR,** President and Chief Executive Officer (CEO) of Oak Valley Health (formerly Markham Stouffville Hospital)

In reading this wonderfully written book I became aware of how hungry my soul was for, not just good news, but transformative action. Jennifer and her global team congregate annually in Ghana to make a difference in the lives of so many. It is really about the Good Samaritan... on steroids.

~ **PETER JENSEN, PH.D.** Canadian Olympic trainer; Sports Psychologist; Authority on leadership; Speaker; Author; Adjunct Professor at Queen's Smith School of Business and SC Johnson College of Business, Cornell University. Founder of Performance Coaching Inc. and Third Factor

A rare and beautiful chance to see inside a remarkable, true story told with tremendous clarity and love. So many inspiring individuals, acts of generosity, moments of courage, and tributes to a tenacious, inspirational drive to serve. All told in a clean, simple style filled with the power of the human spirit. So good to have one's faith in humanity restored or affirmed. Have a box of Kleenex nearby.

~ **Sandra Stark**, Co-founder, Third Factor

Grant Us Tomorrow is a beautifully written account of several different types of journeys: the multiple travels to and from Ghana; the author's personal path into medicine and later into developing leadership skills and abilities; the particular journeys of family growth and those of developing and maturing friendships; the pilgrimage of personal faith; and the remarkable journey of improving health infrastructure and health outcomes in Northern Ghana.

I enjoyed this engaging and moving book immensely. It made me very proud that Jennifer is a McMaster graduate and that her educational experiences here prepared her for such an impactful career.

~ **Paul M. O'Byrne, MB, FRCP(C), FRSC**
Dean and Vice-President
Faculty of Health Sciences
Michael G. DeGroote School of Medicine
Distinguished University Professor
McMaster University

Jennifer Wilson has given us a compelling story that inspires hope in every one of us. This is a story of responding to the call of God. This is a story of the hands and feet of Jesus at work in our world. This is a story that is real—punctuated with healing, disappointment, humour, courage, life, and death, but above all inspiration. Read *Grant Us Tomorrow* and let Jennifer's story ignite a spirit of sacrifice and service in your life.

~ **Michael B. Pawelke, DMin**
President, Briercrest College and Seminary

Wonderfully written. A beautiful interplay between medicine, spirituality and humanity. An inspirational read, with lessons for us all.

~ **Matthew Anderson,**
President and CEO, Ontario Health

Grant Us Tomorrow is an inspiring story. It reminds us that we are all part of a story larger than ourselves. It is a weaving of many lives and stories into a beautiful tapestry to create a picture for a better, more sustainable future. This book is filled with examples of people in Africa, and around the world, who were willing to step out with courage, hope, collaboration, prayer, generosity, and perseverance for the sake of others. It is a modern-day demonstration that the Living God continues to see and hear the cries of humanity—and that he brings people and resources together for good, doing more than we could ever ask or imagine.

~ **Sharon Simmonds BA, MA, DMin**, Author,
Director of Programs, Arrow Leadership

In this book, Wilson describes her journey from the McMaster University Health Sciences Building, to the National Family Medicine Forum, and on to ever-deepening healthcare service commitments in the west African nation of Ghana. I have been privileged to work together with Jennifer via the Institute for International Medicine (INMED), where her contributions in teaching Helping Babies Breathe newborn resuscitation have been especially powerful. But Dr. Wilson's vision is much broader and includes the alleviation of poverty and transforming Ghana's poorest communities today through collaboration with Northern Empowerment Association (NEA).

Grant Us Tomorrow is an inspiring account for those contemplating a career serving the world's most marginalized people.

~ **Nicholas Comninellis, MD, MPH, DIMPH**
President & Professor at INMED,
the Institute for International Medicine

This is a story about falling in love with a people and a place where "nothing is taken for granted"—and of the doctor and growing team who flew halfway around the world to offer "what they had in their hands." With the vulnerability and wisdom of a skilled storyteller, Jennifer draws us into the heart of this community, sharing compelling cases of illness and injustice as well as sacred moments of compassion, generosity, and divinity. Both heartbreaking and heartwarming, this book will bless you and change the way you look at the world.

~ **Ellen Duffield,**
Co-founder, NextLEVEL Leadership,
Master Mentor with Real Power Network, Author,
Coordinator of the Paul E. Magnus Centre for Leadership Studies
at Briercrest Seminary

Oct 2022

Dear Bianca,

GRANT US TOMORROW

a medical memoir

jennifer wilson, MD

Grateful that our paths have crossed -- this will be fun!

Jennifer

PIQUANT PRESS

Developmental editor: Patricia Thompson-Boyko
Copy editor: Julie Fitz-Gerald
Line editor, design and layout: Sue Reynolds
Cover photographs: Erika Jensen

Published by Piquant Press
13240 Mast Rd.,
Port Perry, ON L9L 1B5
www.piquantpress.ca

Library and Archives Canada Cataloguing in Publication

Title: Grant us tomorrow : a medical memoir / Jennifer Wilson, MD.
Names: Wilson, Jennifer (Family physician), author.
Identifiers: Canadiana 20220248664 | ISBN 9781927396230 (softcover)
Subjects: LCSH: Wilson, Jennifer (Family physician) | LCSH: Missionaries, Medical—Ghana—Biography. | LCSH: Physicians—Ghana—Biography. | LCSH: Physicians—Canada—Biography. | LCSH: Missions, Medical—Ghana.
Classification: LCC R722.32.W57 A3 2022 | DDC 266.0092—dc23

Printed and bound in Canada

1 2 3 4 5 6 7 8 9 10

Table of Contents

Dedication

To all mothers…especially mine.

FOREWORD

As a white, privileged, Toronto-based, French-Canadian with colonial European roots, and as an academic family physician engaged in the challengingly-named field of global health at one of Canada's largest universities, I received the kind invitation to write a foreword for this book with more than a little trepidation.

Yet, after carrying with me for weeks the wonderfully rich stories of Jennifer Wilson and the wide Northern Empowerment Association (NEA) community, here I am writing these words.

This book prominently features fabric, a fitting metaphor for the rich tapestry woven by the stories it recounts and the threads of humanity that flow with them, with hues of love, courage, doubt, vision, humour, and faith.

Over the past few years, in the formal upper spheres of global health, debates and discussions about how to achieve the ever-elusive goal of health equity have been translated into ambitious goals and proposed pathways with lofty titles, including the Sustainable Development Goals, the UN Special Declaration on Universal Health Coverage, and the Declaration of Astana and its renewed commitment to Primary Health Care.

In many ways, *Grant us Tomorrow* reads like the "illustrative story book" of those normative documents, giving life to the issues that call for those important efforts. It puts a concrete and human face to the expressions of injustice that manifest as disease, and also hints at some of the solutions.

In addition to being entertaining, informative, and often funny, three aspects of this book make it a particularly worthwhile read.

First is the opportunity to discover the people of Northern Ghana and specifically the NEA community. Tragically, neither the specific challenges nor the structural injustices described in this book are unique to Carpenter and the neighbouring villages. One of the special gifts of this book, however, is the way it allows the reader to witness three of the fruitful paradoxes of global health: the tension between difference and similarity, between distance and proximity, and between poverty and richness. After poignantly describing the novelty and "foreign-ness" of her initial encounter with the NEA community, Wilson skillfully goes on to weave through the book reminders of our common human experience: mothers and fathers wanting their children to be healthy, young people wanting to learn and prosper, all of us ultimately striving to live fully in the midst of love, loss, illness, and health. Similarly, descriptions of challenges imposed by physical distance on the movement of people and equipment between Canada and Carpenter, between the villages and the hospital, between the NEA grounds and the airport, are balanced by a sense of proximity and familiarity anchored in the sustained presence of the Mensah family. With roots in both countries, their steadfast leadership and the thoughtful, continuous weaving of an international partnership span more than a decade.

The book also vividly highlights the contrasting co-existence of richness and poverty in Northern Ghana. While the author does not shy away from describing the material poverty that many readers will indiscriminately (and somewhat erroneously) associate with Africa—lack of medical equipment and supplies, the "rough" latrines, the limited financial means of many—she also eloquently conveys the powerful and transformative human, innovative, and spiritual richness of the people of Northern Ghana. Dwelling in these dichotomies in our current times of division and isolation offers a welcome ray of hope.

Also compelling is Jennifer Wilson herself. Leery of so-called "global health heroes," I agreed to read this memoir with an open mind because my brief encounters with Jennifer, first as a graduate student and quickly as a kindred colleague, had convinced me that she had important things to teach and say. I was not disappointed. Jennifer's qualities as a woman, a physician, and as an international partner shine throughout the book. The very fact that as a mother of five, with young twins no less, she translated a "near-midlife crisis" into such a deep, sustained, and fruitful commitment to NEA gives pause to those of us tempted to respond to inner restlessness with a yoga retreat, remodeling the kitchen, or reading a few good books!

The quality and number of people who gravitate to the NEA orbit, near and far, under her leadership (starting with her husband who provides an "inadvertent masterclass" in the art of being a supportive spouse), also speak loudly of her ability to transform individual commitment into collective action.

The book further puts in sharp relief her identity as a family physician. While her training in emergency medicine is often mentioned, her nature as a true generalist, her commitment to continuity, her ability to consider the full person in the context of their unique circumstances, her ability to navigate uncertainty and the never-ending stream of "surprises" and "small-small problems" with poise, expertise, curiosity, and "vocational vigor" constitute a textbook example of the very best of Canadian family medicine. Readers who practice family medicine might be particularly energized by this book at a time when morale in our ranks has been battered by the pandemic, reminded that they too were "born for this."

The candid expression of Jennifer's faith is evident throughout the book and deserves mention, if only because it surprises in our increasingly secular world. Wilson's almost casual but constant weaving of the thread of faith, a thread she shares with the NEA community, carries with it dimensions of connection, continuity, and universality.

Lastly, Jennifer's remarkable quality as a partner and collaborator is worth noting. True, constructive, effective collaboration is demanding even under familiar circumstances. Her ability to listen deeply, to know when to lead and when to follow, to balance observation and action, humility and boldness, and to build, sustain, and cultivate countless relationships and partnerships, across great distances, language barriers, cultural differences, and the vagaries of local and international politics over more than a decade, merits special attention, especially in the context of short political cycles, waxing and waning funding tides, short 140 character text messages, catchy sound bites, and whirlwind change.

This book is about how a moment of existential restlessness and the ability to hear an invitation to engage with the people of Africa, led a mother and family physician animated by deep faith to humbly take effective, sustained action, weaving the remarkable individual that she is, into an equally remarkable collective of friends and colleagues, to address inequity and injustice.

In a world currently marked by conflict, suffering, and Covid-related separation, as Jennifer and the NEA community prepare to launch into a new chapter, the stories recounted in this book give hope. As we, the readers, turn from this book to the reality of our own lives, in the lingering echo of its powerful stories, some may hear floating from the last few pages the whispers of Jennifer Wilson's two important questions: "What can I offer to my global neighbours?" and, most importantly, "Can I bring along a few friends if they're interested in joining me?"

~ **Katherine D. Rouleau** MDCM, CCFP, MHSc. FCFP
Family physician, St. Michael's Hospital, Unity Health Toronto
Vice Chair, Global Health and Social Accountability
Department of Family and Community Medicine
University of Toronto

Grant Us Tomorrow

INTRODUCTION

For These Reasons I Write

I've been compelled to write this book for quite a few years now. Many excuses have prevented me from beginning, but the greatest explanation is that I am no author. I would much rather treat your allergic reaction or your heart attack than figure out how to write a book. This was not a task for which I had any training and I feared I would be incapable of doing justice to such important subject matters. Then a series of events unfolded which compelled me to begin my story.

Firstly, there was a global pandemic. COVID-19 entered our lives and our world unannounced and humbled us. So often through the pandemic, I reflected on the lessons learned during my work in Ghana, West Africa. For so many years, I thought my friends and I were helping our colleagues in Africa to prepare for their future. It turns out, they were preparing us for ours. The people of Ghana taught me about so many beautiful things in life—love, joy, faith, hope, friendship, adventure, service, teamwork, and resilience to name a few. This beauty is too valuable not to record and I believe our world could use a little dose of beautiful right now. For this reason, I write.

In Ghana, storytelling is the way that history is preserved; children grow up knowing the stories of their ancestors by heart. What has taken place in my life, in the lives of my friends, family, and colleagues, and in the lives of our Ghanaian brothers and sisters cannot be lost. There are too many memories, miracles, and accomplishments. These things should be preserved for our children and our children's children, so they know what we once fought for. I can only hope and pray that these stories might inspire other ordinary people just like us to consider their role in repairing the world. In this way, perhaps the privations described in these pages will seem unthinkable for future generations. For this reason, I write.

Finally, I believe that so many wonderful ideas, visions, and plans have died because it was just too difficult to get started. I often wonder what would have happened if my work in Ghana had never begun—if I had been too busy, too cowardly, too faithless, too tentative, too inexperienced, too unsupported, or too ill-funded to start. Mother Theresa said, "Yesterday is gone. Tomorrow has not yet come. We only have today. Let us begin." Since 2007 I have used this quote to encourage and inspire my global health teammates. Indeed, I would be faltering at the finish line if I failed to tell our story now. For this reason, I write.

So, I ask in advance for your forgiveness of any errors and omissions. Time may have altered a few details here and there over the years. It is my heartfelt prayer that the wondrous fabric of this story will eclipse any deficiencies of individual threads of my memory.

Let us begin.

CHAPTER 1

Code Trauma

The massive orange sun hovered on the edge of the horizon as our team bus sped back to the compound. A day of caring for hundreds of patients in a remote Ghanaian village clinic always ended before dark; African roads can be dangerous places after nightfall.

We often sang on the team bus at the conclusion of our day. Nothing—not heat, hunger, or fatigue—could suppress the enthusiasm of my teammates. But as the bus came to an abrupt halt before a mangled motorcycle lying in the middle of the road, the singing stopped.

Before us was an ominous stillness. No movement. Nothing. Not from the man lying twisted behind the motorcycle, not inside the small vehicle tangled in the long grass of the rural roadside. For a long moment, it was like the paralysis of a dream—then the adrenaline kicked in.

Our team of physicians and nurses descended on the hot African road and instinctively transformed it into an emergency room. Our exhaustion disappeared in the face of this crisis.

The man lying beside the motorcycle was still alive, but his blood pressure was critically low, and his heart rate was dangerously high. He was in shock, agitated, and blood was spurting from a gaping wound on his head. Our trauma resuscitation checklist instantly took priority and we did what we were trained to do.

Insert two large IVs. Stabilize the spine. Secure the airway. Ensure no punctured lung was contributing to his shock. Control external bleeding with pressure. Control internal bleeding by binding the broken pelvis tightly in a cloth. Administer pain medicine. Begin blood transfusion.

We have no blood for transfusion.

My friend Dr. Doug Wu interrupted my racing deliberations.

"Jenn, there's another victim in the ditch."

That patient was less critically ill, but his leg was broken, and the bone had pierced through the skin. He was losing blood fast. Our nurses administered pain medicine and Doug's team splinted the leg using a piece of wood that a volunteer found in the bush. I whispered a prayer of thanks that our pharmacist had stocked our trauma bag with IV antibiotics and Tranexamic acid (a medicine that stops bleeding).

A deep, strong baritone spoke close by my ear. Charles, one of the Ghanaian pastors who had been riding behind us in the truck full of volunteers, reported that his team had secured the environment and were standing by to assist. They had set up roadblocks on either side of the accident to protect us from oncoming vehicles. He also assured me that the other pastors, who had been our translators during the village medical clinic, were praying earnestly on the side of the road. It was always their first response to a crisis.

I explained to our volunteers that I needed a backboard or stretcher to stabilize the man's spine. They disappeared towards the roadblock and returned carrying the back seat of a taxi and a roll of duct tape.

As the sun set, the road was now in complete darkness, except for the headlamps of our Canadian and Ghanaian team. The doctor and two nurses working with me were from my emergency room at home. In this crisis we easily slipped into our familiar "Code Trauma" rhythm.

The outcome for our patients now depended on getting them to a hospital immediately. They needed blood transfusions, CT scans, and operating rooms to have any chance of survival.

I called out to the team. "Who can call 911 and tell me the ETA of the ambulance?" Everyone froze—no one reached for a phone. The pastors looked up from their prayers.

What is going on? Why is no one answering me?

Back home, as the trauma team leader, it is my responsibility to initiate transport protocols. In Canada, I would make one phone call to CritiCall, a central intake system. Within minutes, the dispatcher would connect me to a highly-skilled trauma team leader at a specialized hospital in Toronto while simultaneously mobilizing the ORNGE helicopter or land ambulance to my site.

The silence greeting my request snapped me out of checklist autopilot, and the sudden onslaught of helplessness almost overwhelmed me. My hot sweat turned icy.

The truth of our situation returned to my consciousness. We were not on a Canadian roadside. We were not in the Uxbridge Hospital emergency room. There was no cell service. There was no such thing as 911. There were no ambulances in this part of Ghana. The nearest hospital was many hours away. There was one CT scan in Northern Ghana, serving a population of 3.5 million people, and it had been broken for months. There was a handful of excellent neurosurgeons in the country, but they were in the capital city—a day's travel by car.

This new reality sank in. We were in the middle of a hot, dark, dirt road in Northern Ghana with a dying man strapped to the backseat of a taxi.

Canada felt so very far away.

Chapter 2
I was Born for This

"The two most important days in your life are the day you are born and the day you find out why."
~Mark Twain

Becoming a physician had been a dream for as long as I could remember. I've always loved emergencies. As a primary school student, fire drill days were the highlight of my month. Clipboard in hand, shoulders back, I longed for the responsibility of leading my peers to safety. As a Brownie and Girl Guide, I was the first to complete any first-aid related badges, and my projects were notoriously over the top.

I loved going to the doctor's office. I was curious about every question asked, every piece of equipment used, and every decision made by my doctor. I distinctly remember, as a very young girl, asking Dr. Petrie in Stouffville, Ontario why he wanted me to cross my arms in front of my chest while he placed his stethoscope on my back. "I can hear your lungs better when you move your shoulder blades out of the way," he replied. I think I wrote that tip in my diary.

Hospital visits (although I had few) were oh-so-exciting. The pain of my eight-year-old knee after a ski accident was well worth the chance to be inside an X-ray machine and watch the emergency doctor hold an image of my knee up to the Lite-Bright box on the wall.

As a teen, I couldn't wait to become a lifeguard. I lived for the training scenarios where I would sit in my lifeguard chair, conscientiously overlooking the pool, waiting with my whistle at the ready for the simulated emergency to begin. I couldn't get enough of these practice scenarios—the more challenging, the better. I wanted to be the best.

Once I became a lifeguard, I wore my National Lifeguard Service badge with great pride. However, I was still not satisfied; I wanted more training. I went on to receive my certification in Aquatic Emergency Care from the Royal Life Saving Society of Canada. I cherished that wallet card and still have it to this day. I would diligently prepare for each shift, rehearsing possible scenarios in my mind, carefully checking that all equipment was in place. I'd lifeguard before school, after school, and all summer long. If no emergency happened, I was grateful, but also secretly disappointed. I was, as my kids express it, "extra." This is the term that people who love you substitute for "nerd."

One summer afternoon, when I was sixteen, I was sitting on a lifeguard chair, wearing my SPF 0 baby oil (because that is what we did in those days). I was overseeing the pool at Fair Havens, a conference and retreat centre in Ontario's cottage country. From my perch I could see Highway 48, and suddenly the unmistakable sound of a motor vehicle crash travelled across the golf course to my ears. I stiffened, instantly suffused with adrenaline. This was not a practice scenario.

With three emergency blasts of my whistle, I cleared the pool, called 911, grabbed my first aid kit, and raced down the lane to the scene of the crash. I had no idea what I was about to see, but I knew that whatever it was, I wanted to help. Five words accompanied my pounding footsteps—I WAS BORN FOR THIS.

My arms and legs tingled, and my heart pounded. It was the same feeling I get to this day when the three loud beeps go off in our hospital's emergency room, signaling the impending arrival of an ambulance with a critical patient. I remember seeing broken glass everywhere. I remember hearing people crying. I remember telling an injured woman on the other side of a crumpled door frame not to move, and that help was on the way. I heard the sirens and watched the paramedics work furiously and confidently to stabilize the victims. I felt like part of the team that helped save lives that day even though I was just a young girl, with a whistle around her neck, holding a first aid kit. That accident was a signpost on the path that would, one day, lead me to the Uxbridge Hospital Emergency Room, where I have practiced for over two decades.

But a few years after that accident, I fell off my path.

While my dream of becoming a physician was deeply rooted in

my heart, I gave up on it after my first year of university. I had set off to McMaster for my undergraduate science degree, but things did not go as planned. I suppose it was the classic case of a big fish in a little pond; I suddenly became a tiny minnow in a vast ocean of brilliant kids all wanting to become doctors. Perhaps I could also blame it on the fact that this particular minnow was swimming her heart out seven days a week, morning and night, with the varsity swim team. I was too exhausted to study in the evening, and I couldn't keep up academically. Whatever the reasons, I started to drown.

My marks were not strong enough to get into medical school. I barely passed first-year calculus. I lost my confidence; I wasn't smart enough to become a physician. I figured I had misunderstood my calling.

Weeks before my second year was due to begin, I officially gave up on my dream. I was too embarrassed to tell anyone, so rather than quit outright, I said I was taking a one-year leave of absence from my degree. As far as the world was concerned, I was taking a gap year, but I had no intention of returning.

During that year, I worked, saved some money, and spent as much time as possible with my boyfriend, Graham Wilson, a strong, young farmer with a great sense of humour and a red Kawasaki Ninja 900 motorcycle. One night, as my gap year was coming to an end, Graham and I went out on a date and when he kissed me goodnight on my doorstep he said, "I'm really going to miss you when you go back to school."

"About that," I said. "I have some great news to tell you! I've decided I'm not going back to school after all. I'm going to stay right here and maybe we can get married sooner than we had planned!" I beamed at him as I waited for his response.

What I got was an incredulous stare and a "…Seriously?" A frown appeared on his face as his eyes searched mine. Slowly he said, "What about medical school?"

I began to cry. I was not expecting that reaction. Many friends and family members from our rural farming community were already getting married and starting their families. I had assumed he would be happy that I was giving up on many years of education so we could get on with our lives, and I could become a good farm wife.

Confused and dismayed, Graham gathered me into his arms and

said, "Jenny, what on earth is going on?"

Between sobs, I came clean. "You don't get it. I don't have what it takes to become a doctor."

As I poured out how challenging I had found my last year in school, Graham said very little. When my hiccupping and shuddering stopped, he finally spoke with a maturity that I am still staggered by, considering he was only twenty-one at the time: "I think you have everything you need to get into medical school and to become a great doctor. And I'm not going to be the reason you give up that calling."

Looking back, I can see that until that point, I had not experienced failure of any consequence. I didn't yet have the skills to learn from my missteps and rebound. But as this wise, young farmer kept talking, planting seeds of hope and nourishing my confidence, I felt purpose take root in my soul once again. And with his final words, I felt certain about the next steps I should take.

"There will be lots of time to get married and I'm not going anywhere."

It was as if his faith in me snapped me out of my nightmare. I decided to return and fight for my dream. I knew it wouldn't be easy. I would need to get almost perfect marks for the next three years to make up for my poor start, but I was determined and excited to go for it.

Just before resuming my second year, derailment briefly threatened me one last time. In conversation with a mentor in my church—someone who had guided me during my teenage years and who I trusted—I shared the news that I was returning to university to pursue my dream of becoming a physician. His face fell, and his response was, "You would have made such a great mother."

I was speechless. I wish now that my nineteen-year-old self could have countered with a quick and intelligent response, but back in 1990, gender justice was not yet part of my vocabulary.

Startled by his comment, I wondered just what made a mother "great." My thoughts turned to my own mother.

Born in Macedonia in 1943 as Ristana Mirtsou, she was five years old when she, along with approximately 28,000 Macedonian children, were evacuated from their homes in northern Greece to "safe zones" outside the country during the Greek Civil War. After the war, my grandfather, Nickola Micheff, set out to search for his family and found my then-seven-year-old mother in an orphanage in Yugoslavia. When she was ten years old, the two of them immigrated to Canada, and her Macedonian name was changed to Christina Micheff. There, she was left in the care of a kind neighbour for three years while my grandfather returned to Macedonia to continue the search for his wife and son. Soon after his departure, another neighbour invited my mother to attend her Sunday School class at the local church. She was introduced to the Christian faith and welcomed into a community who loved and cared for her.

In 1956, the Red Cross found my Grandmother Mary and Uncle Louie in Poland and their family was reunited in Canada, where my Aunt Vicky was born. A few years later, my grandmother was sent away to a sanitorium with tuberculosis after which my grandfather developed serious mental health issues and was institutionalized. My mother had no choice but to quit school in grade eleven, find work in a typing pool, and become the primary caregiver for her siblings. Life was extremely difficult. Her trials as a new immigrant to Canada forged both a strong faith in God and a fierce determination that her own children would one day receive the education that she was deprived of. For her, being "a great mother" meant instilling these values of faith, education, and loyalty to family in me and my siblings and then supporting our journey every step of the way.

From a Christian point of view, I found my mentor's comment about my future motherhood equally perplexing. I am no theologian, but the moment those words came out of his mouth, I was convinced he was wrong. The hairs on the back of my neck stood up, my heart started to pound, and I went into fight mode. I knew in my heart that being a doctor and being "a great mother" could not be mutually exclusive if they were both what I was called to do. It was not the God I knew, the one who had placed this vocation in my heart, who spoke these words to me. I felt like I was in a battle.

In battle mode, I was mad. I was angry at myself for listening to internal and external voices that were not speaking the truth. I was mad at myself for listening to people who believed that women could not pursue a professional career and still have a meaningful family life. I stepped—no, I leapt—back on my path, returning to McMaster and spending every waking moment of the next three years pursuing my calling.

I adjusted my schedule and my study habits. With God's help, support from Graham and my family, along with good old-fashioned hard work, I completed my degree and applied to medical school. Graham and I were married on May 14, 1994, and just after returning from our honeymoon at my parents' condo in Florida (the price was right), I received my acceptance to the medical school of my choice: McMaster University.

Not only was I back on my path, but my path was now "our" path, as we began our married life together.

On a crisp September morning, four months later, I made my way to the auditorium of the Health Sciences Building at McMaster University in Hamilton, Ontario. We were an eager and excited bunch of first-year medical students in the Class of 1997, and we hailed from many walks of life and educational backgrounds. I remember looking around the room and wondering if there had been some mistake. Surely, I was not smart enough for this program. Surely, someone was about to walk through that door, call my name, and explain that I had been accepted into medical school by accident. With hindsight, I'm certain I wasn't the only person in the room suffering from a phenomenon known as the "Imposter Syndrome." It was not the first, nor the last time I would experience it. Our professor approached the podium and chose a remarkable theme to usher us onto our path. His words were a gift that I continue to treasure and be guided by to this day.

There are so many things that one could say to a group of "extra," over-achieving, goal-oriented, type-A medical students ready to don their white coats and take on the world. Our wise and discerning professor, from one of the best universities in the world, chose to tell us a parable. I didn't take notes, but from across a span of over twenty-five years, I remember it like this:

> *Once upon a time there was a village. Through this village ran a river with a dangerous current. Each year, lives would be lost as villagers fell into the river, got swept away in the current and drowned. So, the village went to work, devising increasingly elabo-*

> *rate technologies to rescue and revive the victims. They even built a hospital at the base of the river, but they couldn't keep up with the endless influx of victims. They added more beds, a more sophisticated intensive care unit, and smarter doctors. Still, the impact was minimal, and the cost was great. So focused were these heroic villagers with rescue and treatment efforts at the base of that river that they didn't think to ask a fundamental question: "Why were people falling into the river in the first place?"*

The speaker acknowledged that most of us would spend our careers doing important downstream work—rescuing and treating.

And then came the challenge as I received it. "If you want to make a difference in this world, you must remember that upstream and downstream are all parts of the same river. As this story illustrates, downstream rescue and treatment efforts without attention to upstream preventative efforts will be fruitless."

The truth of this parable, given to me on my first day of medical school, would end up shaping not just my life, but the lives of my family and my friends from all over the world.

CHAPTER 3

Three Sacred Chairs

"All I know is that every time I go to Africa,
I am shaken to my core."
~Dr. Stephen Lewis

The ballroom housing the 2004 National Family Medicine Forum was silent, except for the zip, click, and rustle of purses and pockets that people were rifling through to find a tissue. Hundreds of family physicians had gathered in Toronto for this conference, and Graham had encouraged me to be there.

Six months earlier, our twins, Joshua and Jessica, had been born into our family, which was already bustling with three daughters: Olivia (six), Claudia (four) and Amelia (two). The kids' full slate of extra-curriculars, plus the demands of infant twins, required all the partnership efficiency my husband and I could muster. Happily, we had been best of friends since I was sixteen, so there had been plenty of opportunities to refine our teamwork.

Halfway through my one-year maternity leave, however, I was getting restless. It was an adjustment to go from running a family practice and emergency room in our hometown of Uxbridge to being on full-time mom duty with five kids under the age of six. It was all this task-oriented gal could do to grab a shower on any given day before one of the twins needed to be fed or changed—again. With my mind absorbed by newborn feeding schedules, diaper changes, and piano lessons for my older daughters, I began to worry that I was forgetting my medical knowledge.

One night, at 3:00 a.m., I was getting myself set up to tandem nurse Joshua and Jessica on the settee outside our bedroom while Graham fetched them from their cribs. As he handed them to me, I began to sob. "How will I ever go back to being a doctor? I think I forget everything!" Graham sat with me and when the babies were done feeding, he tucked them and their weary mother back into bed. The next morning, he brought me my coffee and said, "I think you need to get out of the house. Isn't that conference that you love coming up soon in Toronto? We can get someone to watch the older girls and Josh, Jess, and I will come with you and hang out in the hotel room. When the babies need to be fed, I will page you." (This is an age-betraying sentence, I know.)

With my parents in charge of Olivia, Claudia, and Amelia, off we went to Toronto for the College of Family Physicians of Canada's annual Family Medicine Forum with playpens, diapers, and the double stroller in tow. It was just what the doctor's husband ordered.

The keynote speaker for the conference was Dr. Stephen Lewis. He was the UN Secretary-General's Special Envoy for HIV/AIDS in Africa, and he spoke passionately about the HIV pandemic and highlighted its effects on women and girls. He told story after story of the men, women, and children he had met during his work there. I especially remember his stories about the grandmothers left to care for their grandkids as a generation was lost to HIV/AIDS. He shared how the suffering he witnessed had impacted him. I remember him saying, "Even a little help from each of you would bring solace and hope to so many." His words wrenched my heart.

When my kids were little, they sometimes asked me, "Mommy, how do you know if God is speaking to you?"

Though I've never claimed that I could hear God's voice talking to me out loud, on that day at that conference, listening to Dr. Lewis's words, it felt like I was receiving a divine message. Dr. Lewis's keynote address awakened something fundamental in me. I realized that I had become so focused on the needs of my family and my community that it never occurred to me that the men, women, and kids in other parts of the world were part of my responsibility too.

From a faith point of view, the greatest commandment after loving God is to love your neighbour. So how was it that I had never considered how I could show love to my global neighbours, like those in Dr. Lewis' stories? My tears flowed, and I knew I needed to accept this challenge in some way. It was time for me to step outside my community and my comfort zone.

I wasn't sure what this revelation might look like in practical terms, especially with five young kids and no formal training in international medicine or global health. I was a mom and a wife and a busy rural family physician, still early in her career. I had no answers, but I had questions—the first one being, *"What can I offer to my global neighbours?"* As I was processing all of this and drying my tears, my pager went off.

I remember reading somewhere that timing is essential in a marriage. That when you have something important to communicate to your spouse, you should consider things like timing, setting, and delivery to give your important communication the best chance of being heard correctly.

I in no way followed this nugget of marital advice as I burst into the hotel room, tears streaming down my face, and proclaimed in my very "extra" way, "I'm going to Africa!"

I'll never forget the look on Graham's face. He was in the middle of what we called the "double diaper change." This is a lifesaver for parents of twins. It involves lying the babies down side by side, lifting the inside leg of each twin with one hand while using the other hand to remove the dirty diaper, wipe, and insert a fresh diaper. It requires skill, coordination, and a bit of luck, but Graham was an expert.

You might think two wailing babies and a weeping wife announcing she was moving to Africa would throw him off his game just a little, but no. He looked at me calmly and said, "Sounds great. Tell me all about it while you feed these hungry babies."

While I didn't book a plane ticket to Africa that day, the seed had been planted. Over the next couple of years, I began to explore how I could responsibly engage in global health as part of my life and career. I started every day by praying God would guide and prepare me, and I read everything I could about medical missions. I began investigating different humanitarian medical groups that might be a good fit, but it was very challenging to find one that was right for me. I didn't feel it would be responsible to enter a high-risk situation that could very well leave my young family motherless. Furthermore, I had professional responsibilities to my family practice and hospital which would prevent me from making any long-term service commitments. I genuinely wanted to "help," but became increasingly concerned about the pitfalls, critiques, and ethical concerns that medical missions are vulnerable to. As a health professional, I took my oath to "first, do no harm" very seriously.

In 2007, I decided to apply for a position on a one-month medical mission trip to Peru. The organization was reputable, but Graham wasn't sure I could handle the donkeys. Yes, donkeys. The mission involved riding donkeys into the Peruvian interior each day. I felt perfectly capable of donkey riding—Graham wasn't convinced.

A few weeks later we attended a Sunday morning service at the Uxbridge Baptist Church. On that morning, Dr. David and Brenda Mensah were visiting from Ghana, West Africa. Brenda (née Paisley) was originally from our neighbouring community of Stouffville, and Graham's family knew the Paisleys very well. In fact, one of Graham's first tasks after receiving his driver's permit at age sixteen, was to transport a Holstein cow in the big farm truck to the Paisley farm.

David had been born in Ghana and had grown up an orphan in a remote, impoverished northern part of the country. After his father died, his childhood was full of suffering. As custom dictated, he was forced to leave his mother and was sent to live with his abusive uncle in Yaara Village far from his home. Fearing death, he escaped, but then fell into the hands of another uncle who was a widely feared tribal witch doctor. Against all odds he again escaped death, found new friends, was introduced to Yesu, and left Africa to study in a distant land—Canada. There, he and his fellow Ghanaian friends resolved that they would do whatever it took to get their education and return to help their people climb out of poverty. He completed his education, including his PhD, and while he was in Canada, he met Brenda. They fell in love, married, and returned to Ghana with their three young daughters. There, they began a Christian community-based development non-governmental organization (NGO) known as Northern Empowerment Association (NEA), which works to alleviate poverty and transform Ghana's poorest communities.

After church that Sunday morning, Brenda asked me for some advice. One of their development staff had terrible asthma. During Harmattan (the dry season when the wind blows the sand from the Sahara Desert all over West Africa) he struggled to breathe every day.

"What puffers is he on?" was my first question.

She looked at me, eyes wide, and shook her head. "None. Puffers aren't available at all in Northern Ghana."

I pictured the cupboard in my office that was full of samples of asthma puffers and I made arrangements to send some with her.

Once our pew-side consult was complete, she asked me, "So what is new in your life?"

I updated her on the family, then told her that I was planning on going to Peru with an organization that was trying to establish primary care for a group of remote villages. "I'm not convinced that this is the right global health opportunity for me," I confessed. "And Graham is quite concerned about my donkey-riding abilities."

Her eyes lit up. "How would you like to have a little chat with us about some of the health care needs and challenges we are facing in Ghana? No donkey-riding skills are required!" she said with her famous, almost mischievous, smile.

A few days later, I met with these two remarkable individuals in the pastor's office at the church. I knew little about David's and Brenda's work, so they spent the next hour introducing me to sustainable, community-based development and poverty alleviation. They told me all about NEA and beamed like proud parents as they talked about their incredible staff.

They explained the projects that NEA was engaged in: clean water, sanitation, education, agriculture, peace, and conflict resolution. They were also training pastors, building churches, supporting orphans and widows, and creating women's initiatives, like peanut farming. These projects were playing a pivotal role in the prevention of illness and death in the region. The Mensahs' work was transforming the communities where David had grown up and suffered so profoundly.

However, medical needs in this region of Ghana were unmet. The health-care system was inaccessible to most and inadequate for those who could access it. Children were dying at alarmingly high rates, and they were losing far too many mothers during childbirth. Needless deaths were a part of everyday life in their communities. They had a vision and had been praying that someday, perhaps, one international doctor might come and partner with them.

"We believe you are that doctor," David said. "Would you consider coming to Ghana on an exploratory mission to help us brainstorm how our organization might begin to promote health and address the local health needs of the population we serve?" asked Brenda. You bet I was!

They didn't need to say another word. I knew this was the opportunity I had been waiting for. This was my time. This is what I was born to do. I thought of the river story on my first day of medical school. I thought of Dr. Lewis' challenge. I thought of the words of Christ, asking me to love my neighbour and care for the poor, the widow, and the orphan.

I instantly loved David and Brenda. I trusted them. I believed in their ground-breaking upstream work. I knew we would work well together.

That one-hour meeting with the Mensahs felt more productive than a year's worth of hospital administration meetings.

Did I feel too young and unqualified? Yes. Did I feel inadequate? Most definitely. But as we concluded, David and Brenda prayed that God would direct our collective steps and bless the work of our hands so that justice would flow to the people of Northern Ghana. I felt a deep peace and excitement about this future that was suddenly unfolding.

I was just about to leave the room when I paused with my hand on the doorknob. I turned to look back at those three sacred chairs and asked David and Brenda one of the most important questions of my life: "Can I bring along a few friends if they're interested in joining me?"

Chapter 4

Graham's Banana Bread

"I'm not the smartest fellow in the world,
but I sure can pick smart colleagues."
~ Franklin D. Roosevelt

Within a few days, Graham and I, together with Mensahs, decided that I would travel to Ghana in November of 2007 and spend two weeks with the team at NEA as they began the process of engaging in health care. I was excited and overwhelmed, but I knew exactly how I wanted to start: with a team.

I've always loved the feeling of working towards a common goal with a group of people. Some of my favourite high school memories centre on being part of the band and the student council. I've always been a wholehearted team player. If proof is required, my kids will gleefully point out the "1988 Most Enthusiastic Band Member" plaque that hangs in our house today. I'm not sure why that plaque disappears whenever their friends are over.

Athletic teams have also been a big part of my life. I was a competitive swimmer throughout high school and university, but the relay teams were my absolute favourite. I was recruited for the McMaster women's water polo team after retiring from swimming, and I loved my coaches Mark Fingland and Heidi Sheppard, my teammates, and everything about this demanding, aggressive team sport. I continued to compete for McMaster throughout my medical training and residency. Our daughter Olivia became our team mascot and Graham was our number one fan. His Wilson cookies (chocolate chip with a secret ingredient) contributed to the enjoyment of most of our road trips.

Through all of these experiences, I learned lessons that greatly influenced the leader I would become. I discovered that I am energized by team dynamics, and that I receive tremendous satisfaction when I can combine my unique, God-given skills with those of others. I love the camaraderie of training, travelling, and performing with a team. I love celebrating success, sharing disappointment, and learning from failure with my teammates. I love putting on a team uniform or team jacket and wearing it with pride. Teams give me the courage to accomplish things I would never have dared to try on my own. Teams make me brave. Most of all, teams teach me that when a group of committed individuals bring their whole hearts and whole selves to the pursuit of a common purpose, they can be unstoppable. All of these truths are congruent with who I am and with the principles of my faith. So as my attention turned to the invitation to travel to Ghana, it was natural to want to bring a small team with me. That is, if I could persuade anyone to join me.

I advertised a community information night to be held at the Uxbridge Baptist Church for anyone who might be interested in a health care mission to Ghana, West Africa. The pool of possible teammates was from my circle of influence—the community of Uxbridge, Ontario.

According to Graham, I am still a "newcomer" to Uxbridge, having only arrived with my parents and two siblings in 1978. Our town of Markham was multiplying, and my folks decided to move their young family to "the country." I started third grade at Goodwood Public School in Mrs. Beatrice Harper's class. I like to tease her that she made me cry twice: the first time when she gave me a B+ in penmanship, which spoiled my straight As, and the second time when I lost the class spelling bee over the word "maybe." (I mixed up the "y" and the "b" and still feel the sting of defeat every time I write that word.) I now realize that minor academic disappointments like these were healthy for a young perfectionist to experience. And my handwriting and spelling deficiencies notwithstanding, I'm honoured to have been Mrs. Harper's family physician now for over twenty years.

My younger sister Rebecca, brother Matthew, and I flourished growing up in Uxbridge. Our parents encouraged us to be involved in everything our community had to offer, as long as our academics didn't suffer. My mother was home full-time and poured her heart and soul into running her household well. She encouraged and modelled a heathy lifestyle and was "organic" long before it was trendy. Cleaning products were homemade and processed food was nowhere to be found. Saving money for our future education was always a priority: leftover wallpaper was used for wrapping gifts and milk-bags were recycled into lunch bags. (Today we'd be cool environmentalists, but back then I just really wanted a Charlie's Angels lunch box and matching thermos). Our S.O.S Soap Pads were cut in half to make them last twice as long, and when we went to the movies, my mother smuggled in homemade popcorn with only a touch of butter and salt. Her spare time was devoted to church and community involvements. She was always the first to respond in practical ways when someone was in need.

My father, Earl, was a successful businessman who founded and ran his own insurance adjusting company, despite never finishing high school. He retired young when a British company, looking to expand their operations in Canada, bought him out. My father is a modest man who prefers the unadorned things in life over anything fancy or pretentious. His spare time was spent baking on his Findlay Oval wood stove or building homes for our family. When one home was finally completed, he'd get bored, start all over again, and we would pack up and move. During his lifetime he designed and built multiple homes in Uxbridge, as well as two cottages. My father always approached problems and difficulties with a light touch and a fabulous sense of humour. His only rule was that we never dated a boy who drove a motorcycle. Sometimes, he would place pictures of motorcycle accidents (from his insurance case files) on our dinner plates just to make his point. Somehow, Graham was exempt from this rule. Perhaps dad had overheard the number of times my mother decided whether or not I could attend a party on the basis of one question: "Will Graham be there?"

My parents provided us with everything we needed, but not necessarily everything we wanted. When I informed them that I "needed" my own horse or my own baritone saxophone to reach my full potential, there was very little discussion—it was a firm "no." My parents were wise enough to recognize that the interests of children change quickly over time and they were determined not to waste a cent that could be saved towards our post-secondary education. There were no all-inclusive trips for our family. Holidays involved road trips to the beach in Florida where we would eat-in except for one or two fantastic nights when we dined at a restaurant. My siblings and I loved those holidays so much that we have all continued the same tradition, to the same beach, with our own families.

Every year on my father's birthday, June 30th, our family moved to our small A-frame cottage that he'd built as a teenager in Bolsover, Ontario. Summers were carefree and unstructured. We had the freedom to create fun with our summer friends as long as we were home for dinner. My grandparents had a cottage next door and had been the first cottagers on the lake. My grandfather was the handyman on the beach, and my Nana was famous for her fish-cleaning abilities and for her green lipstick that turned red when she put it on. My siblings and I were invited over when our Nana needed euchre partners or when the Toronto Blue Jays were playing. We watched the game on her muted television, while listening to it on the radio—she believed that radio commentators were far more skilled than television commentators, who were chosen on the basis of their good looks rather than their abilities. My father loved his cottage on Canal Lake so much that he made us promise that we would never plan our weddings on a long weekend in the summer. If we did, he wouldn't be there.

Holidays were spent at our home with both sides of the extended family, and often with families who were in need. My Macedonian grandmother, "Baba," was famous for her mouthwatering zelnic and baklava, which were fixtures throughout our childhood.

As we grew and matured, my parents gave us more and more independence. We always had reasonable rules and boundaries, but they gave us space and trusted us to make our own decisions and deal with our mistakes. They supported my siblings and me in whatever way they could—until the day we each got married. Once married, we were immediately "off the books," as my dad loved to say.

I always knew I wanted to return and practice medicine in my hometown of Uxbridge, and I geared my training to ensure that I would be prepared for this responsibility.

Graham is a third-generation Uxbridge resident. His grandparents, Hilliard and Ruby Wilson, purchased a 100-acre farm on April 30, 1927, for $5,500. Their seven boys were raised in the farmhouse. Graham's father, Lloyd, was the baby of the family. In 1971, he and his wife Ollie took over the ownership of the farm, where they raised their five children: Sharon, Graham, Craig, Dawna-Marie, and Stephanie. They had been married for nineteen years when Lloyd passed away from cancer at the age of forty-five. Ollie was left to raise five children and run the family auction business that Lloyd had started. Graham and his brother Craig ran the dairy farm while finishing high school and both became auctioneers. It was around that time that I fell in love with Graham, although I wouldn't quite realize it until about four years later.

It happened on a Friday night. We were both at a party and Graham told me that he needed to leave to check on a cow. I had no idea what "check on a cow" meant, but it sounded like more fun than the party, so I accepted his offer to tag along. I was not dressed for "cow checking," so as we stepped inside the back door of his farmhouse, Graham gave me a pair of work boots and his dad's big leather coat. In hindsight, that was the closest I came to meeting my future father-in-law—he was sick upstairs in the last months of his life.

Graham explained that a cow was due to have a baby and might need his help. I didn't realize that farmers did obstetrics. We walked together to the very back corner of the field, where a brand-new baby calf was lying on the ground beside its mother. It was a cold night and Graham wanted to move the calf to the barn. Now, I'm not sure if this was Graham's usual practice, or if the wide-eyed teenage girl watching him might have influenced what happened next. He proceeded to hoist this eighty-pound calf over his shoulders, cradled its front and back legs around his neck, and set off up the hill like some cowboy in the movies. I had never seen anything like it. As we walked past the barn with the mother cow close on our heels, I heard a voice in my head that was as crystal clear as the stars in the Uxbridge sky that night: "*This* is the type of man I should marry. *This* is the type of man who will care for my children and me."

Years later, Graham and I would purchase that very farm from his mom, practice the piano with our five kids in the room where his father was born, and spend many hours walking our beloved dogs, Teddy and Frankie, in the same field where I fell in love with him. The way the threads of my life have been so beautifully and divinely woven together is a mystery and a marvel to me.

On a cold winter evening in 2007, I was preparing to leave the house for my first Ghana information meeting. I remember asking myself, "What if no one wants to go with me?" As I hugged Graham goodbye, I whispered, "I don't think anyone is going to show up."

Graham could see that I was losing my nerve and that I needed a pep talk. "Jenny, you've got this. Let me pray for you." When his prayer was over, he handed me a loaf of his homemade banana bread and said, "Have fun, babe."

With renewed confidence, I set off, clutching that single loaf like a battle shield, ready to face whatever would happen. I arrived early, set up a few chairs in the overflow room, put twelve pieces of banana bread on a plate, and waited.

People started to arrive—colleagues with whom I worked every day in the office and the hospital. Doctors, nurses, administrative staff, X-ray technicians, and pharmacists rolled in. Then paediatric nurses, child life specialists, chiropractors, and volunteers from the church and the community arrived, too. Many brought their families. The overflow room was jam-packed, forcing us to move the meeting into the sanctuary of the church. By 7:00 p.m., the pews were filling up, the banana bread was long gone, and I was realizing something fundamental: I was not alone. There were many people just like me who wanted to serve globally and were just looking for the right opportunity.

The pit in my stomach disappeared and my hands stopped trembling. I walked up to the front of the church and began to speak. Though I had yet to set foot in Ghana, my voice was filled with a passion that surprised my own ears as I told my story and shared the Mensahs' vision publicly for the first of many times.

"I don't believe in coincidences. I know I was meant to be at that conference, to hear those stories, to reflect on my life and the responsibilities that come with my privilege, and to respond. Perhaps you will ask yourself, too, if your being here tonight is no coincidence."

As I concluded I said, "There is a lot I do not know, but I trust God, David, and Brenda to guide our steps. This will be no holiday, but, unfortunately, you will have to pay your own way as if it was." I smiled apologetically. "Applications are at the back of the church."

Someone had to run and photocopy more application forms; they were disappearing faster than the banana bread.

Two weeks later, the inaugural Ghana Health Team was announced and our plane tickets were booked. The community of Uxbridge had responded to the call. My friends and I were going to Ghana.

With my siblings, Rebecca (Harding) Ferguson and Matthew Harding, in the first house my father built in Uxbridge, Ontario.

My family in the second house my father built

Graham's Family: Dawna, Stephanie, Lloyd, Ollie, Graham, Sharon, Craig

Graham and his younger siblings with their father (Lloyd) and grandparents (Hilliard and Ruby Wilson)

<

In Mrs. Harper's Grade 3 class (where I got a B in penmanship and lost the spelling bee)

>

Trying on my costume the night before coming down with chickenpox

At Fair Havens with my good friend Graham, and best friend, Tracey Wilkinson (also pictured is Tracey's friend Laurie Teggart)

RLSSC LEADERSHIP
FORMATION DES CADRES SRSC
NATIONAL LIFEGUARD
SAUVETEUR NATIONAL
POOL
JENNIFER HARDING
86 11 ON

CANADA

THE ROYAL LIFE SAVING SOCIETY CANADA
LA SOCIÉTÉ ROYALE DE SAUVETAGE CANADA

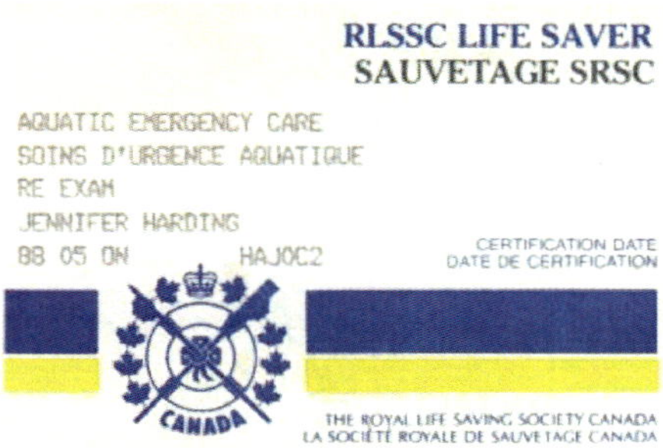

RLSSC LIFE SAVER
SAUVETAGE SRSC

AQUATIC EMERGENCY CARE
SOINS D'URGENCE AQUATIQUE
RE EXAM
JENNIFER HARDING
88 05 ON HAJOC2

CERTIFICATION DATE
DATE DE CERTIFICATION

CANADA

THE ROYAL LIFE SAVING SOCIETY CANADA
LA SOCIÉTÉ ROYALE DE SAUVETAGE CANADA

Senior Prom (I dyed my high heels purple to match Graham's bow tie)

"Sally"— Grand Champion at the Ontario County Show. Graham pictured here with his siblings, Craig and Sharon (who was the 1985 Ontario County Dairy Princess)

Here's why Graham Wilson uses a John Deere Hay System

'Using John Deere hay equipment lets us cut our alfalfa faster, dry quicker and bale faster'

Graham Wilson, Uxbridge, Ontario

My boyfriend, the John Deere model

ATHLETES OF THE WEEK

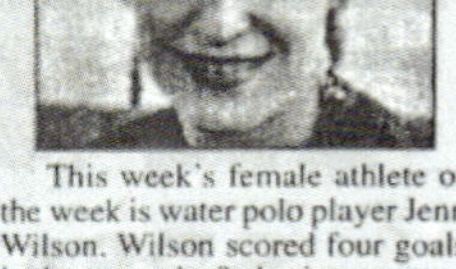

This week's male athlete of the week is basketball guard Titus Channer.

The fourth-year Geography student averaged 23 points in a pair of victories over Lakehead this past weekend.

The two-time all-Canadian is considered a front runner for CIAU player of the year honours.

"It's in the back of my mind, but I try not to think about it," admits Channer. "If I think about awards, it will affect my game."

This week's female athlete of the week is water polo player Jenn Wilson. Wilson scored four goals in her team's 8-1 victory over Brock this past weekend.

The third-year Medicine student hopes the team can build from such victories in preparing for the upcoming OWIAA championships.

"We had a great game," she admits.

"It was a big game for us. It guaranteed a spot in the finals."

Playing water polo for McMaster University

<
*My grandmothers,
Mary Micheff and
Mabel Harding,
on our wedding day,
May 14, 1994*

*Graham with
the wonder twins,
Joshua and Jessica*

^
2004
The year of the Family Medicine Conference with keynote speaker Dr. Stephen Lewis: Claudia, Olivia holding Jessica and Joshua, Amelia

<
2007 Just before I left for Ghana: Me holding Joshua, Graham holding Jessica with Amelia, Olivia, and Claudia in the front

CHAPTER 5

Sharpening the Axe

"Give me six hours to chop down a tree,
and I will spend the first four sharpening the axe."
~ Abraham Lincoln

Preparing to take a medical team to Ghana felt like one of the most important things I had ever been asked to do. I threw myself into the preparations with my whole being.

My training at McMaster University had ingrained in me the need to establish objectives against which we could measure our performance. We knew our team would be visiting a district hospital, followed by five remote villages in Northern Ghana, but I didn't know what our hosts expected of us.

I'm sure David had a chuckle when I asked him to please send me the "objectives" of this mission. This was the first time that my "minority world" approach would contrast with his "majority world" approach. It is worth pausing to explain these terms. The term "majority world" refers to the majority of the world's population who live in parts of the world, like Africa, that are traditionally referred to as "developing" or "third world." The term "minority world" refers to countries, like Canada, that are traditionally called "developed" or "first world"—countries where, in fact, the minority of the world's population reside. Some may say this is just semantics, but these semantics represented a fundamentally important shift in perspective for my teammates and me.

It is characteristic of David that in those moments when our two worlds collided, he always responded with openness, graciousness, and a great sense of humour. He never made me feel stupid or naïve. He welcomed all of my ideas and perspectives with open arms and an open mind, and on occasions when he could have rolled his eyes at me with justification, he instead looked at me with love and gratitude.

David and Brenda obligingly provided our team with four objectives:

1. To be exposed to the needs of Northern Ghana;
2. To follow the command of Jesus to visit the sick;
3. To work alongside Ghanaian health professionals using skills and medicines available to address the medical needs of patients; and
4. To support NEA's goal of improving health on a consistent basis.

Their objectives became our cornerstones.

It is overwhelming for any health professional to agree to work in a rural, remote part of the world which lacks infrastructure, electricity, and basic health care. It is less overwhelming, however, for them to agree to simply expose themselves to need, visit the sick, work alongside global colleagues, and plan for sustainability. These actions required no specialized training—just courage.

Armed with these basic objectives, we set to work. Together with three teammates, Dr. Doug Wu, nurse Elizabeth "Betsy" Convery, and pharmacist Susan Fockler, we took off to Kansas City for a conference on "Exploring Medical Missions" put on by the Institute for International Medicine (INMED). This event equips health professionals with the necessary professional, cross-cultural, and personal skills to serve the world's most marginalized people. We immersed ourselves in courses on medical missions and humanitarian relief programs, learning everything we could about providing responsible care in low-resource settings. We returned from this conference invigorated and empowered, ready to share all we had learned with our teammates.

The support from our community of Uxbridge during our months of preparation was incredible. Businesses in town put tin cans on their check-out counters to collect donations. The Rotary and the local churches got involved. There were bake sales and concerts; young children started requesting contributions to our team instead of gifts at their birthday parties. We quickly raised the $30,000 in funds we needed to purchase our medications and supplies. We connected with an organization called Health Partners International

Canada (HPIC) which provided us with kits containing $5,000 worth of essential medicine to treat 1,000 patients for only $550 per kit. Donations of vitamins, Tylenol, and toothbrushes poured in from our town. Everyone wanted to do what they could. John, the owner of Uxbridge Shoes, offered our teammates a discount on a hearty, closed-toe sandal for the trip. And my patients—I have to say that the 1,300 patients that I have the privilege of caring for in my family practice were tremendously supportive of my work in Ghana. Many of my senior patients booked appointments in the week or two before I left just to say goodbye and make sure I knew they needed me to come back. The outpouring of support was incredible.

As for me, my preparations were three-fold and involved preparing myself as a physician, a team leader, and a mom who needed to say goodbye for a while. I read everything I could find on global health, international medicine, and diseases of poverty. I became well-versed in conditions we rarely see here in Canada such as malaria, intestinal worms, and onchocerciasis. My most essential preparations took place early every morning when I would sit quietly and think, read, and pray that God would help me become a wise, capable, and effective leader. I read the Bible, and I read every book on leadership I could get my hands on. I became very interested in what distinguished healthy teams and healthy organizations from unhealthy ones.

I made a leadership pledge to myself and God:

My Personal Leadership Pledge:

1. I am responsible for causing a vision and mission to have tangible results in the real world. Our team needs to create an impact that the people we serve can count, measure, and feel.

2. I am responsible for the experience of my teammates. I want to help bring out the best in them, equip them to do what they previously would not have thought themselves capable of, and cheer them on as they advance.

3. I commit to self-leadership and constant improvement as a leader.

Before departure, our team gathered for multiple meetings. I brought in guest speakers to teach us about effective teamwork and cultural competency. We learned together, and we also played silly team-building games. Gathering for a common purpose, sharing a meal, and planning together allowed us to establish ourselves as a unit before our departure, so that when we arrived in Ghana, we could hit the ground running. Part of our preparations also involved applying for temporary privileges to work in Ghana. The Medical and Dental Council of Ghana had a thorough application process, including letters of references, to ensure we were appropriately qualified to care for their people.

I loved every minute of those preparations. Graham would often remark that even though I was dog-tired after a long day working in the ER followed by the evening routine of feeding, bathing, and tucking in the kids, I would sit down late at night to start my "Ghana work" and be completely energized. No coffee or chocolate was required. That's what happens when passion meets purpose.

For me, the hardest part of preparing for the mission was leaving my kids. It wasn't easy for them, knowing Mom was heading so far away. I worried they might grow up to resent me and the health care profession. No cell phone coverage and no internet meant I would have minimal ability to communicate with home while we were away, so I decided to prepare them some love notes. Each morning, they could open one envelope and read a message from me that described a quality that I loved about them. Reading those notes now reminds me of just how young they were when I set off for the first time:

> *Olivia* (age nine), *you are the most responsible nine-year-old I know. Thanks for always looking out for your brother and sisters, Liv. I'm thankful for all your help and the added responsibilities you take on while I'm away. I love you.*
>
> *Claudia* (age seven), *you are one of the most organized seven-year-olds I know. I love the way you keep track of everything on your clipboard and how capable you are. Dad might need some help organizing (and cleaning) while I'm away. I love you.*

Amelia (age five), *I love how you are learning the sounds of your letters and reading short words! You are so smart! Pretty soon, you will be reading chapter books like Liv and Claudia! Thank you for being such a great little mom to Josh and Jess while I'm away. I love you.*

Joshua (age three), *great job skating, Josh! You will be a great hockey player one day. I promise to stay away from the snakes! I love you.* (That year, Josh handed me a piece of paper as I was leaving with four wiggly black lines on it. When I asked him to explain his fabulous drawing he said, "It says, watch out for snakes, Mommy.")

Jessica (age three), *you are so full of love. I love how you cuddle us and care for your family. Give Daddy some extra cuddles today, ok? I love you Jessie-bear.*

One week before our first mission, I had readied myself, my team, my practice, and my family for our departure when I received this email from David and Brenda: "When we met with the local medical personnel here in Ghana to plan for the program for the five different locations, they estimated the turnout of patients to be around 5,000 people from over sixty villages. What started as a small idea is becoming something more than we ever dreamed. We believe that this journey will be a powerful message of God's love to the earth and our people that they are cared for. It is a wonderful application of practical work as described by Jesus, 'I was sick, and you looked after me,' Matt 25:36."

Five thousand patients? Sixty villages? Gulp.

There was no turning back. We had prepared to the very best of our abilities and now it was time, ready or not, to put our feet on the ground. Our axe was as sharp as it was going to get.

CHAPTER 6
Entering Mo Land

"Life is either a daring adventure or nothing."
~Helen Keller

On my thirty-seventh birthday, our team departed for Africa. I was surprised by the paradoxical emotions that I felt that day: fear and courage, uncertainty and peace, anguish and delight. I had faith in our hosts, and in God, yet the weight of ensuring that my team members returned home safely rested on my shoulders.

That morning at breakfast, my family threw me a birthday party that included Graham's famous chocolate sheet cake covered in colourful sprinkles. The kids were delighted that they were allowed to eat cake first thing in the morning and gathered around to help me blow out my candles.

Claudia, missing her front tooth, looked up and lisped, "What did you wish for Mommy?"

Tears began to burn behind my ears. My throat constricted with love for my children and with grief for the goodbye that was about to take place.

Clearing my throat to hide the crack in my voice, I answered, "I'll tell you, but I have a gift to give each of you first." I presented my four young daughters with a keepsake locket that bore half of a silver heart. At age three, Josh already loved to puzzle, so a puzzle piece hung from the chain around his neck. Then I showed them the necklace I had been hiding under my Ghana Health Team shirt. From it hung the matching halves to their four hearts and the puzzle piece that interlocked with Josh's.

Through my tears I said, "My birthday wish is for each of you to remember that whenever family is separated from one another, we're still connected. We carry each other with us wherever we go. If you miss me while I'm gone, just reach up and touch your necklace and know that I'm still with you and that I love you very much."

Our group hug—sobbing together over the uneaten birthday cake—lasted a long time. Then my sweet husband stood over us and prayed that God would bring Mommy home safely.

As they walked out the back door enroute to Grandma's house, I could see them trying so hard to be brave—to hold back their tears and smile—but their tears continued to flow. They loaded into Graham's big van, all but one choosing a window seat facing me (that's how big Graham's van was) and fifty small fingers waved goodbye to Mommy.

As I turned back into the house feeling crushed by the anguish in my heart, an accusatory voice whispered in my ear. *What kind of mother leaves her five young children to go to Africa?* I clutched my keepsake necklace and bowed my head.

I slept as much as possible on each of our two flights, knowing that we were in for a very tiring two weeks. Being an emergency room physician, I have trained myself to sleep when given the opportunity—anytime, anywhere. I always carry a pair of earplugs and an eye shield which *usually* make for a great "Do Not Disturb" sign. Consequently, you can imagine my surprise when I was startled from a deep sleep by one of my teammates. Had I missed an announcement for an in-flight emergency? I had not. Instead, a passenger had noticed our team t-shirts and requested to meet the team leader.

Seriously? Now? I stumbled to the front of the plane in the dark.

A tall, distinguished-looking man rose from his seat wearing a t-shirt with an "Operation Hernia" logo. Despite the late hour, he looked impeccably groomed. I looked down at my own wrinkled team t-shirt. He was surrounded by men and women wearing the same uniform. "Professor Andrew Kingsnorth," he said, in a lovely British accent. He shook my hand vigorously.

I introduced myself.

"What a delight to meet you Dr. Wilson! My team and I are enroute to Takoradi, on the southern coast of Ghana, to teach hernia repair to local physicians. I am most passionate about reducing the burden of hernia around the world!" He handed me his business card.

I instantly liked this kind, gentle, and very sophisticated Professor Kingsnorth. We chatted briefly about hernias, avoiding the irritated gaze of passengers trying to sleep. When the flight attendant asked me to kindly return to my seat, the professor said in parting, "Dr. Wilson, please do let me know if you Canadians discover a lot of hernias in the north. Perhaps we could expand our program if there is a need. Cheers now!"

I smiled politely and put his business card in the back of the small Moleskine journal which was always in my fanny pack (yes, I carry a fanny pack). I didn't give the encounter much thought. Nothing had led me to believe that hernias were a significant health issue in Northern Ghana.

Twenty-four hours after leaving home, our team bounded down the steep airplane steps into the hot, thick night. We were on Ghanaian soil for the first time.

Formerly known as the Gold Coast, Ghana is bordered by the Ivory Coast to the west, Burkina Faso to the north, Togo to the east, and the Gulf of Guinea and the Atlantic Ocean to the south. At over thirty-two million, Ghana's population is similar to the population of Canada, yet its landmass is only a quarter of the size of my home province of Ontario. Gaining independence from Britain in 1957, Ghana has a proud history of becoming the first sub-Saharan nation to break free from colonial rule. Along the coast, ancient slave castles and forts remain, bearing witness to humanity's capability for atrocity. Today, Ghana is considered one of the more stable countries in West Africa since its transition to multi-party democracy in 1992.

The southern half of Ghana thrives, with large cities, growing infrastructure, and industry. It is well-endowed with natural resources like cocoa, timber, and gold. The savannah land of Northern Ghana, where we were headed, is not so rich. Frequent rains come from May to September with the remainder of the year persistently very dry. Poor soil conditions and the long dry season result in a lower standard of living. Farming is the primary means of livelihood. Peanuts, yams, corn, and rice are the principal crops.

In Northern Ghana, a large percentage of the population is extremely marginalized and lacks the necessities for life. Although Ghana was one of the first sub-Saharan countries to introduce universal health coverage in 2003, the average rural Ghanaian cannot afford the USD$2 to $10 it costs per year. Even for those who have the funds to pay for health insurance, health facilities are often understaffed, lack skilled attendants, and are not reliably stocked with equipment or medications. Some facilities even lack running water and electricity.

In 2007, physicians were scarce in the north, with approximately one physician per 100,000 patients compared to 190 physicians per 100,000 in Canada. There are many structural reasons why it is difficult for health care professionals to live and work in the northern areas of the country: the underdevelopment due in part to the legacy of slavery; severe poverty; poor roads and transportation systems; the practice of traditional medicine and witchcraft; and corruption.

Rural areas face many barriers that further impact access to health care, including distance, lack of transport, and lack of decision-making power for women. As a result, needless deaths are an everyday reality. Around the time of our first mission, eighty out of every 1,000 kids did not live past their fifth birthday. Women died in childbirth at the alarmingly high rate of 409 deaths per 100,000 live births (compared to seven deaths per 100,000 live births in Canada). The top four causes of death were malaria, anemia, pneumonia, and diarrhea—all preventable and all easily treatable.

These factors make understandable the Northern Ghanaian phrase for "goodnight" which translates to, *"May God grant us tomorrow."*

As our team entered the small airport in the capital of Accra, we were welcomed into the line normally reserved for diplomats and treated like VIPs by Ghanaian authorities. We wheeled our hockey bags out the front door of the airport through a large, curious crowd. The NEA staff greeted us and quickly loaded the truck. The night air was hot, and we were all sweating profusely as we were whisked off to the hotel for a cold shower and a few short hours of rest. The final leg of the trip would begin at dawn.

After a lovely breakfast of fried plantain, baked beans, eggs, and fresh papaya, it was time to begin our journey to the north. NEA's church bus was not what we were expecting. It was a compact, eight-row bus with four seats across. The middle seat was a "jump-seat" that folded up out of the way to create an aisle. Riders needed a strong back and core to survive sitting on one of those minimally padded, non-shock-absorbing seats!

Our driver's name was Simone, and he was NEA's top driver. Every two weeks he would truck thousands of metric tons of raw shea butter from the north to Accra for shipment to The Body Shop in London. Now, before departing, Simone asked if he could pray for our team. Road traffic accidents were one of the most significant risks of our mission, so I appreciated how seriously he took his job. After a resounding "Amen," we were off, packed in closely, and probably all hoping that the person sitting next to us did not have restless legs syndrome or gas.

The city was full of people, traffic, and entertaining storefront signage such as *"Anointed Plumber," "No Food for Lazy Man Ent.,"* and *"Dry Bones Shall Live Again Haircut."* Women carried huge loads of goods on their heads. Kids as young as four or five years old walked along busy highways with infant siblings strapped to their backs. Trucks with open cargo beds were precariously overloaded with fifty people plus livestock. We passed through large markets; every time we slowed to a stop in one of these, local vendors would approach our windows with large trays on their heads bearing fruits, vegetables, or household items. I passed some Cedis out my window to purchase enough fresh plantain chips for my team. They were fantastic.

As we entered the Northern Region, dirt paths replaced paved roads, and mud huts with grass roofs replaced the cement block dwellings with aluminum roofs of the south. Despite evident poverty, we saw brothers playing with homemade toys, sisters lovingly attending to their young siblings, and women carrying huge bundles of firewood or big bowls of water on their heads.

Twelve hours after leaving our hotel, we crossed the massive Volta River and entered what is known as Mo Land—the land of David Mensah's people. A few kilometres later, Simone's prayer for our safe arrival was answered, and our bus slowed as we approached our destination—the village of Carpenter. On our left, a tall, black cast iron fence came into view, behind which sprawled a compound with multiple buildings and well-manicured lawns. On the front yard of this facility, two flags welcomed us—one Ghanaian and one Canadian—flying side by side. The sign read:

NORTHERN EMPOWERMENT ASSOCIATION PARTNERS IN DEVELOPMENT WITH GRID (CANADA) CARPENTER

Our bus turned off the main road as the grinning NEA security team opened large gates. We proceeded up the laneway lined with beautiful trees, passed an Aquaculture Research and Training Centre, and drove past a well where kids were hand-pumping fresh water into large containers. Just past a massive mango tree, in front of a grand, thatched-roof gazebo, the bus came to a stop. When the noisy engine shut off, the enthusiastic clapping and cheering of our hosts filled our ears.

The entire NEA staff were waiting for us, and we were greeted with a warmth that rivalled the weather. David Mensah's arms were in the air and his feet jumped up and down on the red earth as he greeted each member of the team. Brenda, wearing her long, yellow Ghanaian skirt, was easy to pick out from the crowd with her fair complexion. Joy and relief flooded over me when I embraced her. Next in line was Noah Ampen, the NEA Project Manager, whose smiling eyes were full of tears as he raised his arms, cane in one hand, to welcome us.

Most of the children over the age of two reached out to touch our hair and our skin. They kept brushing at my arms until I finally realized that they were trying to clean off my freckles. Children who looked to be under the age of two cowered from us behind the safety of their mothers. If we got too close or tried to interact with them, they would scream in fear. We stood in a big circle, our hosts sang songs of welcome, and David prayed a prayer of thanks to God for bringing us safely there. He had just arrived back from the village of Yaara, where, he reported, people from far-off remote villages were already camping out, waiting for our clinic, which was to be held the following week. *Oh my.*

My residence was called Akwaaba House. Akwaaba means "welcome" in Twi, the language that is spoken by many people in the Southern part of Ghana. Our rooms were spotless and consisted of two single beds, two mosquito nets, a ceiling fan, and a desk. We had flush toilets and outdoor shower stalls. As I was admiring my new home away from a home, a sudden movement on the wall caught my attention. It was a pancake-sized, fast-moving, hairy spider. Involuntarily, I began to scream for help, like some maiden in distress. Help came running but when the Ghanaians saw the object of my horror, they politely suppressed their mirth, explaining that I had nothing to fear. I never did lose my dread of encountering those spiders, but instead of screaming when I saw them, I would try to calm myself by singing that old Raffi song "There's a Spider on the Floor, on the Floor."

While the team was unpacking and setting up the pharmacy, I was introduced to some of the local health care professionals who would be working with us throughout our mission. Ernestina Yobo was just over five feet tall, but I recognized her strength from the moment I met her. She was a nurse, midwife, and medical assistant who had spent her entire career in Ghana.

"Doctor, I am here to support you by all means!" she assured me.

Under the beautiful outdoor gazebo, we gathered for dinner, and that was where I met Abraham Sayibu for the first time. He was smartly dressed in a spotless chef's coat and had a kind and gentle demeanour. Abraham was one of NEA's many scholarship students who had been sponsored to complete his post-secondary training in hospitality. He had returned to NEA to complete his National Service (a one-year mandatory employment program for all tertiary graduates). Brenda had hired a famous chef from a local game reserve to cook for our team and Abraham was set to be her apprentice. A couple of weeks before our mission, the renowned chef cancelled.

At the heart of NEA's philosophy is their belief that young leaders can be empowered to reach their potential, so when the famous chef cancelled, Brenda called Abraham and another NEA scholarship recipient, Patience Doni, to a meeting on her front porch. Brenda explained the situation and proposed that Abraham take on the lead chef role. He accepted this opportunity, believing that Brenda, God, and Patience would help him. And he needed their help: planning meals, shopping, and providing safe and healthy food for a team of twenty-five is no small feat when there are no grocery stores. When Brenda suggested that they keep the meal plan simple and straightforward, Patience beamed and replied, "Madam, we will surprise you!"

So there Abraham stood, with Patience by his side, as confident as any Master Chef, announcing the menu for our first dinner in Ghana.

His staff had prepared spaghetti with meat or vegetarian sauce, salad garnished with vegetables from the NEA gardens, and fresh bread from the NEA ovens. He wanted us to enjoy familiar comfort food for our first meal so far away from our loved ones. It was delicious. As dinner concluded, Abraham had one question for us: Had we remembered to pack the large tins of Tim Horton's coffee that Brenda had requested? With his soon-to-be famous smile, he suggested that we were going to need it.

After dinner, we were summoned to greet the Chief of Carpenter village. In Ghana, protocol dictates that you must greet the chief and elders and receive permission from them before any work can begin in their village. Like many West African nations, even though a democratic government runs the country, there are traditional, tribal chieftaincy structures that still hold authority at the local level. David held high positions of honour in the tribe as the Chief of Development for North Mo and as a Divisional Chief in South Mo. In Ghana, even on the NEA compound, protocol dictated that he be addressed as Director Mensah or Dr. Mensah or "Naa Tibalakala, Gyasehene of the Mo Traditional Area." While our team referred to him as "Dr. Mensah" during interactions with staff or formal speeches, the rest of the time he was simply, and fondly, referred to as "David." (Naa Tibalakala, Gyasehene of Mo Traditional Area just didn't work during a volleyball match or a talent night parody.)

Our desire to honour customary and respectful forms of address was complicated by the differing practices and individual preferences among our multinational team. In the UK, for example, it is usual to call physicians "Dr." and surgeons "Mr./Miss/Ms./Mrs.," but the hernia surgeon I had met on the plane had introduced himself as Professor Andrew Kingsnorth, a title bestowed by a university based on significant academic and research accomplishments. For us, formality was always secondary to promoting a culture of teamwork in the field, where we valued a flat hierarchical structure and operated on a first name basis. The exception to this was our Ghanaian friends, who, out of an abundance of respect, consistently referred to physicians as "Doctor."

Even though David was the "Chief of the Chiefs," he was still expected to follow the greeting and permission protocol with the local village chiefs and so he led our team on foot into the village of Carpenter. It was already dark, as the sun set at 6:00 p.m., but little fires burned everywhere. In the chief's compound, chairs had been set up in anticipation of our arrival. It appeared that the entire village had gathered to watch the proceedings.

Chief Solomon was dressed in traditional fashion, enrobed in a long, colourful orange smock and sitting on a jewel-encrusted chair. His elders sat to his left. David led the way as we shook hands with them all, being careful only to shake with our right hands. In Ghana, your left hand must never be used to greet someone because it is used for hygienic purposes. Hugging and shoulder slapping were also definite no-nos. We were greeted with the phrase "Jamo" which means welcome.

Prior to our trip we had practiced and learned several phrases in the Deg language. Thanks to David's daughter Deborah, we were prepared. So, when we heard the word "Jamo" *(welcome)* we responded with "N-jamnia" *(thank you for welcoming me)*.

Upon hearing our response, the village elders paused, then their eyes and their faces lit up with surprise and delight. They started to laugh, though whether in delight that we knew the correct response or at our pronunciation I'm still not sure.

When the receiving line was finished, David and I were ushered to chairs at the right hand of the chief. I was suddenly very nervous. As the team was taking their seats, David whispered in my ear, "I forgot to mention that you should be prepared to give a speech at any given moment."

Good to know.

He then proceeded to greet the chiefs and elders and explain our mission. He translated his powerful and passionate words into English for our benefit. Then he turned and gave me a nod.

"Any given moment" had apparently arrived and so, with shaky hands and a voice cracked with emotion, I gave my first ever speech in Ghana. I was aware of my teammates' rapt attention and felt them silently cheering me on.

The chief then gave a memorable welcome address to our team. When he concluded, his eyes turned to me and David sent another nod in my direction. I was now expected to respond to Chief Solomon's address with another speech! Protocol is very important to Ghanaians; it was a very steep learning curve for me.

As the weight of the chief's message set in, it was difficult to find the words to respond. He had explained that most of his people had never seen a doctor in their lives and that all of them had lost loved ones due to lack of access to basic health care. He wanted us to know that they could not believe that health care was being delivered to their very doorstep. "We no longer feel forgotten by God or by the world!" he proclaimed.

I responded from my heart. I explained that my teammates, our families, communities, and hospitals had been invited by NEA to share our time, resources, and expertise with them—our global neighbours. I expressed our desire to learn from them, and from the local health professionals who understood best what their communities needed. I told them that we would partner with NEA towards their goal of building sustainable health care.

The ceremony concluded with the chief granting our team permission to begin our mission.

I always meant to ask David what would have happened had permission not been given by one of the village chiefs, but, thankfully, it never came to that.

There was palpable excitement and what I would describe as hope—yes hope—in the air on the NEA compound and in Carpenter village that night. We were just beginning to understand the magnitude of the moment. Our team had landed in this village with more health care professionals, supplies, and medicine than had formerly existed in this entire region of the country.

Although I was exhausted, sleep was hard to find under my mosquito net. A chorus of unfamiliar nighttime noises broke the stillness of the hot, heavy air. I tossed and turned with a nervous excitement for what tomorrow would bring. Hand on my necklace, I willed sleep to come.

A few short hours later, the roosters announced that it was time to begin our work in Mo Land.

CHAPTER 7

A Drop in the Ocean

"Too frequently we think we have to do spectacular things. Yet if we remember that the sea is actually made up of drops of water and each drop counts, each one of us can do our little bit where we are. Those little bits can come together and almost overwhelm the world."

~ Desmond Tutu

It was a beautiful morning as the NEA compound rose to greet our first day. The African morning air was still. Even the Ghanaian and Canadian flags hung in expectation from their poles, ready for the wind to awaken and launch them. From my room in Akwaaba House, I could hear Abraham's beautiful voice singing in the kitchen as his team prepared our breakfast.

At 7:00 a.m., everyone made their way to the large, thatched-roof gazebo where our team had been invited to attend morning devotions. The gazebo was overflowing with the smiling faces of the NEA staff and their spouses. As I entered, Ernestina enthusiastically motioned me towards the empty chair beside her. David welcomed us and explained that staff devotions were an important part of NEA's work. Every morning they gathered together to thank God for the new day, learn a lesson from the Bible, and commit their work into God's hands. He thanked us for joining them.

Grinning, Pastor Jacob then stepped to the centre of our circle. "This is the day that the Lord has made!" he announced. And with that, the gazebo exploded into song and dance. There were no instruments, but it sounded like a full band was backing up our hosts as they worshipped. For me, the thirty minutes that followed, where we bore witness to the faith of our new friends and their devotion to God, was moving and grounding. My constricted throat and the recurrent shivers up my spine affirmed that this was a sacred time.

With a powerful prayer spoken first in English, then translated into Twi, David commissioned our team and committed the entire mission, our health and safety, and our families back home into God's powerful and loving hands. When devotions came to an end, Pastor Jacob asked us to rise for the "Grace." We all stood as the Ghanaians—in unison—lifted their hands in the air, closed their eyes, and recited in English: "May the grace of the Lord Jesus Christ, the love of God, and the fellowship of the Holy Spirit be with you all today and forevermore." The "AMEN" that followed was so resounding that it made me jump.

As I looked around the gazebo at the faces of this massive team, I felt an incredible sense of purpose, peace, and anticipation.

Our initial plan was to spend our first day in Ghana unpacking, setting up, and touring the compound. At the last minute, Brenda Mensah, with a twinkle in her eye, asked if I would consider running a small afternoon clinic for the NEA staff instead. She thought it might be wise to test our operations and logistics with a smaller crowd before leaving the comforts of the compound.

Having lived and worked in Ghana for twenty years, Brenda had an extremely valuable perspective. She understood the needs in Ghana, but she also understood the needs of her fellow Canadians. Brenda knew that the next two weeks would involve long and treacherous journeys that would introduce us to some of the most severe illnesses we would ever witness. She also knew we would soon be caring for large crowds of patients in the extreme heat while dealing with obstacles that were entirely foreign to us: lack of electricity, running water, and toilets just to name a few. A "soft opening" on the compound with smaller crowds and greater control would be a perfect initiation for our team. But she didn't tell me any of that.

I loved Brenda's idea of prioritizing care for the NEA families—I had already been noticing that some of the staff kids had coughs and rashes that required attention. I thought of the emergency airplane protocol that advises passengers to put their own oxygen mask on before assisting others. Caring for our Ghanaian teammates and their loved ones first felt like the right thing to do.

Joining me in Ghana were my extremely efficient and capable

office manager Robin Belanger, and Uxbridge Hospital ward clerk Lesley Joosten. They registered every patient and gave them a medical record and deworming medication. (Mass deworming together with access to clean water, sanitation, and hygiene play a crucial role in interrupting intestinal worms, which is a neglected tropical disease with significant health impacts.)

Once registered, patients were assessed by our triage nurses and treated for minor ailments or referred to the physicians for more serious conditions. All children passed through a station to record their temperature and weight, which served two essential purposes: any child with a fever received an automatic malaria test before seeing the doctor, and establishing the weight of the child allowed us to calculate the correct dosage of any medication they might need. Patients then received a consultation with the physician.

The gazebo where morning devotions had been held was transformed into a nursing station run by my Uxbridge emergency room nurse Cindy Marsh and her team. Here, our nurses would dress chronic wounds, administer intravenous (IV) medication for our sickest patients, treat asthma attacks, and perform minor procedures. The final stop for our patients was a fully-stocked pharmacy designed and run single-handedly by our founding pharmacist Susan Fockler.

We anticipated the health of the NEA staff would be better than that of the general Northern Ghanaian population; however, we were surprised by what we saw that day. We were busy until after dark dealing with acute and serious conditions such as malaria, pneumonia, and complications of pregnancy. We also saw many chronic illnesses such as uncontrolled hypertension, asthma, and diabetes.

Ernestina, our local expert, cheerfully circulated throughout the clinic all day guiding us as we made our diagnoses, treated our patients, and arranged necessary follow-up for chronic illnesses. I quickly appreciated something about Ernestina that remains true to this day. Whenever I asked her for help, she would respond with a smile and the same three words—"BY ALL MEANS!"

One of my last patients that day was Noah, the NEA project manager. He had waited until all of his staff had been seen before seeking care for himself. Gloria Ross, who was the X-ray technician at my hospital back home, assisted Noah as he limped into our clinic with his cane. Noah handed me some recent X-rays of his ankle, which he had broken many years ago. Noah smiled at me expectantly as he expressed his gratitude to God that our team had come to relieve his suffering. His pain prevented him from farming, and as a result, he couldn't provide for his family. He could not believe that we had come with our "special medicine" to restore him to health.

As I placed the X-ray film up to the window, Gloria and I were speechless. We could barely recognize the ankle joint due to the deformity and arthritis.

My heart sank. I knew there was nothing I could do for his ankle. Even in Canada, ankle replacement surgery is difficult to access, and it was definitely not an option in Ghana. Trying hard to disguise my anguish, I moved him to the examination table. I checked his blood pressure, heart, lungs, and finally, his ankle joint, which was swollen and deformed. I brought him back to my consulting desk and explained that he had a condition called advanced arthritis. I told him that even in Canada, we had limited options to cure this problem. Still, we could use medication and therapy to help control the pain. I prescribed him a year's worth of arthritic medication, topical anti-inflammatories, and gave him some daily exercises. I told him I was so sorry for the suffering that he had to endure.

While I waited for my translator to break this bad news, I could only guess what his response would be. These so-called "experts" came all the way from Canada to give me Tylenol and exercises?

As tears filled Noah's eyes, I wanted to crawl into a hole.

Then, to my shock, he stood, raised his arms in the air, and began to thank God. My translator interpreted with the same passion I could hear in Noah's voice. He told me that he was so grateful for my thorough examination and my explanation which helped him understand why he felt pain. Often in Ghana, spiritual meanings can be assigned to pain which make it even more difficult to cope. He was confident that this medicine would allow him to farm again, and he now had hope for tomorrow. He asked God to bless me and my children and my children's children, and to replenish my efforts many times over. Then he stood and, grinning, limped out the door bringing our first clinic to a close.

That night, we fell into bed exhausted and grateful that we had the opportunity to care first for our new teammates at NEA who we would be working with so closely over the next two weeks.

The next day NEA arranged for us to make the long journey to visit Wenchi Methodist Hospital, the closest hospital to the project site. The Bishop of Wenchi, C.K. Konadu, had been a teacher who took David, a young, orphaned boy, off the street and into the school many years before. During the day, he taught David math. After school he taught David about God, and how to run like the track star he would become.

When we got to the hospital, Bishop Konadu, the hospital administrator Mr. Botwe, and all the hospital staff were waiting to greet our team. We presented them with supplies from home, including two incubators that our teammate, Luanne Evans, had obtained from the Uxbridge Hospital.

The next two days at Wenchi were undoubtedly the most challenging days of my life up to that point. Our team of twenty-five people poured heart and soul into working alongside our hospital colleagues as an endless stream of men, women, and children arrived, bringing their concerns to us.

On the first day, our paediatric nurse, Carolyn Wilson, came running towards me with a bundle in her arms. She tried to speak but all she could say was, "This baby…" before her voice cracked with emotion. I lifted the blanket to reveal an infant whose wide eyes were sunken into her head. Her hair was sparse, and her cheek bones were abnormally prominent. Based on her size, I initially wondered if she was premature, but Carolyn informed me that this tiny girl was over six months of age. My hands shook with horror while conducting the rest of my examination.

The baby was profoundly malnourished. Her mother's breast milk had dried up and without money to purchase formula, she was forced to feed her watered-down porridge. I was astounded by this child's tenacious will to survive. Arrangements were made to admit her to the hospital's refeeding program.

At day's end, Carolyn advised me that she and Ernestina were making a quick visit to the children's ward to check on the baby before our team departed. A short while later, they returned looking bewildered.

"They're gone!" Carolyn cried out when she saw me.

Ernestina explained that the baby's father would not grant permission for his wife and daughter to stay at the hospital. He insisted that they immediately return to their village. Also, the mother had many other children at home to care for, and there was no money for the extra fees required to stay with the baby.

We were devastated by this unexpected turn of events and brought the situation to the Mensahs so they could "fix" it.

David and Brenda listened to Carolyn's frantic report, but didn't look surprised. Neither did they look like they were ready to spring into the action we thought this situation demanded. They simply nodded their heads and placed a hand on Carolyn's heaving shoulders as she spoke.

David said, "Thank you, Carolyn, for all you have done, but there is nothing more that any of us can do right now. NEA will try and gather more information about the situation and see if the father is willing to accept help for his family. Now, it is time for you and your teammates to get on the bus and return to the compound."

Our second day at Wenchi Hospital was barely underway when I heard someone yelling "Code Blue, Code Blue!" At first, I thought the forty-degree heat was playing tricks on my ears, but I quickly realized that wasn't the case. A woman had gone into cardiac arrest just outside our pharmacy. The team sprang into action. Cindy began performing CPR and Betsy called for someone to bring the hospital defibrillator. To our dismay, it was broken. So was the stretcher we fumbled with to transport her to the ER. Despite our best efforts, she passed away.

That night, as I reflected on our first "Code Blue" in Ghana, I wasn't sure what we would have done had she survived—angiograms, angioplasties, and cardiac intensive care were unavailable in the North. Was there even a point in attempting a resuscitation in the first place?

While some of the details of those two days at Wenchi have faded with time, there is one face that remains etched in my memory: the forlorn face of a thin, young woman slumped against a pole wearing a blue bucket hat. Each time I left my consultation room to speak to our nurses or our pharmacist, I saw her sitting there so very still, her wide eyes tracking me under the rim of her hat. When I realized that she was not being attended to, I asked Ernestina if we could assist her.

Ernestina helped the woman into my consultation room. She was emaciated, weak, and had a chronic cough and diarrhea. My translator spoke with her for quite some time, leaning very close in order to hear her voice—barely above a whisper. His translation from what seemed like a very long conversation was one short sentence: "She heard that Canadian doctors were visiting and made a very, very long journey in search of help."

This was my introduction to HIV and AIDS in Africa. This woman did not know her diagnosis, and she did not know that HIV treatment was free in Ghana. Ernestina took charge and immediately connected her with the hospital's infectious disease nurse who admitted her to the hospital.

As the woman in the blue bucket hat was led away, Ernestina saw the distress on my face and said, "Don't worry, doctor. She will be strong and healthy when she returns to see you next year!"

I didn't believe her.

The next day our team packed into our little bus for another beautiful journey to the remote village of Nyamboi. NEA had been actively working in this village for several years providing a water well, school building, and new health clinic. Brenda's title in the village was "Queen of Development," and so she sat on a special stool during the welcome ceremony. The Chief and elders were seated in a semi-circle, ready to greet us as we arrived.

The Chief spoke: "I have been around for a long time, yet I have never seen anything like this." He waved his arm in a broad arc towards the sky and proclaimed, "That you people would come through the air to deliver health care at our doorstep is unimaginable to us."

After the eloquent and moving speeches, we were granted permission to begin our work in the recently built health centre as a massive crowd gathered out front.

We saw things we had never seen before that day, but despite the seriousness of the problems we encountered, the Ghanaian staff and the patients ensured that our clinic was full of laughter and joy.

One of my favourite moments was when a five-year-old boy wanted to show me how fast he could run on his club feet, which were at ninety-degree angles to his legs. His mom was so proud of him as she explained how he made the one-hour walk to school every day. His family could not afford the surgery to correct his condition, but with extra funds in our budget we were able to refer him to an excellent paediatric orthopaedic surgeon in Ghana.

I scribbled a note in the Moleskine journal in my fanny pack—NEED TO RAISE MORE FUNDS FOR REFERRALS!

Nyamboi also provided us with our very first experience using pit latrines.

NEA had recently built these simple and inexpensive toilets for the village. A pit latrine generally consists of three major parts: a hole in the ground that collects human feces, a concrete floor with a small hole, and a shelter. The user squats over the hole (this takes more skill than you might think) and urine and feces enter the pit. When properly built and maintained, pit latrines can decrease the spread of disease by reducing the amount of human feces in the environment from open defecation. This decreases the ability of flies to transfer pathogens between feces and food. Pit latrines are a low-cost solution to the world's massive sanitation crisis. According to the United Nations (UN), 4.2 billion people still live without safely managed sanitation and 673 million people still practice open defecation. Lack of sanitation is a major cause of death in our world today, causing an estimated 432,000 deaths due to diarrhea every year and contributing to diseases such as intestinal worms, trachoma, and schistosomiasis. The UN estimates that 297,000 children under five years of age die each year from diarrhea as a result of unsafe drinking water, poor sanitation, and lack of hand hygiene.

As darkness began to fall after our full day in Nyamboi, this warm, vibrant village held a ceremony for us. Hundreds of villagers gathered, and the chief and elders sat in a semi-circle. They spoke eloquent words of gratitude and presented us with gifts of yams, fresh bananas, eggs, guinea fowl, and a majestic white ram.

As health care practitioners, we were not used to being the recipients of such gratitude and I could not hold back my tears. Neither could many of my teammates. When the ceremony ended, we loaded our bus and just as we were about to depart, David boarded and asked for our attention. "I want you to know that I am shocked—really shocked. The significance of a white ram is profound. It is usually reserved for most important guests, like the President of Ghana." And with that, he climbed down from the bus, leaving us to ponder the events of that remarkable day.

We were full of joy—deep joy—to have had the opportunity and privilege to care for the people of Nyamboi. Our bus was full of laughter and song as we drove off into the night, until suddenly, we came to an abrupt halt in front of the horrific motorcycle accident described in the opening pages of this book—our first African "Code Trauma."

I knew the man lying motionless in the centre of the road would almost certainly die. Even at home, I'm not sure he could have survived his injuries. But here, in Northern Ghana, strapped to the backseat of a taxi by our "Code Trauma Team," hours away from a hospital that may or may not have had a doctor in it, he had no chance of survival.

I remembered the accident that I witnessed as a teenager twenty years ago, eager to help but having only the training of a lifeguard. Today, I had the skills to possibly save this man, but there was no 911 to call and no emergency room to send him to. For the first time in my life, I was faced with a reality I had not fully understood—that many citizens of our world do not have access to health care. The implications of this inequity were borne in on me—on that dark, bloody African roadside—in a way that statistics never could.

If there is one thing I can say about health care professionals, it is that they know how to quickly reset and continue working despite tragedy and difficult cases. After all that had occurred over the past four days, and the terrible accident the night before, I was concerned about how my teammates would cope. However, the next morning they were all up early, looking refreshed, sipping the Tim Horton's coffee that Abraham had brewed, ready to head to the village of Bamboi where NEA had built a health centre. As our bus pulled out of the driveway, I hummed a famous old hymn that speaks of the mercies of the morning.

The local health care team welcomed our assistance warmly. These hard-working staff and the patients at the Bamboi clinic opened my eyes—and my mind—to many things over the next two days.

Midway through our clinic, a honking pick-up truck approached our health centre and came to a dusty halt just outside the entrance. A woman was lying in the back of the truck, screaming. She was about to deliver a baby. I was surprised that the crowd barely batted an eye at this interruption, which was a show-stopper for all of our team.

She was carried into the small, dark delivery room of the clinic. The midwife of the clinic asked me if our team could deliver the baby so that they could observe our technique. We kicked into action. Our maternity nurse Dale Heywood coached the mother and compassionately held her hand and wiped her brow through each contraction. Dr. Michael Damus and I prepared for the delivery, and our paediatric nurses Carolyn Wilson and Laura Molyneaux prepared to assist the newborn if required. Thankfully, a beautiful baby girl came out screaming, and we breathed a collective sigh of relief—until the mother started to hemorrhage.

Postpartum hemorrhage (PPH) is the leading cause of maternal death worldwide, with an estimated mortality rate of 140,000 women per year, or one maternal death every four minutes. Thankfully, PPH is easily preventable and treatable with an inexpensive medication called oxytocin. We called for the oxytocin and the midwife ran to the refrigerator, only to return empty handed with a panicked look on her face. Their supply had run out.

In Canada, if oxytocin is ineffective at controlling the bleeding, every labour and delivery unit and every emergency department has a Plan B, C, D, and E. In the Bamboi clinic that day, none of those options were available. After aggressive uterine massage, combined with the frantic prayers of everyone standing on that blood-soaked floor, her hemorrhaging slowed to a trickle and finally—it stopped.

The horror of that moment brought to life the statistics that I knew in my head. Had this woman remained in her village and delivered without a skilled birth attendant, she certainly would have died. Even though she had attended a clinic to deliver, she had still almost died due to an unreliable supply chain of inexpensive, life-saving medication.

I made a note in my Moleskine journal to add oxytocin to our bag of emergency equipment.

Another patient who further opened my eyes to the painful realities of this new world was a woman my age, with five children—just like me. She had been sick with a fever for several days and had been treated for malaria but had not improved. Her abdominal pain had become unbearable, and death appeared to be imminent. Then the family received word that there were physicians visiting the Carpenter area from Canada. They strapped her to the back of a bicycle and made the day's journey hoping to find us. She was semi-comatose when she arrived.

We discovered she had a perforated bowel from a condition called typhoid fever, which often mimics malaria. Salmonella typhi bacteria, found in contaminated food and water, causes this disease. This woman's village did not have a clean water supply—they drank from a dirty river. My nurses Margaret Van Dyck and Heather Wilson helped me resuscitate her with IV fluids and antibiotics after which NEA provided the necessary funds to urgently transport her to Wenchi hospital. Our colleagues there took her straight to the operating room.

One of the most memorable patients from all my time in Ghana was seen that day in Bamboi. He was a boy of about ten years old, so thin and frail that his family had to carry him into my examination room. His parents lifted his pant leg to reveal a wound that I can still see and smell as I type these words; his entire leg was being eaten away by a tropical ulcer called Buruli.

The family was from a remote village, and despite the attempts by a local herbalist and witch doctor to treat the ulcer, it now consumed most of his leg. I knew immediately what it was, due to its characteristic appearance, and I knew he would soon die without intervention. Ernestina and the medical assistant from the clinic agreed with my diagnosis despite the fact they had seen very few of these ulcers in the past—especially one this extensive. (When cases like this arrived, Ernestina would often exclaim, "Our people are hiding their diseases from us, but have chosen to share them with you!")

I was so relieved when the clinic staff informed me that there was a treatment centre in the southern part of Ghana that specialized in Buruli. There, the boy could get free treatment, including skin grafts or amputation. A lengthy discussion ensued in the local language between the health professionals and the family. Quite some time later, Ernestina summoned me back to the room with the boy. "Doctor, this family wants me to thank you for your care for their son and for making arrangements for his condition, but they have decided to return home to their village."

I could not believe my ears.

With her voice devoid of the emotion that I could see in her eyes she explained, "They need to return to their five other children and their farm. They will not be able to afford the cost of transportation and accommodation in the city while their boy receives treatment—it will plunge the entire family into poverty. You see, Doctor—they cannot sacrifice their whole family for the sake of one child."

The local health workers kindly shook their heads at my feeble attempts to find a solution. "Their decision—it is final," one of them whispered into my ear.

I will never forget that boy; I will always remember his pain. I will never forget the way he looked at me; I will always remember the impossible choice that those parents had to make. I prayed that the medicine and supplies that we sent home with them might bring some comfort to his last days.

I returned to my consulting room and laid my head down on the desk to try and regroup. I felt a tap on my shoulder. A young girl who was about eight years old appeared beside me with a large tray of food on her head. I had seen this young entrepreneur earlier, happily selling her food to the large waiting crowds. She knelt down beside me and in halting English said, "It will be okay Doctor Jen-i-fa. This will make you feel better." And she handed me a dried fish. An entire fish. Complete with eyeballs.

Ernestina chuckled softly behind me and placed her hand on my shoulder. "It is time to get back to work, Doctor."

I did.

When Sunday finally arrived, our team was relieved of all clinical duties and enjoyed a very sweet day of rest, leisure, and fun. We experienced our first Ghanaian church service and witnessed the joyful, authentic faith of our hosts once again. Testimonies were given from patients we had treated over the past week. They spoke of healing and restoration and hope for the future. We also had the privilege of taking a tour of the NEA project site with David Mensah as our guide. We visited the cassava plant, the fish hatchery, the ostrich farm, the corn-drying facility, the gardens, the bakery, and more. We heard how these sectors of development were being replicated in remote communities, putting a dent in poverty. Because of these initiatives—along with NEA's water and sanitation programs, peace-building initiatives, education facilities, and church planting—health was improving and communities were being transformed. It was astonishing, this glimpse at how health care delivery could integrate so naturally into the other development sectors.

The moment we took a break from our work, I suddenly missed my family terribly. It hit me like a tidal wave each time we had a day off. When I had unpacked, I discovered twelve envelopes that Graham had secretly tucked into my suitcase. He didn't know that I had done the exact same thing for the kids. Each envelope contained a precious handwritten letter with a word of encouragement as well as something to make me laugh—one for each day. Graham is not normally one to put pen to paper when it comes to matters of the heart, so I appreciated those love notes so much.

During that trip, a small Ghanaian cell phone that our hosts had given me could occasionally get a bar of signal (if I stood under a particular tree and held it in the air at a certain angle). Every few days that signal appeared long enough for me to get a choppy update through to Graham and at least hear that the kids were okay. After my calls, Graham would send an email update to our families. In true

Graham fashion, he tried to alleviate their worries with some trademark comic relief:

> *...The team is exhausted and got to bed relatively early tonight. Tomorrow they are off to Yaara for two days after which they will run their final clinic in Carpenter. NEA has planned a dinner party for their last night. Rumour has it that one of the rams is going to take one for the team. That should be interesting as Jenn doesn't do well knowing her meal before she eats it—I'm not sure about the rest of the team...*

Those calls to Graham were the only contact our team had with home during our two weeks in Ghana—no one else had a cell phone.

The morning after our day of rest, we set out on our longest journey yet to the most remote and deprived region of David's tribe. After leaving the main road, we travelled along a dirt path, in places eroded by washouts, to the village of Yaara. This was the village that David had been sent to as a young child after his father died. There, he'd been severely mistreated until he could escape on foot through the bush back to the Bamboi area. David recounts this harrowing story in his book *Kwabena: An African Boy's Journey of Faith.* One of the most remarkable things to me about David Mensah was that he returned unflinching to the site of his childhood trauma, determined to alleviate suffering for future Davids.

When we arrived, there was a full-on party taking place which ushered in two of the most memorable days I spent in Ghana. The women of Yaara danced in a large circle to the beat of the village drum, wearing vivid, colourful dresses. In the centre of the circle sat mounds of fresh fruit, eggs, guinea fowl, chickens, and—another white ram.

No one had briefed me on this dancing circle so, culturally oblivious, I joined in. My teammates joined in too, much to the pleasure of the crowd.

The women were tremendous dancers, and I'm sure we looked

absolutely ridiculous—we had great difficulty even finding the beat. The kids were roaring with laughter watching us.

David's older brother, Joseph, was the Chief of Yaara village and he presided over the welcome ceremonies before we began our work in the primary school. He spoke eloquently about the mission's significance and presented us with gifts of thanks before our work even began. He apologized that they could not give us even more food for our stay, but a drought had significantly impacted their farms that season.

Amongst the thousand patients who attended our clinic that day, there were two unexpected groups. A large group of men had somehow skipped the triage process and were gathered outside my consultation room. I asked Ernestina who they were and why they were there. She quickly addressed the crowd after which they all pointed to their groin regions. She turned to me and said, "Hernia. They all have a hernia."

Hernia is a condition in which the contents of the abdomen bulge through a weak area in the groin—they can be dangerous because the abdominal contents in the hernia sac can twist off and become trapped, requiring an emergency operation to prevent death. Hernias in Canada are usually the size of a grape; sometimes they're so small that we need our patient to cough or bear down to feel them.

But as I examined these grapefruit-to watermelon-sized bulges, I was shocked. I quickly realized how such pain would dramatically affect their ability to do the manual farm chores required for their survival. I was dumbfounded. Why on earth are there so many hernias in this village? I remembered Professor Kingsnorth, the British hernia specialist I had met on the plane, and wished I hadn't been so quick to dismiss him.

That day was my introduction to learning that the incidence of hernias in Ghana and in most of sub-Saharan Africa can be up to ten times greater than in high-income countries. This may primarily be due to genetics. This high incidence combined with an extremely large number of unrepaired hernias (due to lack of surgical resources) leads to large hernias which can be complicated by incarceration, strangulation, gangrenous bowel, and death. The economic toll due to disability from hernia is massive, but has not been well quantified. On a practical level, this means that young, healthy men and women cannot work on their farms to provide for their families. Many die an early death—all from a hernia. In Ghana, hernias and poverty co-exist in a vicious cycle.

As I looked out my classroom window at the large crowd of hernia patients, my heart sank just as it had when I'd seen Noah's arthritic ankle. I had nothing—nothing to offer these people and the countless others who would attend our clinics during the remainder of our mission. All I could do was record their names and tell them that we would do our best to work with NEA to find a solution. But I could make them no promises.

That night, our team stayed over in Yaara village as our commute back to the compound would be too long. Chief Joseph's family moved out of the extended family compound that David and Brenda had built them, and our team of twenty-five moved in. There was no running water, so it was there that we learned the art of the "bucket bath" which involved a bucket of cold water, a bar of soap, and a cloth. Pure delight.

But despite my refreshing "bath," I didn't sleep a wink that night, and it was not due to lack of hospitality on the part of our hosts. Neither was it due to the oppressive heat. All I could picture was the group of hernia patients pleading with me to help them. The middle of the night can be a dangerous time to process emotions—I wanted to escape and go home.

Thankfully, the next morning's mercies brought renewed perspective and strength, as I watched Brenda and the women on the compound prepare a hearty breakfast of porridge, eggs, and fresh fruit. Even our Tim Horton's coffee had made the trip to Yaara. After breakfast, David took us on a tour of the village. He started with the tiny one-room house he had lived in as a young boy. Then he showed us the home where the village witch doctor, who was the keeper of the town idol, had once lived. As we approached the house, David explained that we would see animal skulls hanging outside the hut and asked us to avoid making eye contact with them. "I have many stories I could tell you that would be very hard for you to hear—you don't understand or appreciate the dark side of idol worship. After my father died from a hernia and I was sent here to Yaara, the witch doctor told my uncle that our family needed to provide a dog for sacrifice—it may have been for spiritual protection or something my family had done to offend the idol." David's face fell. He paused, and looked to the ground. "My uncle chose my childhood dog and only companion as the sacrifice." He then went on to explain that hundreds of dog skulls—including that of his own dog—still hung around the perimeter of that witch doctor's hut. I felt a wave of acid rise up from my stomach to my throat.

A hushed silence fell over our group—no one said a word. Then David smiled and gave a little jump in the air saying, "But today we serve the living God and these idols hold no power over us!"

And our group of wide-eyed Canadians, eyes firmly fixed on the ground, moved on.

The tour ended on a happy note when David showed us the drilled well that NEA had recently provided to the village. "This well saves the women and girls of this village countless hours every day—hours that they used to spend walking to the far-off, unclean river," David explained. "More girls are now in school simply due to the presence of this very well." The heaviness of the previous night lifted a little as I pondered that gain.

The second set of patients who I was not expecting in Yaara was a small group of "Jennifer's Women" as they would soon be called. These were women with infertility. Because I was the only female physician on the team that year, the village nurses brought them all to me. Ernestina explained that the inability to have a child in Ghana was a death sentence. If a woman was unable to conceive, it was considered her fault and was grounds for divorce. Worse than that, she would be banished from her village, never to marry, destined for a life of poverty. So, you can envision the looks on the women's faces as they waited to see me. I had seen desperation in the past, but not like this.

I felt helpless and sick to my stomach as I worked. Infertility is a complex medical condition requiring advanced testing and expensive therapies unavailable in Ghana. I was a family doctor not a reproductive endocrinologist! I followed my routine: take a good history and examine my patients. I soon discovered that most of the women had chronic, untreated pelvic infections. I couldn't be sure that this was the cause of their infertility, but it was all I had to go on. Using the World Health Organization's syndromic approach to gynaecological infections, I offered them—and their partners—treatment. I also gave the women the best prenatal vitamins Canada had to offer. Knowing their potential fate, I made a habit of briefly placing my hand on their shoulder and offering a silent prayer to God for my treatment to work, and their life of deprivation to be averted. I confess that my silent prayer was lacking in confidence that this impossible reality could change—but I offered it anyway.

We said goodbye to our new friends in Yaara village and wondered if we would ever see them again. Our bus made the long, bumpy journey back to Carpenter, where we would remain for the rest of our mission.

Our time in Ghana wrapped up with a final clinic, just across the road from the NEA compound in the primary school of Carpenter village. Brenda planned it this way knowing we would be exhausted from our travels. The ongoing needs we witnessed as the villages around Carpenter funneled in began to weigh so heavily on my heart that I started to wilt—I was not sure I could finish the mission. It felt as though anything we did was such a tiny drop in the bucket.

But a few things happened during the last two days that altered my perspective.

I was called out of my consultation room by David. He led me towards a group of people standing by a bench. A woman with a baby in her arms sat there. It was the woman who had nearly died of postpartum hemorrhage after delivering her baby in the Bamboi clinic five days prior. She was surrounded by both her family and her husband's family, who had travelled a great distance to Carpenter that day.

The two grandmothers announced that they had named the baby "Ama Jennifer" to thank and honour our team. Ama referred to the day of the week on which she was born—Saturday. They went on to explain through the translator that years in Ghana are not marked by numbers (i.e., 2007). Instead, they are characterized by events. They wanted us to know that their village would mark the year of Ama Jennifer's birth as the year that the first NEA medical team came to Ghana. They also wanted me to appreciate how many women in their village had died of postpartum hemorrhage. Because their daughter's life had been saved, they would now encourage all the women in their village to deliver babies at the health facility rather than in their huts. David gave me the nod to make a speech, but my throat was so choked with emotion I could not utter a word. He did a great job covering for me.

Soon after that, our last clinic ended and Chief Solomon of Carpenter village addressed our team. As he presented us with gifts—including our fourth ram—he said, "Even though the raindrop is so small compared to the vast ocean, the ocean always accepts it." He asked that we Canadians, who have as much as the ocean, accept their raindrop of a gift.

It was a profound moment for me. I felt that our work was such a small drop in the vast ocean of their need. He felt that his gift of thanks was a small drop in the sea of our plenty.

His words and the visit by Ama Jennifer's family gave me much to consider. Then, that evening, a pile of yams was delivered to the NEA gate by the family of the mother of five who had arrived on the back of a bicycle with a perforated typhoid bowel. She had survived her surgery at Wenchi and was now back home with her five children. David also told us that this woman and her entire community would soon have clean water—NEA was going to dig them a well.

On our final night in Ghana, the NEA staff planned a party. Abraham's team prepared a great feast, fit for a wedding reception, and we dined under a canopy of stars with all of the NEA staff and their families. Brenda and David presented the women on the team with a dress and the men with a shirt made of colourful Ghanaian cloth. We took a picture of us all in our new clothes in that multi-purpose grand gazebo which had served faithfully as our dining room, our nursing station, and our church for devotions.

The morning of our departure was bittersweet. I missed my family and longed to get home. I was physically, mentally, and emotionally exhausted, and certain that I was utterly incapable of seeing even one more patient. On the other hand, recognizing the unspeakable needs and the many injustices that existed in this region, I wanted to do more to be part of the solution. I had no idea what to do next.

As if sensing my conflicting emotions, the pastors sang a song for us. Their harmonies, their wisdom, and their perspective echoed across the compound in the still morning air.

"Unto the Lord, be the glory
Great things he has done.
Unto the Lord, be the glory
Great things he has done.
Great things, he has done
Greater things he will do
Unto the Lord, be the glory
Great things he has done."

Our hosts were not conflicted about the value of a drop of water in a bucket, or the ocean. They were not feeling paralyzed by the overwhelming health care needs in Northern Ghana. They were full of celebration and thanksgiving for the great things that had taken place on this mission: for lives saved, for skills transferred, for knowledge gained, for relationships with village leaders strengthened, for partnerships forged, for ripple effects unknown. They were marking, not just the moment, but the entire year by what we accomplished together, and they were confident that God would do even greater things in the future.

As I was about to board the bus after a tearful goodbye, I was stopped by Noah. He set down his cane and handed me a package wrapped in brown paper. Written on the outside was a message. It said, "Doctor, Thank you for all you have done for me, my family, and my people. May God bless you and take you home safely. Noah Ampen." Inside that package—from a man who was concerned about having enough money to feed his family—was a full-length gold and blue dress with a pair of matching sandals. They were a perfect fit.

The words of the pastors' song rang in my mind during our ten-hour bus ride and two flights home. I, too, was grateful for the great things that we were privileged to be part of and I had a strong sense that our time in Ghana was the beginning of something even greater. The problems were complex, and the barriers to health and health care were many, but I returned home resolved to embrace my role and my responsibility to be part of the solution.

I had more questions than answers, but one thing had become crystal clear to me by the time we landed at Pearson International Airport—I had to find that business card belonging to Professor Kingsnorth and his hernia organization.

Departure Day birthday breakfast

Inside the church bus

^
Two flags on the NEA compound

>
Our Master Chef, Abraham

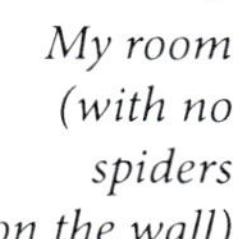

>
My room (with no spiders on the wall)

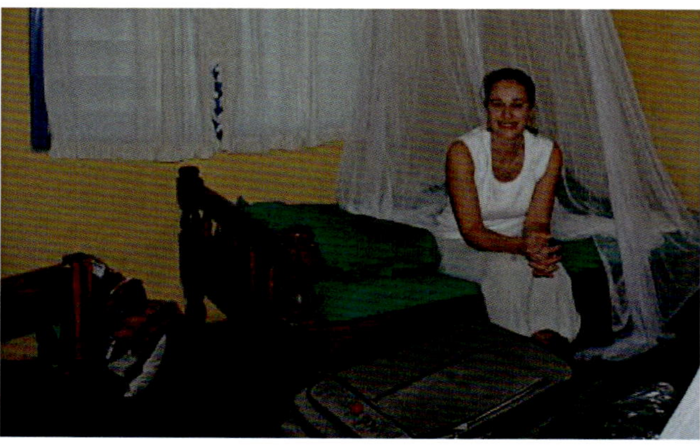

Akwaaba House, our first accomodations
v

Devotions under the gazebo

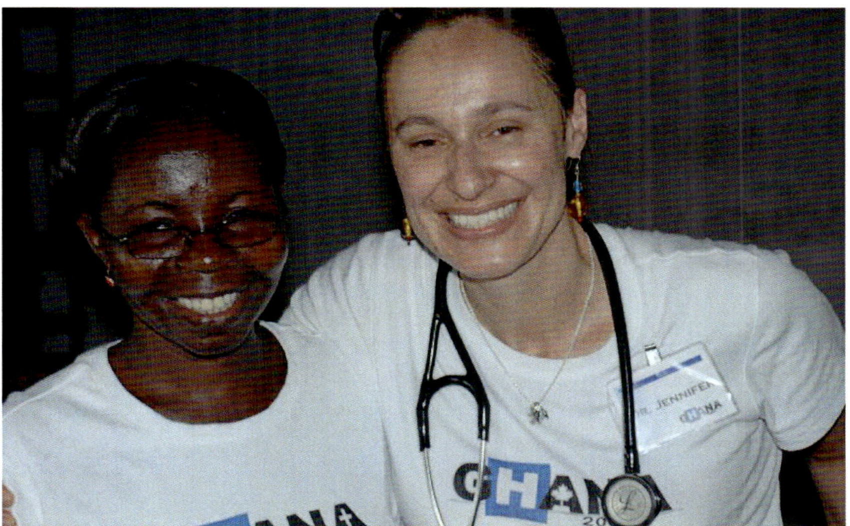

Ernestina and me

Greeting village chiefs and elders

^
Lesley and Robin registering patients

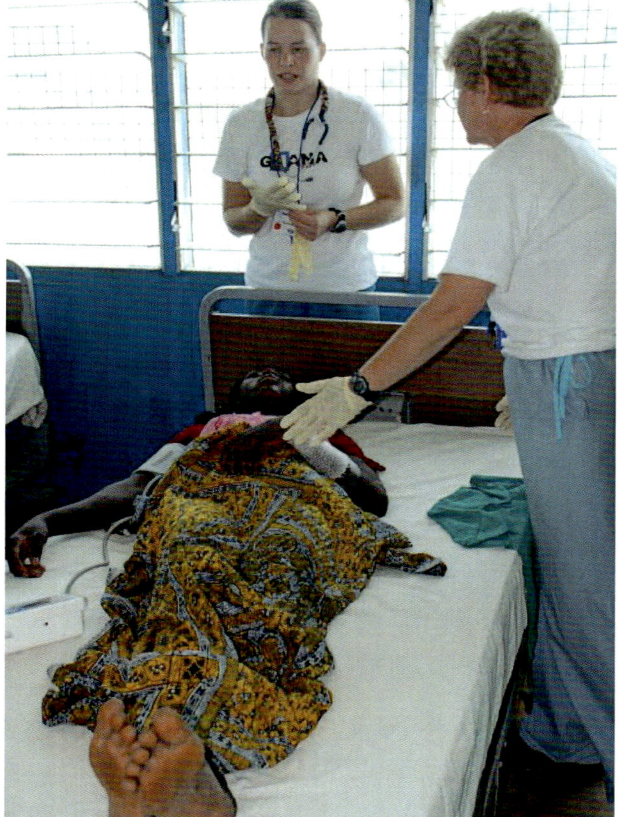

<
Woman (with five children) critically ill with typhoid fever being resuscitated

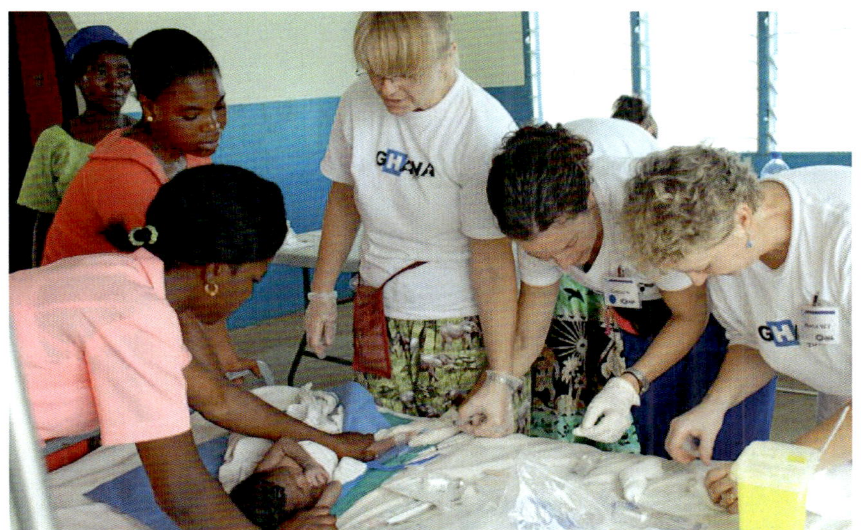

^
Team nurses resuscitating a sick infant with village nurses

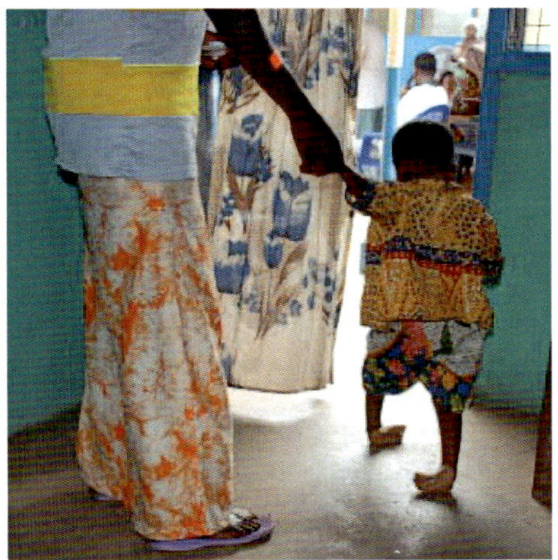

<
Club feet

The heavy rains (that stopped the day prior to our arrival) washed out portions of our road. Marion was not deterred!
v

Chief Joseph at the Yaara welcome ceremony

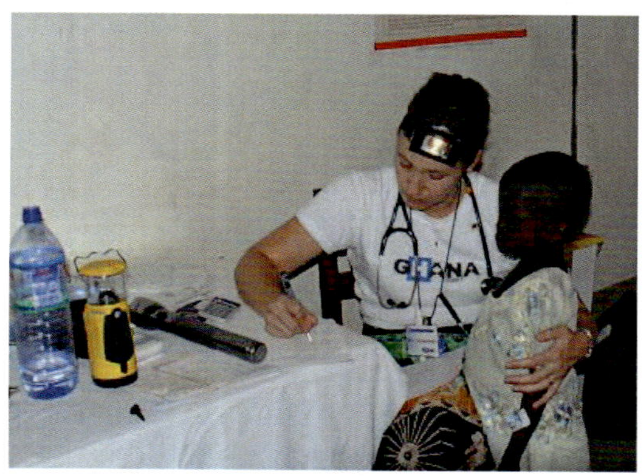

^
David and Brenda accepting our first white ram, tubers of yams, guinea fowl, and basket of fruit

<
My little patient

David's childhood home in Yaara village

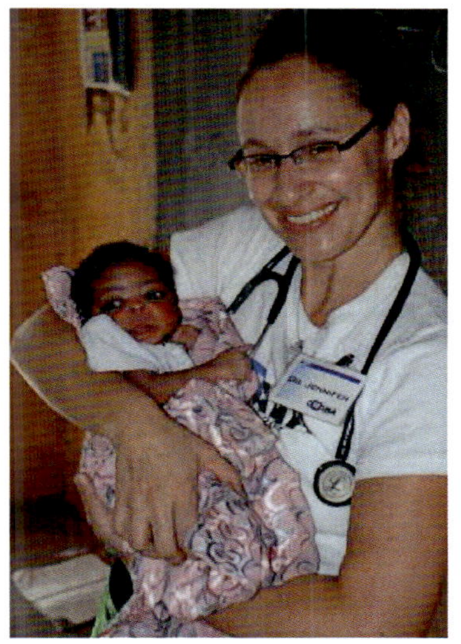

^
The baby named Ama Jennifer in honour of our team who helped to save her mother's life after a post partum hemorrhage

Meeting David's mother, Abena, for the first time

Church service

Gifts of thanks given to the first Ghana Health Team

Robin Belanger organizing the crowds

Ghana Health Team 2007

Graham and the kids were waiting for me at the airport when I returned. Graham had them all dressed to the nines and they had balloons, flowers, and homemade "WELCOME HOME MOMMY!" signs. It was a sweet and precious reunion as our family of seven clung to one another in relief. We stopped at Jack Astor's for dinner on the way home and it was in that bright, loud, and rowdy restaurant that I first realized that I might face a few physical and emotional challenges transitioning back to my life in Canada.

A wave of residual motion sickness assaulted me during dinner and I had to make a few runs to the restroom where I had never been so thrilled to see flush toilets.

My first night at home didn't get much better. The kids were so eager to tell me everything that happened over the past two weeks, but by about 7:00 p.m., my jet lag hit hard and I had trouble keeping my eyes open. That night, I awoke in the dark of night with a scream, having no idea where I was or who was lying next to me. Graham's comforting voice reminded me that I was back home in Uxbridge.

With five young kids and a busy medical practice, there was not much choice but to dive back into life as I had known it. However, even though I was in Ghana for only two weeks, my worldview had changed in a dramatic way. I would rise early to ponder this shift in my life and try to journal what I was feeling and thinking. I would pray for God to give me insight and wisdom as to the next steps I was supposed to take.

Everyone wanted to know how the mission had gone. I had two speeches prepared—a longer version for those who were genuinely interested, and a short elevator pitch for those who were just being polite by asking. Some people, like my sister-in-law Stacy and brother-in-law Will, surprised me when they were not satisfied even with my long version—they wanted the full in-depth report complete with pictures.

At times I felt so conflicted. I would embrace my five healthy children and think of all the mothers who had lost so many of their kids. I would wander through my home and think of the huts that most families in Ghana lived in. I would sit on my toilet and think of the lifesaving pit latrines that most of rural Ghana used. I would look at my closet, overflowing with clothes, and think of the one dress that a village of women shared for special occasions. My unearned privilege and their unearned oppression weighed heavily on me.

At work, my Ghanaian patients were never far from my mind. During my first shift back in our emergency room, I had a patient with a heart block who needed an emergency pacemaker. Then I had a multi-system trauma patient that we stabilized and flew to Sunnybrook Health Sciences Centre for surgery. Both patients were out our door within one hour. Neither of them would have survived in Ghana.

Many of my patients in my family practice felt the need to apologize for the reason they came to see me. "This must be so minor compared to what you witnessed," they would say. Interestingly, I never felt that way. I knew that regardless of where you live, your health and the health of your loved ones is one of life's most precious resources and highest priorities. I never wanted my patients to feel that their concerns didn't matter to me. The only thing that did bother me from time to time was when people complained about having to wait in our emergency room for two or three hours over a very minor problem when we were busy with serious emergencies. Graham suggested I post panoramic photos of our African waiting rooms just to remind people what incredible health care resources we have in Canada, even if waiting for them is inconvenient at times.

A short time after returning home from Ghana, I was at the Uxbridge Baptist Church when in walked the Mensahs' oldest daughter Elizabeth. I can't remember her outfit, but I do remember she was wearing the cutest pair of high-heeled shoes. When I saw those shoes, I knew I needed to talk to her.

After church, I cornered her and she asked me how I was doing after returning home from her beloved Ghana. My eyes welled up with tears and all I could choke out was, "How is it that you are still able to wear your cute high heels?" Realizing my question had nothing to do with her shoes, she suggested we sit and chat. She shared with me how she has spent her entire life going back and forth between Ghana and Canada, and that perhaps she could offer me a little advice.

I didn't have my Moleskine journal with me so I cannot quote her directly, but I remember the lessons I took away.

She spoke about how, in her opinion, God protects us in such a way that it's possible to learn to fully embrace life and work in Ghana and in Canada without feeling burdened or hypocritical. She encouraged me to focus on the blessings of Canada that can be used to support Ghana, and on the blessings in Ghana that can be applied to life in Canada. Each world has so much to offer the other. She affirmed that straddling these two worlds can be done well with God's help and would, in fact, become very natural over time if my calling was to serve in both places. I was so grateful for that conversation. It gave me clarity that I was indeed being called to return to Ghana knowing that I could slip back into my Canadian life—and shoes—when I returned.

By early 2008, preparations had begun for our second mission. This time we had assembled a team of forty-one friends and colleagues from Canada, the US, and Europe. Miraculously, no recruiting was necessary. When our 2007 team members returned home and shared what they had witnessed, and how the mission had impacted them, friends and colleagues stepped up. I was particularly delighted that many of my staff from the Uxbridge Health Centre and the Uxbridge Hospital were joining us. Our communities rallied behind us, and the necessary funds poured in for our medication and nursing supplies. I was in awe.

While mission preparations were underway in Canada and the UK, NEA built a small surgical facility on the NEA compound in Carpenter. Nestled between our team residence and the ostrich farm, it contained theatres (the British term for operating rooms), recovery rooms, consultation rooms, and a ward. NEA designed the entire surgical centre in such a way that it could be used for other purposes during the fifty weeks we were not in the country. At the centre of the building, a beautiful tree sheltered a sizeable open-air courtyard. This tree, soon to be known as "the surgical tree," provided shade and rest for the hundreds of patients and health professionals who would congregate on the wooden benches underneath its massive branches. All of the equipment for this facility was gathered by Professor Kingsnorth's team in England and was packed into a shipping container which set sail for Ghana well in advance of our mission.

As our Canadian team finished boarding the British Airways flight to London in November of 2008, I popped in my earplugs, lowered my eye shield, and reclined my seat-back for a relaxing pre-mission rest.

This trip, I was not woken up by a team member introducing me to the world's most prominent hernia surgeon. Instead, it was a panicked voice on the overhead speaker. "If there is a medical professional on board, please press your call button and alert the flight attendant immediately." Like stars in the night sky, little lights pierced the darkness as my team, all wearing their white team t-shirts, rose to their feet. The look on the flight attendant's face was priceless.

A man with a heart condition was unconscious in his seat. Within moments, the aisle, and then the tiny airplane galley, became our emergency room. My Uxbridge ER nurses, Cindy and Betsy, expertly inserted an IV from the plane's medical kit and after a quick announcement, passengers searched their carry-on bags and found the medicine we needed.

Dr. John Simpson, who practiced family and emergency room medicine with me in Uxbridge, was also at my side resuscitating this man. I'd known John for many years. When Graham and I purchased our first house in Hamilton during my medical training, we decided to turn our basement into an apartment to help pay the mortgage. Young John, just beginning medical school, answered our ad when his future bedroom still housed an oil tank. He and Graham had both grown up on dairy farms and they instantly forged some sort of "male farmer bond" as they talked cows and pedigrees and the future of the dairy industry in Canada. John signed a rental agreement before renovations even began. I realized in that long ago moment that he was a man who could catch a vision before it became a reality. Now here he was, many years later, embracing another vision—building health care in Ghana.

Once we stabilized the patient, the pilot informed us that emergency protocol required him to land the plane at the closest airport.

Since we were not yet halfway across the Atlantic, that meant we would need to turn back to Canada. The plane made a U-turn and we spent the remainder of the night caring for our patient.

Thankfully, the man survived the trip back to Canada and was offloaded by paramedics in Newfoundland. While we waited on the tarmac for take-off, the pilot made an announcement. "Unfortunately, the plane will need to stay overnight in Newfoundland as the crew has reached their maximum hours of flight duty." It got worse. "The bad news is that there is a major convention taking place in the city this weekend and there are no hotel rooms available. The good news is that the Red Cross will be available to meet you in the terminal."

As we entered the airport, we were approached by a compassionate and enthusiastic team of Red Cross volunteers proudly wearing their red vests and ID badges. Their arms were full of blankets, pillows, food, water, and toiletries for us. Oh, the irony. A humanitarian medical team en route to Africa was stranded in a Canadian airport being cared for by the Red Cross. What a way to start our mission! The hospitality of Newfoundlanders made the situation less painful for us all, and we were treated to a bus tour of St. John's.

Over the next twenty-four hours, our teammates and luggage finally arrived in London, where we had missed our connecting flight by a wide margin. The next available flight to Ghana could not accommodate our entire team, so we were forced to divide ourselves up and take multiple flights connecting through Germany or Nigeria. With no communication with one another along the way, by a miracle of God, we all arrived in Accra within a few hours of each other. Unfortunately, our luggage didn't fare as well on that Amazing Race—twenty-eight pieces were missing. Thankfully, our exceptionally detailed nursing and pharmacist leaders had planned for this exact scenario; they had divided and separated every medication and every supply into two or three different bags in case some got lost. As a result of their foresight, we had everything we needed to run our first three clinics while we hoped and prayed the rest of our bags could be located. The next morning, our beleaguered team travelled to Carpenter to catch up with our surgical colleagues.

One day behind schedule, our bus pulled into the NEA compound, and we immediately noticed something special. On the front lawn, a third flagpole had joined the collection. Standing majestically beside that of Ghana and Canada, was the flag of the United Kingdom. The three waving flags, the entire British hernia team, and all the NEA staff enthusiastically welcomed us. Side by side, united and strong, vibrant and colourful, those flags were symbolic of a future that was higher than our best prayers and thoughts.

We were eager to unpack our supplies and medications, but first, NEA informed me that there was a "small-small" problem (this is a term that my Ghanaian friends routinely use for situations that I would label as full-blown crises). The container of surgical equipment, shipped months earlier, had not yet arrived. It was held up at the port in Accra. NEA was working to have it released and was confident it would come "soon-soon." In the meantime, there was much work to be done to prepare the surgical facility and our mobile clinic, which we began after we enjoyed Abraham's traditional first-night-welcome spaghetti dinner.

That evening, there was a commotion outside the training centre—the type of commotion that one can immediately sense is an emergency. A family had come to the gate with a sick patient in the back of a truck. We quickly evaluated her and realized that she had a strangulated hernia—a surgical emergency in which the blood supply to the portion of bowel that is trapped in the hernia is cut off. Within minutes, our surgeons assessed the situation and agreed that she needed an operation to save her life. We looked at each other in horror as we realized that our world-class hernia surgeons had no equipment or supplies—they only had their hands. Forced to act, the anesthesiologist sedated the patient with drugs from our medical trauma bag. Once fully relaxed, the expert hands of these surgeons were able to manipulate the hernia and reduce it back into the abdomen, restoring blood flow to the bowel and delaying the need to operate.

Ernestina was the first to speak: "Your team has arrived at just the right time!"

Brenda wanted us to take the next day off to rest after our long journey, but my team politely declined her kind offer. We wanted to get to work and begin the NEA staff clinic. The NEA staff, in turn, politely declined our offer to run their clinic, deciding that the remote villages needed us more than they did. They were willing to wait until the next year, if necessary, to receive our care. I tried to protest, but they were politely intractable.

The next morning, right on schedule, we set out for Nyamboi village, leaving the surgical team behind to unload the container whose arrival we anticipated at any moment. We had a wonderful reunion with the leaders of the village, and, after a moving welcome ceremony, we got to work alongside the village nurses. Based on the evaluation of our first mission, our team had made some exciting changes to our mobile clinic.

The first significant change was the addition of dentistry.

When I shared the dental needs in Ghana with Dr. Michael Banh, who worked in the suite next to me at home, he signed up immediately. Lesley, who had served as one of our administrators in 2007, was also trained as a dental assistant. They, together with Professor Kingsnorth's good friend, Dr. Bernie Jukes, formed the first dental team introduced to Northern Ghana. To illustrate how serious I am when I say, "first dental team," it's necessary to understand that when our NEA volunteers approached the Nyamboi crowd to gather patients for the dental clinic, they suddenly realized that there was no word for "dentist" in the local language.

The second change was an expansion of our pharmacy program. Pharmacy is the most complex part of a mobile clinic. When pharmacists receive a prescription from the doctors, they need to locate, prepare, and label the medication, and then counsel the patients on how to take it properly. It is a very time-consuming process and must be executed with accuracy and safety in mind. With double the physicians on this year's team, Susan knew she had to create efficiencies. She brought three exceptional pharmacists with her—Alice Watt and Ardith Knechtel, who work at my home hospital, and Karen Prosser, who is my husband's cousin. Susan also brought a fully automated dispensing system, designed by her team, that could run on generators. They pre-packaged much of the medication ahead of time to save that step in the field.

Susan realized on our first mission that many of our patients could not read or understand the usual instructions we place on a pill bottle. Determined to find a more culturally relevant label, Susan used computer-generated pictures of the rising sun, the midday sun, the setting sun, and the moon to indicate the time of day that patients should take their medicine. Later, our pharmacy team conducted a small study to look at the effectiveness and relevance of this approach to the local population. These efficiencies allowed us to provide the highest quality of care to as many people as possible, and they helped our team get back to the compound every day before dark. Preparing this two-week pharmacy was a twelve-month labour of love.

NEA fired up the generators, and our pharmacy was open for business.

After a hot and gruelling day of delivering care, teaching, and training, we were excited to return to the compound to see how the surgical centre was shaping up. As we pulled into the gates, there was still no sign of the container, though NEA continued to predict its "soon-soon" arrival. But when we returned to the compound the following day with our first white ram from Nyamboi village, the container was still nowhere to be found.

Meanwhile, unknown to me at the time, the surgical patients staying in the local primary school were planning their exit. They were already extremely fearful of surgery, and the delay in the container's arrival had unnerved them. They began to interpret the delay as a sign from God that they should go home. NEA was doing everything humanly possible to fix the situation. Our leaders from Canada, the UK, and Ghana, met together that evening and agreed to give it one more day before sending the surgical team and their patients home. In the interim, we invited the surgical team to join us in Yaara village, knowing the crowd would be enormous and that we could use their help.

We almost didn't make it to Yaara village the next morning, as a section of the road suddenly disappeared and turned into a large pond. We all rolled up our pants and waded through with our equipment on our heads. We understood the risk of contracting schistosomiasis (an infection caused by the larva of snails that penetrate the skin during contact with standing water), but nothing would stop us from getting back to Yaara. The village welcomed us as if we were royalty. The women were dancing around a large collection of fruits, vegetables, yams, eggs, guinea fowl, and a ram, and we joined in again (although we weren't any more successful at finding the beat this year than we had been the previous visit).

Chief Joseph also presented me with my own pile of yams and a chicken to thank me for my leadership. After the ceremony, a sweet boy approached me and, in excellent English, offered to babysit my chicken while I went to work.

Our surgical team, eager to contribute, jumped in to assist our medical and dental teams. They helped wherever help was needed—weighing babies, administering acetaminophen, testing for HIV and malaria, and assisting in the nursing station and pharmacy. The surgeons examined a large crowd of over 100 hernia patients and put them on the waiting list for the following year. Bolstered by our expanded team, we had an incredibly productive day, caring for over 500 patients.

One case still stands out in my memory. A young man in his twenties had a disfiguring growth on the back of his neck. It was a benign lesion, but this growth prevented him from getting married and even from finding a job. I introduced the patient to Professor Kingsnorth who, assisted by his surgical nurse, turned the dim school classroom into his theatre and removed the mass under the light of his headlamp. That man's life was forever changed, and the surgical team bore witness to the impact they could have. The man expressed his profound gratitude to God that we arrived in his village at just the right time.

We didn't make it home before dark that night. On the way home, Simone uncharacteristically stopped the bus in the middle of the dark road and asked us to get out. He told us to look up, and then he shut off the lights on the bus. With zero light pollution, a massive canopy of stars exploded into our visual fields. It was a sight that will be forever imprinted in my memory. How could this be the same sky that we gaze up at in Canada or in England? Beauty, majesty, and a renewed perspective defined the moment and those that followed. Although he never admitted it, I'm certain Simone planned that stop for a reason. I believe he was trying to prepare our hearts and minds for what was to come next—the container had not arrived that day. The port authorities had finally released it, but now the shipping company was insisting that NEA pay an unconscionable sum of money for them to deliver it. The amount being requested could have crippled NEA's development work for years to come and, just as importantly, set a precedent for any future containers we might want to send.

There was nothing more anyone could do. It was time to accept that our dream of bringing hernia surgery to Northern Ghana was over. The next morning, the hernia patients would be released back to their villages, and we would say goodbye to the surgical team, who would return home to England. As for our medical team, our missing bags had not been found and we had barely enough medication to run even one more clinic. Looking to the majestic night sky once again, I realized how little control I had over what tomorrow might grant us.

Chapter 9

At Just the Right Time

"We must stop regarding unpleasant or unexpected things as interruptions of real life. The truth is that interruptions are real life."

~C. S. Lewis

When I was in grade one, I auditioned for a role in my school musical. I loved to sing, even though singing is definitely not my greatest strength. To my delight, I was given the role of a gypsy (a word whose pejorative connotation we were oblivious to in 1976). I couldn't wait to wear the costume my mother made me: a red and white polka-dot skirt with a matching kerchief and a colourful beaded necklace. The best part was the red hoop earrings that clipped on to my yet-to-be-pierced ears. Opening day finally arrived, and I awoke covered in spots from head to toe. I had chickenpox, and I was devastated. My mother sat me down and said, "Jenny, this is called a disappointment, and you will have many of them in your life." She didn't try to fix it, nor did she try to distract me from it. She could have so easily compared my disappointment to those of her traumatic childhood, but she didn't. She taught me to name what I was feeling, accept it, and move on.

It would be an understatement to label the delayed surgical container and subsequent collapse of our hernia program a disappointment. Abraham and Patience prepared a beautiful farewell dinner for our surgical colleagues, but no one was hungry. A sudden commotion from outside the dining room snapped us out of our melancholy and sent us running. A group of men were frantically pushing a lopsided wheelbarrow towards us while screaming for help. In the wheelbarrow was a woman, writhing in distress and vomiting, with a strangulated hernia. She was one of the hernia patients, brought to Carpenter for an operation that we were forced to cancel. The team quickly transferred her to the surgical theatre, now filled with tension, but still empty of equipment. The anaesthetist administered a sedative to relax her. Grasping the bulging pouch of dying bowel, the surgeons worked together using only their hands and their God-given skills to expertly untwist the bowel and manipulate it back into the abdomen. Relief flooded the ill-equipped operating room. The hernia was temporarily fixed and her life was saved.

This became a defining moment in the history of our Ghana Health Team for two reasons. Firstly, our surgical team had now saved two patients without any equipment. Through these lives saved and their experience in the village of Yaara, our surgeons came to understand the impact their care could have. In witnessing the suffering of the people of Ghana, solidarity and a commitment to assist NEA was growing. They didn't want to go home.

Secondly, word spread quickly that, even without their container of equipment, another needless death had been prevented by our surgical team. Trust and confidence grew amongst the patients, their families, their villages, and the entire tribe. The surgical patients no longer wanted to go home either.

And then—cue miracle—a message arrived. Word began to spread throughout the compound and the entire region that the container was on the move, travelling north, and due to land in Carpenter early the following morning. Just like that, reality had changed. The dream of a surgical program was resurrected. No one was going anywhere!

The next morning, I woke very early, too excited to sleep. I went for a walk on the compound and marvelled over all that had taken place. I found myself standing in front of the NEA ostriches who seemed bemused by my presence. I loved watching these fascinating birds, and I visited them frequently—they were so full of personality and so important to development. A single ostrich egg could provide a protein-rich meal for an entire family.

When I arrived at the dining hall for breakfast, a celebration was taking place. Our twenty-eight pieces of missing luggage full of medication and supplies had arrived intact and just in time for our long trip back to Yaara. With the team now aboard the bus and about to turn off the main road, our driver, Simone, pulled over and pointed ahead with a smile on his face. Tears sprang from his eyes. Lumbering along the road towards us, in a grand processional with flashing lights and fluttering orange flags, was a transport truck bearing our surgical container. It passed us and continued on its triumphant way to Carpenter. I'm told that it pulled through the NEA gates, past those three jubilant flagpoles, and up the driveway where every staff and team member, along with every hernia patient, greeted it with raised arms and voices. They said that even the trees seemed to extend their arms in celebration, and the birds joined the chorus of praise.

As we carried on, we were temporarily diverted from our joy as a violent stomach bug suddenly made its way through the bus. It was not a pleasant journey. As we approached Yaara, a wave of nausea threatened to highjack me, but I was determined that it would not interrupt my plans. Later that day, working beside John, I tried hard to hide my emergency runs to the bush to vomit in between seeing patients. About an hour later, it became clear that my mind-over-matter approach was not working; John forced me to surrender. After a "Ghana Cocktail" (IV fluids, anti-nauseants, anti-diarrheals, and antibiotics) and a power nap, I was back to work.

That afternoon, David, Brenda, and Ernestina arrived at my consultation room with a young woman. She approached hesitantly, stopped in front of me to make a curtsy-like gesture, and handed me a large bag of peanuts. David explained that this was one of "Jennifer's Women" who had attended our clinic in 2007 for infertility. Concerned about her fate if she did not soon conceive, NEA had enrolled her in their peanut farming co-op. David explained that this program was one of NEA's very first initiatives designed to give vulnerable women the ability to produce food and earn income. "They can have dignity and become a respected member of their community," David explained earnestly.

Brenda nodded. "More than 5,000 women have already graduated from the peanut farming program. They make at least $320 yearly. For this woman, that number is ten times what her annual income would have been prior to the program."

Then the young woman turned around and unwrapped a second beautiful gift. Hiding behind her, strapped to her back by a piece of colourful fabric, was her newborn baby boy. This young mother had travelled over four hours on foot just to thank me. Excitedly, she also explained that many more women facing ostracization—just like her—had successfully conceived in the months after our mission and were now proud mothers. I remembered the moment, one year prior, when I had said a silent prayer for her with my hand on her shoulder. I was moved beyond words. Needless to say, the line-up of "Jennifer's Women" was longer than ever that year.

A very memorable moment brought an end to our special day in Yaara village. One of our team nurses, Linda Stride, was counselling a woman in the pharmacy. After explaining through the translators how to safely administer medicine to her four children, the woman suddenly collapsed at her feet and began to shake. Assuming the woman was having a seizure, Linda knelt down beside her while calling for help. The translator quickly intervened and explained. There was no medical problem. The mother had fallen to Linda's feet in gratitude for the life-saving medicine that Linda provided to her children. She was shaking with tears of joy.

We arrived back at the compound completely knackered (a favourite UK phrase which is so much more descriptive than "exhausted") to find a beaming surgical team. They reported that everyone on the compound, even the patients and the children, had helped unload the container and set up the surgical theatres in no time at all. Ten successful surgeries had already taken place, and all the patients were recovering with no complications. The mood in the dining hall that night was one of relief and deep joy.

On Saturday, while hernia surgeries were underway, our medical team paid a repeat visit to our colleagues at the Bamboi Medical Centre. As we worked alongside the large group of health professionals there, my eyes were opened to two new realities. Firstly, countless patients over the age of forty and fifty complained about their low vision. Women could no longer sew; men were injuring themselves with their machetes; pastors were unable to read the scriptures to their congregation. We came to realize that no one had access to reading glasses. That familiar pit in my stomach returned as I realized we had nothing on hand to help them. I reached for my Moleskine journal and scribbled, "NEED OPTOMETRY. NEED READING GLASSES!"

Secondly, the devastating impact of malaria finally sank in for me. Malaria is a life-threatening disease caused by a parasite that is transmitted to humans through the bites of infected female Anopheles mosquitos. It is preventable and curable. In 2018, there were an estimated 228 million cases of malaria worldwide, and the estimated number of malaria deaths stood at 405,000. Children under five years of age are the most vulnerable group affected by malaria; in 2018, they accounted for 67 per cent (272,000) of all malaria deaths worldwide. The WHO African Region carries a disproportionately high share of the global malaria burden. In 2018, the region was home to 93 per cent of malaria cases and 94 per cent of malaria deaths.

That day, a twelve-year-old boy was carried semi-conscious into the Bamboi clinic. His mother reported two days of high fever, cough, and seizures. Now he was lying on our examining room bed barely alive, with a positive malaria test. Moments like this were genuinely terrifying. At home, we would have run a paediatric resuscitation ("Code Pink"), called the helicopter, and moved the child to The Hospital for Sick Children in Toronto. Here, we did our best with what we had. An IV was started, antimalarials were given, and Ernestina brought a basin of water, reminding us for the first of many times that "water is the best medicine." She compassionately sponged the boy down while humming a tune, all the while assuring this panicked doctor that he would be fine. A few hours later, the boy was sitting at the side of the bed, asking for lunch, flanked by his grateful mother and relieved nurses.

When we returned home that evening, I popped into the theatre to check on the surgical team. They had just finished operating on a man of about thirty years, and David Mensah was standing in the corner of the room with a massive smile on his face. He could not take his eyes off the man on the table.

When David was a young boy, he watched his father die of a strangulated hernia. His family's descent into poverty and suffering were all marked by the very condition that had just been cured by a simple operation. Watching David, I choked up imagining what he was thinking.

In the same way that the NEA staff had sacrificed their family clinic to make up for our lost time, the surgical team worked right through our day off on Sunday while the rest of us travelled down the road to the Bamboi Church. It was a service with so many highlights. The church in Ghana left many impressions on me, but the testimony we heard from a young teenager that morning was one of the most impactful. She approached the front of the church and spoke boldly. When she found out that the surgical container was delayed in customs, she and her friends fasted and prayed to God for five days. When it was released, they stood along the main road, waving their handkerchiefs as it passed through their village. She began to weep as she thanked God for hearing her prayers so that mothers and fathers would no longer die from their hernias.

To say the girl's story humbled me is an understatement. My approach to the delayed container was to fret and try to "fix" things. "Soon-soon" was not soon enough for me. NEA's strategy was entirely different. David and NEA wanted that container in Carpenter more than anyone, yet their response to the crisis was to be patient and call on their people to pray. Meanwhile, they did everything humanly possible and conducted their business in a systematic, calm, discerning, ethical, and sustainable manner. They truly believed and reminded us that, "God's timing is the best timing." I would witness this same approach during every crisis we would face together. I was being schooled in many ways.

When the three-hour church service ended, we returned to the compound for lunch and mandatory naps. As I drifted off into a blissful sleep under my mosquito net, there was a knock on my door. It was David. He had received word that two people were very ill in a small village called Teselima and were not expected to survive until our next clinic. Nap forgotten, John and and I hopped in David's pickup truck. The first patient was a man with high fever, cough, and profound weakness. His malaria test was negative and his right lung was full of crackles. He had severe pneumonia, one of the top three causes of death in Ghana. Going to the hospital was not an option for him, so we started him on antibiotic medications and prayed for the best.

The second visit was to an elderly woman who had been rapidly losing weight over the past number of months. We were ushered into the courtyard of her compound and asked to sit on a bench while the family prepared her for our arrival. While we waited, her adult daughter came to greet us with a baby strapped to her back. The daughter's face lit up, she raised her arms in the air, and then, she began to dance. Seeing the confusion on our faces, David leaned in and whispered, "She dances to thank you for visiting her mother." John and I sat pensively, shoulder to shoulder, mesmerized by the joy on her face and her expression of gratitude.

When the dance was finished, we were ushered into a room where we met an older woman near death. After hearing the details of her illness and examining her, it was clear she had advanced cancer and that she was in her final days of life. We explained the situation to the family, offered our support, and left medications and supplies to keep her comfortable. It was a memorable afternoon and, despite the seriousness of the work we completed, I felt a refreshment that a nap could never provide.

Speaking of those "hut calls" years later, John reflected, "These things form who we are Jenn."

Monday morning, we journeyed back to Bamboi, and it was there that I met a teenager I will call Sarah. She had a condition called neurofibromatosis; a massive tumour distorted her entire face. Due to her disfigurement, she was not able to attend school. She was desperate for help and destined for a life of poverty and isolation. I gave her the treatment she needed for unrelated conditions, and told her I would talk to NEA about options to help her. I was sure that surgery for this condition would not be available in Ghana during her lifetime. My heart ached for her future.

As I was wrapping up with Sarah, Ernestina arrived in my room holding the hand of a young, healthy-appearing woman. I recognized the blue bucket hat—she was the woman with AIDS that I had met at Wenchi hospital on our first mission. Ernestina wanted to show me how strong and healthy this woman had become now that she was receiving antiretroviral therapy (ART).

Our final clinic days were spent in the village of Carpenter. During those clinics we were able to accommodate all of the NEA staff and their families who, when we first arrived, had sacrificially given up their appointments for the sake of the remote villages. That day, a young girl with meningitis frightened me.

At home, we teach our medical trainees to test for neck stiffness as a sign of meningitis and yet we rarely find it. This girl's neck stiffness was visible from across the room. She should have been in a paediatric ICU. I remembered my son, Joshua, who at six weeks of age had also had meningitis. He had been stabilized at our local hospital and transferred to our regional paediatric centre, where he received a lumbar puncture, CT scan, and IV antibiotics. He was then transferred to a tertiary care paediatric hospital where, after a week in the hospital, he made a complete recovery. The best we could do for this girl was to administer one dose of a powerful, long-acting IV antibiotic and acetaminophen for her fever. We sent her back to her family's hut with instructions to return to see us the next morning. I prayed she would survive the night.

I also remember a young woman with four children. This family was from a remote village, and they were all profoundly malnourished. Ernestina immediately engaged the woman in an in-depth discussion. Her husband had died, and she was trying her best to make an income by collecting and selling wood. Recently, her sister had also died, and she was left to care for her baby niece in addition to her own three children. This mother, despite her best efforts, was plummeting into poverty; she could not collect enough wood to feed her family. The NEA leaders and pastors immediately became involved and enrolled her in their peanut farming program for widows. I watched that resilient and courageous mother leave our clinic with a smile on her face and her head held high. NEA would ensure that this family would be okay.

We also began to see more and more diabetes throughout our mission. I was so grateful that Cathy Fockler, a diabetic nurse, was able to help these newly diagnosed patients with the counselling and follow-up they required. This was a health need that would require more attention in the future. I made another note in my journal—"DIABETES."

At about three o'clock on our final clinic day, we heard the sound of beating drums. Everyone peered out from their consultation rooms to see a long line of chiefs dressed in their regalia approaching the clinic with large umbrellas, instruments, and drummers. A news network was setting up cameras. It was time for another ceremony. I remember being surprised and vaguely annoyed by the interruption—there was still much healing work to be done, and this was our last day. Neither our NEA staff nor the local health care professionals nor the patients seemed annoyed at all. Their faces were full of excitement as the processional approached. An event such as this did not happen in the little village of Carpenter very often. This was a powerful lesson for me; I tend to view interruptions as annoyances to my overly scheduled days. My Ghanaian friends and colleagues view unexpected events as welcome gifts and learning experiences. That ceremony was a once-in-a-lifetime opportunity for many, and the delay of our clinic was of no consequence in the long run.

At dinner that night, David congratulated our team on a successful mission, despite the many hurdles and challenges we had faced. As he was talking, a massive crack of thunder vibrated through our bodies, the power went out, and a torrential downpour began. When someone's flashlight finally illuminated David's face, his eyes were brimming with tears. He tried to speak but his voice cracked. David looked to the floor and paused to collect himself, as our team looked on with puzzled faces.

He explained: "The rainy season in Northern Ghana arrived late this year and the rains showed no signs of stopping as the day of your arrival approached. Now, when I say 'the rains,' I mean daily monsoon-like rains that wash out the village roads, making them completely inaccessible. Had those rains continued, you wouldn't have been able to get to the village clinics, and the surgical patients wouldn't have been able to get to Carpenter. In response, we stationed shifts of people in the Carpenter Church twenty-four hours a day to pray that God would hold off the rains. They started praying one week before your mission began and continued every day and every night throughout your mission. The reason I am so emotional is that the rains stopped the day before your arrival, and they held off until this very moment—until your work was complete."

By mission's end, thousands of patients had received medical and dental care. Our surgical team had completed ninety-three surgeries, won the trust of the people, and committed to continuing this program. Despite the challenges, everything we had collectively hoped for and more was accomplished. We got word that the man with pneumonia in Teselima made a full recovery. It turns out that he was a social worker and youth advocate for the entire region. The family of the dying woman sent word that she passed peacefully in her sleep. They, too, were at peace and considered it the highest honour that she and her family received a visit from our team before her death. The little girl with meningitis was seen playing soccer on our final day in Ghana.

Abraham and his team prepared another memorable celebration feast under the African stars. He proudly announced that the main course included one of the NEA ostriches. I'm told he was very delicious.

Our team caught a few short hours of sleep and then began our long journey home. As I made my way back to Canada and reflected on our mission, I thought about Ernestina's words after the first strangulated hernia patient was saved: "Your team has arrived at just the right time."

Whether it was our team, the surgical equipment, our missing luggage, the desperate women longing to become mothers, or the rain, these words were a thread woven through the very fabric of our mission. My Ghanaian colleagues were teaching me about timing and about patience—things that might be harder for me to learn in a country like Canada.

I wondered how many "Plan A's" I had abandoned when faced with interruptions, obstacles, and disappointments simply because "Plan B" or "C" was readily accessible to me. I also wondered how many times I had altered or manipulated the timing of "real life" simply because I had the resources to do so instead of waiting and being still. I was filled with gratitude to God for His timing and intervention during our two weeks in Ghana. I was also thankful to our team who gave their whole hearts to the people of Ghana, despite the uncertainties and challenges.

My heart and my Moleskine journal were full of plans, and now it was up to God and NEA to establish our next steps.

CHAPTER 10

It Matters To This One

"Despite grand debates on world order, the act of humanitarianism comes down to one thing: individual human beings reaching out to others who find themselves in the most difficult circumstances. One bandage at a time, one suture at a time, one vaccination at a time."

~ James Orbinski,
Médecins Sans Frontières

It was November 2009, our third mission in Northern Ghana. I could feel the tears welling up in my eyes. My throat began to close as I tried to lead the resuscitation. The six-week-old baby's name was Joshua—the same name as my son's—and he was in distress. His little forehead was covered in beads of sweat. His eyes were wide and fearful. He was breathing so fast that his chest wall was collapsing in between each rib as he desperately gasped for air. Joshua had pneumonia. My mind flashed back to the cold terror I had felt holding my own critically ill son.

The crowd of thousands who had gathered in Yaara village that November day in 2009 was instantly forgotten. All efforts turned to saving the life of this child. I called for Joan Maguire, a "rookie" nurse on our team. We called her a "rookie" because it was her first time with us in Ghana, but in fact, Joan had graduated from nursing school the year I was born. I met Joan at an information night at Uxbridge Baptist Church when she humbly asked if I thought her skills could be of use in Ghana. Joan was an intravenous (IV) specialist at South Lake Regional Health Centre in Newmarket, Ontario. I could not sign Joan up fast enough.

Joan was about to attempt one of the most challenging but memorable IVs of her career. I held my breath and said a prayer as Joan searched this dying, dehydrated baby's arm for a vein, not by sight but by touch. One attempt was all she needed.

Ernestina looked up at me in amazement and said, "This baby was the reason Joan came to Ghana."

Once he'd been resuscitated with fluids and given antibiotics and inhalers to dilate the constricted airways in his lungs, we prepared to transport Joshua to a paediatric intensive care unit. Until that moment, I hadn't given any thought to accessing paediatric intensive care in the country of Ghana.

I called for David and quickly explained the situation to him.

His response shocked me. "Jennifer, it is not wise to send Joshua to a hospital. He should remain with your team." I was surprised he knew the boy's name.

My natural reaction in moments like that was to assume that I knew better. However, I was beginning to realize that I didn't yet possess the correct lens to see and understand the social, cultural, and historical structures that impact life in Ghana.

As I paused to try and process why David would advise this, my mind jumped back to our first year in Ghana and the severely malnourished baby, who should have remained in hospital, but was taken home to her village instead. I recalled the boy with his leg ravaged by a large Buruli ulcer whose parents had made the decision to carry him home to die instead of to a hospital. Then I flashed back to the man from the motorcycle accident who had been resuscitated on the middle of the road and sent to hospital on the back seat of a taxi. I had learned—though I'd never had the heart to tell my team—that our patient survived the trip to the hospital, but died in a hallway after waiting all night to see a doctor who never came. A few years later, I would have my own first-hand—and extremely traumatic—experience involving a neonatal intensive care unit in Ghana. But that day had not yet arrived, and so it was impossible for this rich, young, naïve, western-trained physician to fully comprehend why David was against sending this boy to a hospital.

A loud commotion brought an abrupt end to my musings. David and the village chief (his brother Joseph) were having a passionate conversation. The two men (who looked like twins) turned, looked at me, and explained that Joshua was their nephew. Their younger brother Peter (Joshua's father) was in Carpenter having his hernia repaired that day. David wanted us to take Joshua and his mom Lydia back to the NEA compound to remain under the care of our team. These brothers understood only too well how serious the situation was; their villages bore agonizing witness to the fifty per 1,000 infants who died in Northern Ghana before their first birthday. They knew many of those kids. They knew many of those grieving families. They assured me that if Joshua passed away on the compound, their family and their village would be at peace, knowing that he was given the best opportunity to live.

Ernestina, always by my side, spoke for me when she realized that I was at a complete loss for words: "By all means, Dr. Mensah. Your nephew will be in the finest hands," she said with a confidence that I did not share.

I made a note in my Moleskine journal: "NEED TEAM PEDIATRICIAN."

My personal reflections leading into that 2009 mission—where we met Joshua for the first time—had been deep. I had continued my morning routine of sitting on the living room couch with my journal and Bible, praying and processing questions about life, death, faith, and global citizenship before my kids woke up each morning. Elizabeth Mensah was correct in that I was starting to feel more comfortable moving back and forth between the minority world and the majority world, but my bank of questions continued to grow.

When I was asked to speak about our mission one Sunday at my local church (in lieu of the pastor's sermon), I wanted to decline. I wanted to say no because I had so few answers to my questions and I agonized—really agonized—over what I could say to my church. I prayed for wisdom, insight, and understanding.

I prepared my remarks as diligently as possible and stepped to the pulpit one Sunday morning with a silent prayer on my lips: "May the words of my mouth, and the meditation of my heart, be pleasing in your sight, O Lord."

I spoke about injustice. I told my congregation about the injustice after injustice that we witnessed in Ghana. I admitted that I had been left with so many unanswered questions: What should be my response as a doctor, a mother, a wife, a Christian, a human? What can God possibly expect of me? What does God expect of the church? I admitted that it was in that place of uncertainty that I could become so easily frozen in passive response to the cry of brokenness on this planet. I confessed that when I got home from Ghana, a part of me wanted to close my eyes to the way that life really is for millions of the poorest people around the world and focus instead on life in Uxbridge. "But my eyes have been opened again through David and Brenda and the Ghanaian people, and I just don't think I can close them and pray that someone else will fix it," I said through my tears.

Then I showed them a slideshow accompanied by a song that spoke about a future where the poor were as much on the Church's heart as they are on God's heart; about a world-transforming faith rather than a world-withdrawing faith; about a world and a church where worship, service, justice, beauty, and compassion belong together. Finally, I thanked them for their loving support of me, my team, and the people of Ghana. The impact of their encouragement, financial support, and prayers could not be underestimated.

Setting my questions and my search for answers aside, I threw myself into our team preparations and everything was proceeding beautifully until a pandemic threatened our plans. The H1N1 pandemic was declared in June of 2009, just five months prior to our mission. Despite the threat, forty-five brave team members answered NEA's call to return to Ghana. This would be the first of three times a dangerous virus would threaten our plans, and we were grateful that a vaccine was developed in time for our mission to proceed.

When we arrived in Ghana that year with ninety hockey bags (donated by Pat Higgins, the owner of Uxbridge Canadian Tire) full of supplies and medications, we received a beautiful greeting from all of our dear friends at NEA. They had a surprise waiting for us. A brand-new, two-storey facility now stood beside the gazebo! The bottom floor was a state-of-the-art kitchen for chef Abraham and his hospitality team. The top floor was an air-conditioned dining room big enough to seat our entire group.

However, the biggest shock when we arrived in Ghana was not the size of the new building, but the size of the crowds waiting to see us. Word of our first two missions had apparently spread far and wide. In addition to the local residents in Mo Land, patients needing medical care, dental care, and hernia repairs arrived from as far away as the capital of Accra and from neighbouring countries such as Ivory Coast and Burkina Faso. The number of people and their many needs were, quite frankly, overwhelming. The volume threatened to paralyze us.

Guided by David, Brenda, Ernestina, and our wise Ghanaian medical colleagues, our team's collective response was to stop looking at the crowd and focus on the individual in front of us. This was not an easy task, but we set out each day determined to give our full attention to one person at a time, one prescription at a time, one dressing at a time, one hernia at a time, one painful tooth at a time, and one pair of reading glasses at a time. I had a professor in medical school who liked to say, "You are only as good as your last patient." This became a mantra for me every time the crowd would threaten to overwhelm me in Ghana (or during my emergency room shift at home).

No matter how busy we were and how long the line-ups were, teaching and transferring skills to the local health professionals remained a top priority. The team at NEA rolled up their sleeves and rallied behind us in every way they could: preparing healthy food for us, doing our laundry, praying for and encouraging us, providing us with security, drivers, translation, logistics support, and coffee—lots of coffee. The new dining hall sported an eighty-cup coffee percolator—which was always on! NEA cared for us with thoughtfulness and kindness, looking after our every need so that we could remain strong and focused on our work.

The year before, NEA and I had identified three significant priorities (noted in my rapidly growing collection of colourful Moleskine journals): "expand our dental program, provide diabetes care, and start an eye program." I was thrilled that our 2009 team was prepared to "begin" to collaborate on all three of these essential health issues. I say "begin" as these plans felt so small in the face of the enormous and complex health issues, but at least they were a start. As Antonia Machado once said, "Traveller, there is no path. The path is made by walking." And so, we began to walk.

When our kids were little, Graham met another father at nursery school drop-off. Dr. Kyle Chin was a local dentist who quickly became our friend, then our family dentist, and before you knew it, a dentist on our Ghana Health Team (Recruitment 101—Wilson style). When Kyle arrived in Ghana for the first time, the tribe honoured our dental team by officially adding a new word to the Deg language—"Nyina Doctor" which translates to "tooth doctor."

There is one dental patient that Kyle often speaks of. A woman from the nomadic Fulani tribe came to see him one day with a serious dental issue. It was a very difficult situation for Kyle to manage with his limited resources and he felt terrible for the suffering she had to endure. The next day, Kyle spotted this woman in his line-up and his heart sank. He knew there was nothing more he could do to help her. When her turn finally came, she did not want to sit in his dental chair. She had returned and waited for hours in the hot sun simply to stand before him and thank him. Kyle was at a loss for words, humbled.

Diabetes is also a serious problem in Ghana. Africa is the region with the highest proportion of undiagnosed diabetes, and 60 per cent of adults who are currently living with diabetes are unaware of their condition. People with diabetes are at increased risk of developing cardiovascular disease (CVD) which is a major cause of death and disability, and a serious barrier to sustainable development. Diabetes specialists in Ghana are few and far between. In 2017, only five certified endocrinologists served twenty-five million people, and they were all located in the major cities of Kumasi, Accra, and Cape Coast.

When one of my consultant colleagues at Markham Stouffville Hospital, who specialized in diabetes, asked to join our 2009 team, I was beyond thrilled. That year, Dr. Laila Bishara, an endocrinologist, was joined by returning nurse Cathy Fockler and pharmacist Martha Bailkowski, both Certified Diabetes Educators. On our very first morning in Ghana, before our devotions under the gazebo, our diabetes team poked the finger of every NEA member and their family to screen for diabetes. Seven cases of undiagnosed diabetes were discovered.

One individual, our friend and driver Simone, was an unexpected patient in our inaugural Carpenter Diabetes Clinic. Simone had been experiencing some blurry vision and lack of energy that he assumed were due to his long hours on the road shipping shea butter. He had no idea he had uncontrolled Type 2 diabetes. For the next two weeks, Simone received one-on-one dietary counselling, monitoring, and coaching from his personal endocrinologist, nurse, and pharmacist. I think he was relieved when we finally went home and his diabetic boot camp came to an end! Along with all of the new cases diagnosed that year, Simone was referred to the closest hospital for ongoing care. Our diabetes team spent time teaching at that hospital and helping them develop their program.

The final addition to our program in 2009 was eye care. Low vision is a barrier to development. If children cannot see, they cannot go to school. As vision starts to decline in middle-age, there are no reading glasses available. As a result, productivity, ability to earn an income, and quality of life diminish. Furthermore, we witnessed many injuries, such as finger amputations, that were simply a result of low vision. As with any need we identified over the years, it was hard to know where and how to begin. I had hoped to recruit some eye doctors to join us that year, but was unsuccessful. I was resigned that eye care would have to wait another year, but one of our nursing team members, Marion Hurlburt, felt otherwise.

Marion was fiercely determined to create a path that was not yet there. On her own initiative, she received training from friends in eastern Canada to run a reading glasses clinic in a low-resource setting. She liaised with the Uxbridge Lion's Club and our local optometry clinics, who responded enthusiastically by running a drive for eyeglasses. Marion cleaned, labelled, and packed 500 pairs of reading glasses into our hockey bags. During our two-week mission, Marion and her Ghanaian volunteer team gave out every pair of those reading glasses. The impact of improving vision for 500 patients was immeasurable. One man had not been able to read his Bible for many years due to declining eyesight. Marion fit him with new reading glasses, and he promptly pulled out his tiny pocket Bible and sat there reading for hours. One woman, a fifty-five-year-old seamstress by trade, struggled to earn an income due to her low vision. With a simple pair of reading glasses, she could resume her work and earn revenue for her family. It was an excellent beginning.

Along with our medical, dental, diabetes, and eye programs, our surgical program also got off to a strong start. With all the equipment on-site from the previous year, the team began operating immediately. Before our arrival, NEA worked with the local medical personnel to screen, list, and prepare 200 hernia patients. Busses were sent to remote villages to collect the patients two days before their surgeries, and they were housed and cared for in the local school. After their surgeries, NEA transported them back to their villages and followed up with patients to document any complications. It was a complex program, but because of NEA's exceptional organizational skills the team was able to operate on about twenty patients each day. They even had time for unexpected emergencies, such as abscesses that needed to be drained and severe burns requiring debridement. Burns were an unfortunate health issue that came to our attention that year. Cooking is done on outdoor fire pits that children play around. This was a definite opportunity for NEA to provide preventative education.

Joining Professor Kingsnorth on the surgical team in 2009 was a man named Mr. Magdi Hanafy. Magdi, a tall and physically imposing man, is an experienced general and vascular surgeon born in Egypt and now practicing in Manchester, England. He had travelled worldwide with Operation Hernia, but was thrilled to be in Carpenter for the first time. It did not take long for me to see what a huge heart this gentle giant had. He wore a smile that engulfed his entire face.

One of Magdi's hernia patients stands out in my memory: a 104-year-old man with a hernia that was so "gigantous" (our definition of a cross between gigantic and enormous) that he could no longer walk. Our surgeons deliberated over what to do. Typically, one would not operate on a man of this age. However, he was otherwise in excellent health and was suffering greatly from this hernia. The patient assured Magdi that it would be okay with him if he died on the table. He would gladly take the chance if it meant he could live without pain and disability from this hernia. The surgery took place.

On our single day off that year, Magdi and the team faced an unexpected emergency. Mr. George Yeboah, the Director of NEA's agriculture sector, was in a motorcycle accident on his way to church. He suffered an injury to his leg, severing a major tendon that joined his quadricep muscle to his kneecap. Without a tendon repair, his leg would be useless. Thankfully, Magdi was experienced in this type of surgery and was able to successfully fix his leg, allowing George to walk again.

Another physician new to our team in 2009 was Dr. Charles Peniston. Charlie is a cardiothoracic surgeon with a famously contagious laugh who wasn't sure if his skill set could be of use in Ghana. He had a strong desire to contribute globally, but recognized that cardiac surgery was not something that would be done in Northern Ghana any time soon. I remember Charlie promising me he would study general medicine all year if he could join our team in Ghana. Sure enough, on the overnight flight to Ghana, while stretching my legs at 3:00 a.m., I found Charlie studying a textbook on Tropical Dermatology under his small overhead light. That moment spoke to how committed he was to the work he was about to undertake. It also foreshadowed something genuinely remarkable that was about to unfold.

On our first day in the villages that year, we began to notice a strange pattern. We were seeing many kids with similar-appearing round sores on their legs. We had never seen these before, and our physician team continued to see similar lesions in all the villages we visited. Consulting with Ernestina, our local colleagues, and Charlie's Tropical Dermatology textbook, we began to wonder if these ulcers could be Yaws. It seemed impossible as Yaws was said to be eradicated in Ghana.

"It is often said that Yaws is found where the road ends," says Dr. Nana Konama Kotey, Programme Manager at the National Buruli Ulcer Control and Yaws Eradication Program, Ghana Health Service. "It primarily affects people in poor communities where access to basic health care is limited."

Yaws is a chronic, disfiguring, and debilitating childhood infectious disease. It is caused by spiral bacteria of the Treponema genus, which also causes syphilis. It mainly affects children under the age of fifteen and those in poor, remote communities. Yaws was one of the first diseases targeted for eradication in the 1950s and today there are only fifteen countries currently known to still be endemic for the disease. In 2009, the prevalence of Yaws in Ghana was only at 0.681

per cent, and so the health care professionals we worked with had never seen it, except in textbooks. Concerned that we had uncovered an unusually high prevalence of Yaws in this region, we kept medical records and photos of eighty-one cases we found from different villages. After our departure, NEA sent a report to the Regional Director of Medical Services. They were so shocked by our data that they sent surveillance teams into these remote villages and confirmed the sores were, indeed, Yaws. As a result, public health teams were sent to undertake mass eradication treatment.

Yaws eradication became an unexpected priority, but we still maintained our goal of focusing on one individual at a time, like David's critically ill nephew Joshua. The day we transported him back to the NEA compound, we were full of trepidation, knowing he was unlikely to survive. Although we had no oxygen supply, our anesthetist, Dr. Perry Board, suggested that we could use his oxygen concentrator to convert room air into oxygen to support Joshua's breathing. We were beginning to appreciate how valuable the collaboration between our medical and surgical program was. We moved Joshua to the surgical ward and, under the watchful eye of our physician and nursing team who made rounds on him day and night for five days, Joshua finally began to improve. He required less and less oxygen, he began to eat, and then his precious little smile returned. What a celebration we had when that little boy was finally discharged home, with his grateful parents Peter and Lydia by his side!

Those who have met David know that he is a master storyteller. Over the years, his stories often helped me to understand the concepts and lessons that were simply too hard to wrap my North American brain (and heart) around. When he told this particular tale about a small child and a starfish, it really helped me process and gain perspective on all that had taken place on this 2009 mission:

> One day a man was walking along the beach when he noticed a child picking some things up and gently throwing them into the ocean. Approaching the child, he asked, "What are you doing?" The youth replied, "Throwing starfish back into the ocean. The surf is up, and the tide is going out. If I don't throw

> them back, they'll die." "Child," the man said, "don't you realize there are miles and miles of beach and hundreds of starfish? You can't make a difference. It is hopeless. What you are doing does not matter!" After listening politely, the child bent down, picked up another starfish, and threw it back into the surf. Then, smiling at the man, he said, "It matters to that one."

David bent down and pretended to pick up a starfish and throw it back into the ocean. He did this over and over again, all the while smiling and saying:

> "It matters to our chief driver Simone."
> "It matters to the man who can now read his Bible."
> "It matters to George who can now walk."
> "It matters to the Fulani woman with the painful tooth."
> "It matters to the 104-year-old hernia patient."
> "It matters to each child with a Yaws ulcer."
> "It matters to my brother Peter."
> "It matters to my nephew Joshua."

He went on and on, with a crack in his voice, naming individual lives that had been impacted by our mission as our tears began to fall. If that wasn't enough, David reminded us that making a difference in one life impacts an entire family's life, which impacts an entire community, and so on. He thanked us for compassionately picking up one starfish at a time to offer it life and, in doing so, helping NEA bring health and hope to an entire region.

For me, 2009 was when I realized that this mission would bring me a gift I had not expected—lifelong friends who were becoming like brothers and sisters to me. That year also taught me some very important lessons. I learned that when individual human beings give their best-but-imperfect offerings to other human beings who are requesting their help, a tangible difference can be made in this big, hurting world.

I also learned an important spiritual lesson that year. On the day of George's motorcycle accident, we all attended the Bamboi Church, where Pastor Jacob gave the sermon. At one point, he began to wave his white handkerchief and said, "We have heard about the Christ, and we have read stories about the Christ. But when you are here, we see the Christ in our midst." I have reflected on that statement many times since and been challenged as to how it applies to my life and the life of the local and global church. With those words, Jacob took a black and white teaching of the Christian faith that I had never truly comprehended and caused it to explode in full colour. I now understood what Teresa of Avila meant when she said:

> Christ has no body now but yours. No hands, no feet on earth but yours. Yours are the eyes through which he looks compassion on this world. Yours are the feet with which he walks to do good. Yours are the hands through which he blesses all the world. Yours are the hands, yours are the feet, yours are the eyes, you are his body. Christ has no body now on earth, but yours.

This understanding added depth, purpose, and meaning to my work. It also provided answers to many of my questions. The critically difficult moments that were yet to come, became sacred.

On the last day of our mission, while we were gathered under the gazebo for our concluding staff devotions, Magdi's 104-year-old hernia patient walked in and sat down wearing a red Chicago Bulls hat. Translated by David, he gave one of the most powerful speeches I have yet to hear in Ghana. He explained to the team that he felt like a young man again and was free of pain. He wanted to thank us but had nothing of value to give. All he had was his tongue to speak. So, his thank you gift was to ask the Most High and Almighty God to bless our children. From that day forward, he wanted us to know that our children would be adopted members of his family.

We were sent home in grand fashion that year. The collection of eggs, chickens, guinea fowl, fruits, and vegetables given to us by many villages was most impressive. David was in his glory with the number of thank-you rams that were welcomed onto his compound. The Chief of Nyamboi penned us a beautiful letter saying, "To all who contributed in diverse ways to make the dream a reality, I say thank you, and may the Almighty replenish thou coffers abundantly." But the most touching thank you came from David's brother Peter—the father of Joshua. During another memorable banquet under the stars, prepared by our dear friend Abraham, Peter stood before us and sang a song of thanks for our team. Through his music, he thanked God for bringing our team specifically for his family—to repair his hernia and save his son Joshua. As a way of honouring our entire team, he announced that Joshua would now be known as my son and I would be known as his mother.

In the end, 5,000 patients received medical, dental, and eye care, and many more received basic treatment with acetaminophen, vitamins, and de-worming. One hundred and eighty-six patients received life-saving surgery for their hernias. The numbers say a lot about the remarkable 2009 team, but the numbers didn't matter to us. What mattered to us were the individual men, women, and kids—the starfish—who could now live stronger, healthier, more joyful lives because of NEA's continued presence among them. Significant challenges still existed, but we saw first-hand the powerful hope blossoming as poverty was alleviated and health restored for individuals, families, and communities. We were learning from our expert hosts that there are no short-cuts on the long road to sustainability. While I lacked clarity about the journey ahead, I was absolutely certain of one thing: stopping to care for the sick and the broken along the roadside was the right thing to do. I didn't want to leave anyone behind.

CHAPTER 11

The Work of Our Hands

"Vulnerability is the birthplace of innovation, creativity, and change."
~ Brené Brown

It really wasn't the first impression I'd been hoping for.

The year was 2010 and I was making a presentation to the Board of GRID's Directors. GRID stands for Ghana Rural Integrated Development, a Canadian charity which has partnered with NEA since 1983, supporting its vision of sustainability and integrated development in Northern Ghana. The list of accomplishments this partnership has achieved are many and diverse. Some of the most impressive include clean water for tens of thousands, food security for widows, chemical-free sustainable fishponds and waterways, scholarship endowments, innovations in farming and micro-enterprises, and the building of scores of health clinics, schools, and churches. Their efforts are perhaps best summed up by the first words found on their website (grid-nea.org):

Enabling People.
Transforming Communities.
For Good.

I was honoured to be asked to join their Board of Directors; this was my first official meeting. One of the reasons I had accepted the invitation was my belief that GRID understood how important it was for NEA to address determinants of health.

Health determinants, I had learned in medical school, are those factors that affect the holistic wellbeing of individuals and communities. They are not limited to physical health but include social and economic factors, the physical environment, and individual behaviour at all stages of life. They do not exist in isolation from each other. As the WHO Constitution puts it: "Health is a state of complete physical, mental and social wellbeing and not merely the absence of disease or infirmity."

The work of NEA and GRID focused on the whole person—their physical, mental, social, and spiritual needs, as well as their environment. They were manifesting an incredible version of the river story that my professor at McMaster University told my class on that first day of medical school. NEA's development sectors were like fences preventing people from falling into the river of ill health in the first place. The moral of that river story was that we, as downstream health care professionals, needed to link hands with upstream organizations in order to have the most significant impact. By joining the GRID Board, I felt I would be doing precisely that.

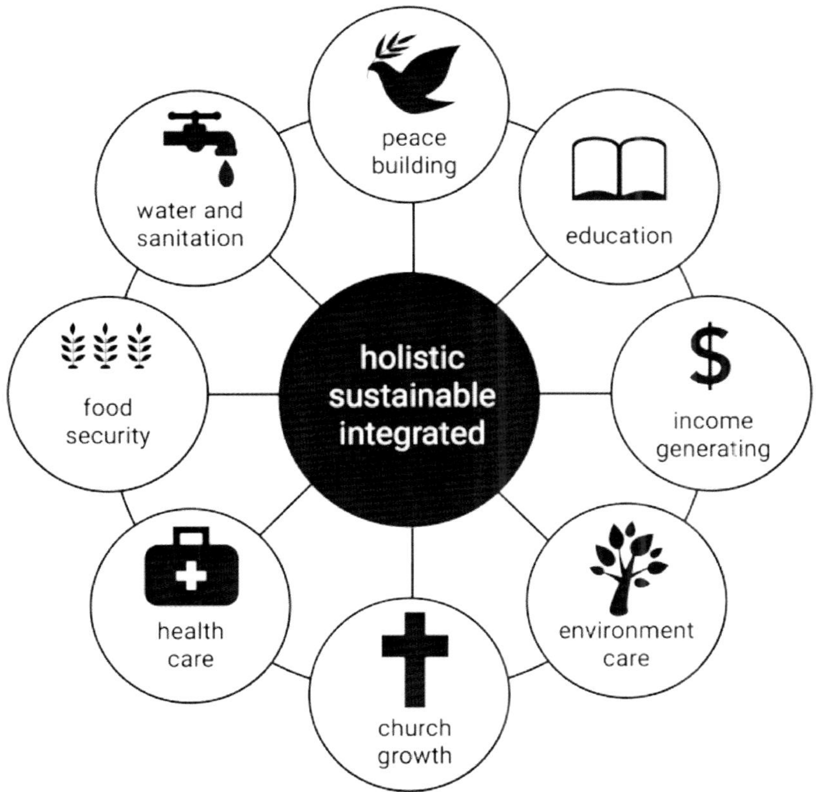

GRID's & NEA's Development Model

I had chosen my outfit carefully (I'm a big believer that important events deserve a thoughtful outfit). Graham had given me a pep talk as I walked out the door. Now, standing in front of the Board, I gave my report, showed pictures, told stories, and concluded with my observations: health needs were great, children under the age of five were dying at alarming rates, moms and babies were dying regularly in childbirth, and malaria was causing too many preventable and needless deaths.

After I concluded, David and Brenda, who were in attendance, gave their report and spoke about their vision for the next season of their ministry. David explained the incredible impact that delivering health care was having on the entire region's overall health. Curing diseases, restoring vision, repairing hernias, and treating pain was catalyzing development and health status was rising. David announced that he wanted the Ghana Health Team's work to be one of NEA's top three priorities. He wanted us to continue to grow our program, train more local health professionals, and help them plan for a sustainable health care solution.

When those words came out of David's mouth, the magnitude of this task hit me afresh. I felt a pit in my stomach, and I began to sweat. Health care planning and delivery were becoming one of NEA's top priorities?

At the time, Graham and I were genuinely running on all cylinders. Our kids were eleven, nine, seven, five, and five, and our household was a flurry of activity. I was a full-time family and emergency room physician in an under-serviced community. Between family, work, community, and church involvement, I was already feeling stretched. Consequently, I did my Ghana Health Team work in my spare time—usually late in the evening or during the night. I had no more time to give and not much gas left in the tank.

When Mr. Jacques Lapointe, the Chair of the Board, asked me to respond to David and Brenda's strategic direction, I could feel my emotions bubbling up. Undoubtedly, David and Brenda had not meant to put any undue pressure on me. Still, I was overwhelmed by so many things—the impact our mission was having, the great need and suffering that still existed in Ghana, the seemingly impossible vision before us all—and my lack of capacity to give more. It felt like a David and Goliath scenario. The giant was health inequity and I felt ill-equipped and inadequate to help NEA and GRID face it. I opened my mouth to respond, and I burst into tears.

In all fairness to me, I had worked all night in the ER before the Board meeting (terrible planning on my part). Nevertheless, tears continued to pour down my mascara-stained cheeks and drip onto my carefully chosen power outfit. By looking at the faces staring at me, I could tell that an outburst such as this was not commonplace around that highly polished boardroom table.

I thought of the quotation by Ziad K. Abdelnour: "Be strong enough to stand alone, smart enough to know when you need help, and brave enough to ask for it." I was not feeling strong, smart, or brave at that moment. Quite frankly, I was mortified. However, the Board got the message loud and clear from my not-so-subtle breakdown: I needed help.

Jacques made quite an impression on me that day. His business career in pharmaceuticals and biotech spanned over thirty-five years. He had held several top executive positions with global responsibilities. Jacques is also a man of faith. One of the things I appreciate the most about him is that he demonstrates so beautifully what I like to call the divine-human cooperative. In all things, he relies wholly on God and uses common sense, while rolling up his sleeves to do his part. He models a wonderful balance of faith, reason, and action.

Jacques was quick to acknowledge the enormity of the Mensahs' statement. He was equally quick to encourage me and assure me that I had the full support of the Board. He asked me to tell him exactly what help I needed to continue as the Ghana Health Team Leader and promised to do his best to mobilize it. Jacques and his wife Brigitte were so committed to this aspect of GRID's work that shortly after that Board meeting, they signed up as volunteers on our next Ghana Health Team.

The first thing I needed was administrative help. The back-room needs of planning this mission, operationalizing it, and equipping a large team of health professionals worldwide was the heaviest weight on my shoulders at that time. GRID found me the help I so desperately needed within a short time; her name was Lynnita Weber.

Lynnita was hired by GRID as a Program Manager and Senior Advisor, but part of her portfolio was to assist our health team. Lynnita is an international development professional who lived in Sudan, worked in Angola, and directed a multi-country relief program. She also happens to be Brenda's niece. Lynnita is the type of team member who knows what you need before you ask for it, and she became immediately committed to using her gifts and abilities to free me up so I could do what I do best—lead and inspire others towards our vision. Her contributions and the deep friendship we developed were a lifeline to me.

I also knew that I needed a leadership team. This mission's planning needs were mushrooming, as were the leadership needs on the ground when we were in Ghana. I had noticed in 2009 that I was being interrupted far too often while I was with patients. Thankfully, working in the emergency room trains you to think and act despite constant interruptions (as does having five kids). Still, too many interruptions can prevent us from giving good patient care. I needed other leaders on the ground who could problem-solve the issues that arose while running a clinic for thousands of people so that I could focus on the patient in front of me. I also knew that sharing the burden of leadership would allow me to lift my eyes up and off some of the day-to-day issues and on to the longer-term goals we were striving towards—capacity building and long-term sustainability. I had clarity as to what this leadership team would look like and who I wanted on it. The process of establishing a leadership team was easy, natural, and an absolute joy.

While Lynnita took charge of all our administrative and IT

needs, I asked a returning team member, Carol Smith-Romeril, to lead our Logistics and Operations. Carol was the Vice President of Patient Care at Ross Memorial Hospital in Lindsay, Ontario. She knew exactly how to run a health care organization, so overseeing the running of all of our clinics was right up her alley. Susan Fockler would continue to lead our pharmacy program and enlarge her team of pharmacists. Three nursing leaders would manage our complex nursing program: Betsy Convery, Margaret Van Dyck, and Joan Maguire. Kyle would continue to lead our dental team and Magdi was excited to take over as leader of our surgical program so Professor Kingsnorth could move on to establish new hernia programs in other parts of the world. Marion agreed to continue leading our eye program and I was on cloud nine that we had finally had an optometrist to join her!

Dr. Martin McDowell, an optometrist from Stouffville, Ontario, knew Brenda from their primary school days when they had attended a one-room school together. They had stayed in touch over the years and he decided the year 2010 was right for him to go to Ghana.

I vividly remember my first phone call with Martin. I had been praying for an optometrist to expand our eye program for three years. Martin was experienced and certainly had the skill set for the job. He informed me that he would come with us under one condition. I was ready to agree to almost anything to get eye care to Northern Ghana, but his request surprised me: "Can you guarantee that I will have fun?" he asked.

I thought I had misheard him. Fun? I remember thinking, "People's lives and vision are at stake, and you are worried about having fun? Seriously?"

Now, I'm not really known as the "fun" person in our family. Graham wins that title hands down with his quick wit and fantastic sense of humour. I am, however, made fun of, on a reasonably regular basis. Don't get me wrong. My family is very kind and respectful. Still, even I can appreciate that I provide no end of material worthy of a good tease: I always pronounce "chipotle" without the "l"; I wear a sun visor and fanny pack with far too much confidence; and I have an apparently unjustifiable belief in my ability to sing harmony. Also, I am your typical "Type A, somewhat intense, always-planning-for-the-worst-case-scenario" type of person. These types are not always that fun to be around. It truly is a hazard of my profession as an emergency room doctor where we see all the disasters. As careful as I am to leave work at work, it inevitably changes how you live, parent, and see the world.

A case in point occurred one evening at a Red Lobster restaurant in Toronto. We finished our meal and the server brought a tray of hard, round candies with our bill. She offered one to our five-year-old, Claudia, who promptly announced to the entire room, "That lady just offered me a choking hazard!" Claudia wanted to make a citizen's arrest. Let's just say, it's a good thing my children have two parents.

Having said all of that, I love to create fun for others. In our family, I am the planner of the parties and vacations. If any of us has a victory, however large or small, a celebratory dinner is planned, and the victor's meal is served on a "CELEBRATE" plate with me singing an out-of-tune version of "For She's/He's a Jolly Good Fellow." I love to entertain and host events (themed events are my favourite), especially for our large extended family. My all-time favourite event was Graham's fortieth birthday, which was a "Back to the 80s Bash"—DJ, dance party, and temporary-tattoo parlour included. Graham used to say to me, "Do you think you might be going a little overboard with this event?" He learned pretty quickly not to question Jenny's vision or budget when she is in event planning mode. I spent many summers directing a summer camp for kids and was even the social convenor for our medical school.

So, irritated by Martin's request and not sure about this first impression he was making, I found myself saying, "I'm all about fun! I promise, you will have the time of your life in Ghana!" I promptly made a note in my Moleskine journal "PLAN FUN," just in case I forgot. That was a crucial conversation. It turns out the good eye doctor may have shone a light on one of my blind spots as a leader.

One other critical event took place in the months before our November 2010 mission. In June of that year, The Muskoka G8 summit was held in Huntsville, Ontario. The G8 plays a leading role in international affairs. In partnership with the global community, it has helped gather significant resources to address critical global challenges. As President of the G8, Canada planned to champion a major initiative to improve maternal and child health in the world's most vulnerable regions. At the end of the summit, Canada committed $75 million to take a comprehensive and integrated approach to address maternal, newborn, and child health. They issued a call for funding for projects over $500,000 to address the leading diseases and illnesses that kill mothers and their children.

To say that this call for proposals caught our attention would be an understatement. The objectives were precisely in line with the needs we witnessed in Northern Ghana and the strategic direction that we all wanted to take. We thought of the woman who almost died of a postpartum hemorrhage in the Bamboi clinic because no oxytocin was available. We thought of Joshua, who nearly died of pneumonia.

Meanwhile, across the ocean, the Mensahs' daughter, Deborah Mensah, was in England completing a Diploma in Public Health from the prestigious London School of Hygiene and Tropical Medicine. During her studies, she read about a successful program in Bangladesh to reduce child mortality run by a physician who is now at The Hospital for Sick Children in Toronto. Having witnessed the needless paediatric deaths while growing up in Ghana, Deborah's interest was piqued. She connected with her professors who had already carried out a similar trial in Ghana. Deborah reviewed the preliminary results in 2010 and suggested to her mom and dad that NEA was well-positioned to implement a similar program in Northern Ghana if they could find some funding.

We knew it was a long shot. The G8 summit would select only a handful of Canadian organizations. We would be up against big actors in the development world. We felt like minnows in the big sea of international development organizations.

Brenda, Lynnita, and Deborah began to work on a proposal, but knew that we would require data to make our submission even more competitive. We needed to prove the health needs in Northern Ghana, but there was very little data coming out of that region. We needed to translate our anecdotal evidence into concrete statistics. We also needed to demonstrate that we could measure the results of any program we implemented. Lynnita was experienced in research and data collection in low-resource settings, and so she arranged for us to use our Ghana Health Team medical records to collect data on our upcoming 2010 mission. She would add this to the application to the Muskoka Initiative as soon as we returned from our mission that year.

During my morning quiet times leading up to our fast-approaching 2010 mission, while praying for my team and the work of NEA, a particular Bible verse from Psalm 90:17 grabbed my attention and my heart:

> *May the favour of the Lord our God rest on us;*
> *establish the work of our hands for us—*
> *yes, establish the work of our hands.*

This verse resonated deeply within me and became a special prayer that I continue to pray regularly. We were embarking on some very serious business—our largest mission ever, a new optometry clinic, and an expanded teaching program. Now we were collecting data to obtain funding to reduce mothers' and babies' deaths. I continued to feel out of my league, but whenever my insecurities, inadequacies, or imposter syndrome crept in, this verse grounded me.

Armed with this beautiful prayer and the support of my family, the GRID Board, and my leadership team, I felt courageous and alive. My hands—open and outstretched—were ready.

CHAPTER 12

This Is Life

*"The only thing worse than being blind
is having sight but no vision."*
~ Helen Keller

Her mother brought her to our clinic because she was sick with a fever. Malaria was causing this usually playful toddler with Down syndrome to lie limp in her mother's arms and we needed to act fast. She was carried to our nursing station, where a rapid malaria test was done to confirm the diagnosis. At the same time, Joan effortlessly inserted an IV and our nursing team descended on her with fluid and acetaminophen, while a new pharmacist to our team, Sherry Doochenko, delivered injectable anti-malarial medications to the bedside.

Within an hour, this little girl was sitting up and asking for food. Our team's nurse practitioner Sandra Skerratt summoned me to the gazebo to reassess her. I was bothered by one persistent abnormality on her examination—there was something most unusual about her eyes. Each eye moved independently of the other. At first, I was concerned that this was a neurological complication of her malaria or even an atypical seizure; however, that no longer made sense as she ravenously ate from her little bag of rice. I suggested Ernestina ask the mother for more details about her unusual eye movements.

It was a short conversation. Ernestina translated, "She is blind."

Globally, one billion people live with blindness or vision loss that could have been prevented. That's around one in seven people in our world who would be able to see today if they had received glasses, surgery, or antibiotics for treatable eye conditions. In places like Ghana, access to any type of eye care is limited or non-existent. From an economic point of view, eliminating avoidable blindness is one of the most cost-effective ways of fighting poverty. For every dollar invested in blindness prevention, more than four dollars is returned in economic terms.

I tried to picture this little girl's future, growing up blind in Northern Ghana. I was quite sure that there were no resources for the blind and likely no opportunity for her to receive an education. I decided to send her to wait in the long lineup outside Marion's and Martin's eye clinic, just in case there was something they could do.

That particular year, in 2010, I was honoured that forty-nine teammates joined me in Ghana. Since the inception of the mission, I had hoped to bring along as many of my friends as possible, and this year was no exception. It wasn't as though I specifically went out and recruited my friends per se. Rather, as our team shared stories about our work in Ghana within our friendship circles, they caught the vision.

Jacques and Brigitte Lapointe from the GRID board arrived in Ghana one week ahead of our team to assist with the massive preparations required to host a group of fifty. On the eve of our departure, Jacques sent me an email: "The groceries are in (two days of open market shopping and two truckloads), the cow has been butchered, the cookies have been baked, the beds are ready, the translators have been briefed, the drivers are waiting in Accra, and that's just a brief sampling of the pages and pages of logistics in place to ensure that as many patients as possible are helped while you are here." He signed off by saying, "And because this is Africa, for every Plan A, there is a Plan B."

Ghana was ready, and so were we! As we gathered in Uxbridge Baptist Church's parking lot before departure, Rev. Dr. Dale Dawson shared from Psalm 139:9-10:

If I rise on the wings of the dawn,
if I settle on the far side of the sea,
even there your hand will guide me,
your right hand will hold me fast.

I was always an emotional wreck after saying goodbye to my kids, so those verses were a comfort to me. I invariably questioned my decision to leave them when I saw them weeping and clinging to their "mom's-going-to-Ghana-and-gave-us-this-in-case-she-doesn't-make-it-back" gift. That year I made them a no-sew tied fleece blanket with a special inscription. It was quite a feat for this non-crafty mother—I'm good at sewing up human beings but can't darn a sock. My kids use those blankets around the campfire pit to this day.

We landed safely in Accra and were welcomed by the Minister of State from the Office of the President, who waved us and our 7,000 pounds of luggage through Customs. An African band played beautiful music while the baggage was loaded onto the NEA trucks. We began to sweat. Two team members—Charlie and one of our pharmacists, Karen Monaghan—promptly started dancing, much to the local crowd's delight. After a short sleep in the hotel, the Department of National Defense escorted us on our twelve-hour journey to Carpenter. The three waving flags and all our friends at NEA were waiting for us on the compound's immaculate grounds. Hugging was not part of the Ghanaian culture, but we were all so genuinely happy to be together that suddenly, without any discussion, hugs were being given and received without a second thought. After the formalities of the welcoming ceremony were over, the children swarmed me. "Dr. Jen-i-fa, you have returned!" "Dr. Jen-i-fa, how is Canada?" "Dr. Jen-i-fa, my favourite subject is mathematics!" "Dr. Jen-i-fa, did you bring any toffee?" My "arrival to-do list" forgotten, the kids and I sat together and had a visit. As I crawled under my familiar mosquito net to sleep that night, I noted in my Moleskine journal that Carpenter was starting to feel like a second home.

The next day, after our traditional first-morning devotions, the team was summoned to the chief's palace, where we were formally greeted once again by Chief Solomon, and I gave my first speech of the mission. After breakfast, while the team of veterans set up for our staff clinic and prepared our operating theatres, we sent most of the first-time team members on a one-hour tour of the development compound with David. Our rookies returned about three hours later, wide-eyed and in awe of all that NEA was accomplishing. They also appreciated how our mission would fit into the larger development context.

Before we began our NEA staff clinic, a contingent of elders from the village arrived with a carload of yams, a white ram, and words of gratitude. It felt peculiar to be recipients of such generosity before we had actually done anything. We hit the ground running, and Charlie was soon consumed with a tragic case involving a young man with necrotizing fasciitis or "flesh-eating disease." By the end of that first day, 260 staff members and their families had been treated, and seventeen hernia surgeries had been completed. Our day ended with a visit from David's mother, Abena Fulamuso, who had arrived from her village of Jugboi to greet us. She was a tiny woman who had never left Mo Land, yet she spoke with a passion and eloquence that moved me deeply. She ended her speech by saying, "Before you were born, you were all destined to be my sons and daughters."

The timing of David's mother's comment was noteworthy, as the next day was the second of November, the day I was born. While Magdi and his surgical team were left behind to operate on the compound, the rest of us headed to Nyamboi village, where about 1,500 people attended my "fortieth birthday party."

I was dreading going to Nyamboi village that year, and it had nothing to do with turning forty. I was afraid to find out the fate of a little boy I had met the year before. He was about nine years old, and his father was the village linguist and a teacher in the elementary school. The boy had had a healthy childhood, but a few months before our last mission, he became so weak that he could no longer hold up his head, swallow, or even walk. Ernestina and I spent time trying to understand what could be attacking this boy's nervous system and wondered if it was a progressive neurological condition, such as muscular dystrophy. It was a heartbreaking case. We explained to his father that his illness was severe, and the only hope of finding the correct diagnosis would be to send him to the capital city. I waited while Ernestina and the father had an intense discussion.

To my shock, Ernestina turned to me with a smile and said, "They will go."

I wanted to be sure he knew how serious this was and that even after making the long and costly trip to Accra, there still might not be a cure.

After Ernestina translated my concern, the father looked at his son with tears in his eyes. Then, this linguist who had such a command of language said simply, "We must go. This is life."

Ernestina bowed her head and quietly stated, "By all means. By all means." I was too choked up to say anything.

As we approached the chief and elders of Nyamboi village who were waiting to greet us, I spotted the linguist and my nervousness heightened. I was sure his child had died and that a great deal of money had been spent chasing his cure.

He smiled at me from ear to ear and shook my hand. "My son is well!"

My breath caught in my throat as he beckoned to a robust, healthy boy who began running towards us.

Ernestina, remembering the father's words from the year before, leaned in and whispered in my ear, "This is life."

It was a hot and gruelling day of work in the village, but it ended with a special patient. He was a boy of about eleven years who was part of the Fulani tribe—an impoverished, nomadic tribe in Northern Ghana who are expert cattle farmers (often referred to as cattle whisperers) and expert jewellery makers. Although very poor, the girls and women wear clothing and beautiful handmade beaded necklaces, earrings, and bracelets. They speak their own language and do not understand any of the languages of Ghana. The translation was always a challenge for us. Often, we would need a two- or three-step process to finally translate their language into English. The children are not educated, and the girls marry very young, often at just fourteen or fifteen. It is a harsh life for these children, and they face many health issues. Discriminated against and marginalized by many in Ghanaian society, NEA was keen to address the needs of the adolescents in this tribe.

Upon hearing that our team would be in Nyamboi village, this smart and resourceful young boy took it upon himself to find a way to get to our health team. He waited in line all day on his own and finally landed in Dr. Lorna Adams' chair. After Lorna completed her consultation and examination, she sent him to our pharmacy to collect the medications he would need for his ailments.

Meanwhile, the hour was getting late, and we needed to get on the road to be home before dark. While the boy was waiting at the pharmacy, Carol and the NEA leaders decided to close up the clinic and ask the remaining patients to return the next morning for their medications. This Fulani boy quickly tracked down his doctor, Lorna, and explained that he would be unable to return tomorrow. He and his herd would be many miles from Nyamboi by then. Without a thought, Lorna commenced "Operation Cowboy," convincing our logistics team that we could not leave unless her "cowboy" got his medicine. She must have given a convincing argument, as our entire team's departure from the village was put on hold for the sake of this one child. The pharmacy team, nurses, and Lorna quickly unpacked bags and got this boy the medication he needed, carefully counselling him on how to take it. As our bus pulled out of the village, we watched the young cowboy secure his medicine in his waist pouch, turn to wave at us, then disappear barefoot into the thick bush where his herd was waiting for him.

At dinner that evening, Magdi, in his new role as our lead surgeon, gave our medical team an update. Their theatres were equipped with bright new lights (we were jealous) and brand-new air-conditioning units (we were very jealous). To avoid confusion between the two theatres, they had renamed them David Theatre and Brenda Theatre in honour of NEA's founders. Magdi was grinning from ear to ear as he reported that his team had successfully operated on twenty hernias that day, with no surgical or anaesthetic complications. He was so pleased that we had two anaesthetists that year: Dr. Ira Bloom from Canada had joined our veteran anaesthetist, Dr. Perry, and our anaesthetic program was becoming more and more sophisticated. We quickly realized how important it was to have two doctors skilled in anaesthesia. If one was down with diarrhea (a condition we fondly referred to as DWD), surgeries could continue. Furthermore, administering anaesthesia in our rustic facility required courage, creativity, and adaptability. In our setting, two heads were definitely better than one for this critical role on which our entire surgical program depended.

After dinner, Abraham made a surprise appearance in the dining hall carrying a big chocolate birthday cake with candles. Dessert is not usually part of Ghanaian cuisine, but he made his first chocolate cake in honour of my birthday. I was so touched. When I finally wrapped up my duties for the night, I tried to reach Graham and the kids, but there was no cell coverage to be found, despite me wandering around waving my arm in the air, willing a small bar of coverage to appear.

Alone in my room, a wave of nostalgia and longing for my family washed over me. I sat alone in my little space in Africa. What a contrast to Graham's fortieth "Back to the 80s" theme party. Then I noticed a piece of folded foolscap paper sitting on my bed. It was a two-page, handwritten birthday message from Brenda. In it, she, like Pastor Dale, shared a Psalm that is still marked in my Bible with the words "40th birthday." Of course, it was from Psalm 40:

> *Many, Lord my God,*
> *are the wonders you have done.*
> *The things you planned for us*
> *no one can recount to you;*
> *were I to speak of them,*
> *they would be too many to declare.*

In this Ghanaian birthday card, she reminded me of the many blessings that I had experienced in my first forty years: my family, my friends, my education, my best friend Graham, my five healthy kids, and my vocation, to name a few. She recounted some of the wonders that had taken place since the day she, David, and I sat in those three sacred chairs: four missions, a growing group of international health care partners rallying around our cause, an expanding medical, surgical, dental, and teaching program, and now, an eye program. She reminded me of the many challenges we had faced together—like the surgical container stuck in the port. She listed some of the lives saved—Joshua, the hernia patients, the kids with malaria. She concluded by saying that she was excited about the wonders we would speak of on my fiftieth birthday, and her hopes that Graham and the children would have made a visit to Ghana by then. It was a lovely birthday gift from a woman who knew only too well the loneliness of being so far from home and family. By reflecting on God's faithfulness and the blessings of the past, and then choosing to look to the next decade with great hope and anticipation, I settled in, content and at peace under my mosquito net. Those sheets of foolscap were worth far more than any fancy card or gift that money could buy (not that there was anywhere one could buy a fancy card or gift even if one wanted to).

Returning to Yaara filled us with excitement, as we knew that adventure was always waiting. That year, the "short cut" (three-hour drive) was not available, so we packed our overnight bags and took the "long cut" for another sleepover in the village. Staying over meant that we could work longer days, not being limited by travel.

Yaara always welcomed us with great flair. The entire village gathered in a circle around the village drummers and all the gifts they wished to present to us. As we prepared to greet the chief and elders, I reminded my teammates of the most important protocol of keeping their left hand behind their back and shaking with their right hand. As I approached Chief Joseph with my right hand extended, I was shocked when he jumped up and gave me a big hug with both arms!

On that first day, we were able to see all the patients who came to the clinic—no one was turned away. One large group had arrived from a far-off village by canoe. One man travelled on foot for days, as he heard that there was an eye doctor with us. He was losing his vision, and Martin quickly discovered that he had acute angle-closure glaucoma in both eyes. His eye pressures were four times more than normal. Glaucoma is the second leading cause of blindness in the world, according to the World Health Organization. Ghana has the highest prevalence of Glaucoma in Africa and the second in the whole world. Glaucoma has been nicknamed the "silent thief of sight" because there are usually no symptoms or pain associated with its onset, and the loss of vision typically occurs gradually over a long period. By the time it is recognized, the disease is usually quite advanced.

With no surgical options to treat glaucoma in the North, our eye team provided eye drops and oral medicine to lower his eye pressure. By the next morning, his pressures were down to almost normal, and he was out of danger. Martin predicts he would have been blind in three days without treatment. Due to the generosity of Canadian pharmaceutical companies, we provided him with an ample supply of costly glaucoma eye drops. Martin was able to refer him to the teaching hospital with extra funds raised by our team. "The blind will see" took on additional spiritual meaning for many eye patients like this man; the eye clinic was held in the local church, underneath a massive wall mural of Jesus Christ who gazed over Martin's consultation station. Martin, however, was troubled by the amount of irreversible blindness caused by glaucoma that he had seen in just six days.

Other Yaara highlights included bucket baths, seeing again the majesty of stars in an unpolluted sky, a village tour, and a big bonfire party. The women of Yaara taught our women a traditional dance, which we tried our best to learn as the village drummers willed us to find the correct rhythm. Charlie and Karen won the prize for most enthusiastic and "creative" dancers—titles they would keep for many, many years. At the closing celebration, I had the extraordinary honour of being introduced to some "baby Jennifers" born to women with infertility before being treated by the 2009 health team. Peter and Lydia presented our team with yams and a guinea fowl to thank us for saving Joshua's life the year before. I held him—my Ghanaian son—on my hip while his father gave a moving speech.

When Sunday finally arrived, we were more than ready for a day of rest. There was no way to sustain our performance and remain resilient under pressure unless we had some time to refresh our minds and bodies. We slept in and, after a leisurely breakfast of porridge, omelettes, fresh fruit, and Tim Hortons' coffee, made our traditional visit to the Bamboi Church. We were challenged by Pastor Jacob Mensah to consider our life and, in all things, love one another and push ourselves beyond what makes us happy. As I looked around at my teammates—my friends—from Canada, UK, and Ghana, it was clear that they were doing just that. They were visiting the sick, relieving suffering, advocating for widows, and giving sight to the blind amid their own sweat, tears, diarrhea, insect bites, and personal sacrifice. They were going way beyond personal happiness; this mission was a powerful demonstration of love on so many levels.

The rest of the day was spent napping, reading, playing games and sports, and just having some good 'ol fashioned fun. Some of us were DWD, but after a day's rest and a visit from our team doctor,

John, we bounced back to good health.

Our medical, surgical, eye, and dental teams were refreshed and ready to face week two on Monday morning. At breakfast, Kyle made an announcement that he needed our help to recruit dental patients. He suggested we ask our patients if they were having dental pain and explained that dental pain is translated as "caca." In Canada, "caca" is baby talk or a slang way of referring to excrement or poop. And so, all day long, the call for "caca?", "caca?" rang out through our clinics, which, quite embarrassingly, hit a funny bone for many of us. We finally had to explain to our translators what was making us laugh, and of course, they too joined in with the laughter. I found it interesting how a little low-brow humour (my husband's favourite kind) could co-exist in a healthy equilibrium with serious and often heartbreaking work.

Over the next week, our four female physicians spent a great deal of our time running a "rapid assessment gynecology clinic." With no family physicians or gynaecologists accessible to Northern Ghana's women, they brought all their issues to us. Taking a standard gynaecological history requires taking a pregnancy history from each woman. We ask them how many pregnancies they had, how many miscarriages or abortions, how many premature babies, and how many live babies.

It didn't take long for us to notice a concerning trend. Almost every woman we interviewed had lost at least one child—most had lost multiple children. Their pain was raw and palpable as they spoke of their babies' and children's deaths, lost souls that lived on in their memories. The causes of death were not a surprise to us. Most of them died of the very things we were treating in our clinics: diarrhea, malaria, and pneumonia. We also discovered that many of these babies died at birth. I understood that neonatal and child mortality was high in this region, but until this mission, I had never processed the impact of these deaths from a mother's point of view. I noted this sombre finding in my journal.

On our second last day, our travelling medical clinic was supposed to take place at the Carpenter village school. The two big trucks carrying all the team supplies and equipment were loaded and ready to depart when word came back from the NEA logistics team that there was a "small-small" problem at the school. It was no longer available to us.

A last-minute change of plans was something that we were learning to anticipate and expect. Someone on the team coined the phrase "TIA" for unexpected situations like this. TIA stands for a transient ischemic attack or mini-stroke; however, on our Ghana mission, TIA stood for "This Is Africa." It was a quick way of reminding ourselves that our first response to a change of plan or disruption should be one of acceptance and adaptability.

I wasn't always privy to why plans changed in Ghana or what the "small-small" problems were, but that did not matter. Our hosts knew best, and they didn't want to burden us with details that were out of our control. Our role was to be ready to pivot on a dime when NEA made the request. Within an hour, Carol, our chief logistician, and the NEA volunteers had created a Plan B for our clinic. They began to unload the trucks—the clinic would be held on the NEA compound.

Spending our final two working days on the NEA compound turned out to be a game-changer. Efficiencies were maximized as we had access to power, running water, and more volunteers. We also had greater control of the crowds, as the compound was gated. Our productivity was further improved as we had no travelling to endure, plus we had all the comforts of the compound (such as bathrooms instead of pit latrines). We even had electricity and air conditioning in our main clinic area, which housed our physician consult area and pharmacy. We had more time for teaching. Our work was invigorated by the proximity to NEA staff and our surgical team. Patients were excited about Plan B as well—being granted access to the grounds of the famous NEA facility was a privilege indeed.

It was wonderful for me to experience our surgical program up-close-and-personal during those final two days. I finally watched a hernia surgery from start to finish, and could really appreciate the incredible skill and dedication of this excellent team of surgeons, nurses, and volunteers. By mission's end, Magdi's team had completed a record number of 206 surgeries, a feat made more amazing by the fact that two surgeons, due to arrive mid-mission, had had to cancel their travel plans at the last minute. TIA.

Our final clinic day arrived, and it was a big one. Knowing it was our last day in Ghana, patients came from far and wide. We started early and worked until long after the sun went down. At the very end of the day, I happened to glance across the room at my colleague, Lorna. I expected to see a look of relief that our work was almost done; however, the expression on her face sent a chill up my spine. I recognized that look—I had seen it before, and I had felt it too many times to count. It was a look of anguish as she and Ernestina counselled a visibly pregnant woman, accompanied by a toddler, with a new diagnosis of HIV.

This pattern—facing a particularly challenging or difficult case right at the end of our mission—would be repeated over and over again on our missions yet to come. At one point, I remember asking God why we had to end our work on such a tragic note instead of a positive one. I never got my answer, but reflecting on it now, I firmly believe it was His way of keeping us humble. These cases prevented us from becoming proud of our accomplishments and reminded us that, although our work was done for the moment, there was much more to be done.

As we wrapped up our mission and dined under the stars, we were entertained by a team of very unique, traditional Ewe dancers (soon joined by Charlie and Karen, of course). As I went to sleep on my last night in Ghana, my head and heart swirled with many thoughts and emotions. Magdi expressed it well in his final mission report: "The life of both providers and recipients of care will never be the same again."

This certainly was true for our little patient with the dancing eyes. She was seen in our eye clinic, where the team of Martin, Marion, Jacques, and Brigitte gave her and her mother VIP treatment. Martin quickly determined that this little girl was not completely blind after all. Rather, her vision was so impaired that her eyes appeared to be "dancing" because they were constantly trying to focus. By a miracle, in the database of 3,000 pairs of eyeglasses, Brigitte found a tiny pair of children's eyeglasses that were a perfect strength and a perfect fit. When the eyeglasses (donated by an unknown family in Uxbridge) were placed on her, the little girl froze, looked up, eyes aligned, and saw her mother for the first time. She began to stroke her mother's tear-streaked face over and over again. Then, she looked down at her wiggling fingers and began to giggle uncontrollably at them—ten playthings she hadn't realized she had. The mother returned to my desk weeping with gratitude for the gift of sight her daughter had been given. Her eyes were finally at rest, but the dance was just beginning.

Magdi's conclusion was certainly true for me as well. This mission forced me to think deeply about the value of human life. It began with my reflections on my milestone birthday and the gift of my life that my mother gave me. Adding to the mixture of my thoughts and emotions was David's mother's speech about us being her sons and daughters, the linguist's "this-is-life" response to his dying boy, and my reunion with Joshua and his family. I thought about the baby Jennifers and the lives they would live. I thought about the toddler with dancing eyes who could now see her mother, and I thought about Lorna's cowboy. I thought about Charlie's young patient with flesh-eating disease whose life, without a miracle, would soon be over. But it was witnessing the pain etched on the faces of countless mothers as they listed their deceased children that haunted me. We would listen in respectful silence to the women recounting the details of their child's death: a beautiful name, a tender age, and a description of an unimaginable circumstance. When the translator concluded, there would be a grief-filled hush. Then, to our horror, the same mother would begin again with the details of another child. This memory ignited my musings. Every mother's nightmare—losing a child—was a reality for most women I had met that year. How was that possible? My experiences affirmed my belief that every life is of value, every life matters, and every life is worth fighting for.

As I nestled into my seat on the plane, relieved that my teammates were safely on their way home to their loved ones, Martin approached. In the way that the sombre and the joyful often went hand in hand in our work, he bent down to whisper in my ear before moving on. "You were right. I did have fun. Let's do it again next year."

I was unable to suppress a fist pump to which the stranger beside me responded with a pleasant, if curious, thumbs-up. I settled in for the long journey home. Our vision of a preferable future for Ghana's people was slowly coming into greater focus, and I couldn't wait to see what would happen next.

CHAPTER 13

Arise and Come Forth

Emergency: the emerging of something unexpected; from the Latin word emergere meaning "arise, bring to light" and emerge meaning "I arise or come forth. I emerge. I surface."

My passion for emergency medicine has only grown stronger since the terrible motor vehicle crash that I witnessed when I was a young lifeguard. After twenty-two years in the Uxbridge Emergency Room (ER), I still look forward to every shift with the amazing team I am privileged to be part of. Working in a rural ER is not for the faint of heart. We do not have the same human resources as larger hospitals do, yet we must be prepared for anything and everything.

Rural ER physicians need to be comfortable with what we call "HALO procedures"—HALO stands for High Acuity Low Opportunity which refers to life-threatening procedures that are rarely performed. We rely heavily on teamwork—our nurses, administrative clerks, lab and x-ray technicians all play key roles during moments of crisis. We also rely on our physician colleagues to drop everything and rush in from home to assist us when extra help is needed. My work in the ER equips me to better care for my family medicine patients and the practice of family medicine makes me better equipped as an ER physician. It is a wonderful synergy. To this day, I still spend most of my continuing education and conference time staying up-to-date with the vast, exciting, and ever-changing field of emergency medicine.

In 2011, after my first decade in the ER, I felt it was time to refresh my knowledge and skills, so I decided to prepare for and sit my Emergency Medicine (EM) certification examination. I had been trained as a family physician, but back in 2000, when I graduated, rural family physicians had a broad scope of practice and were expected to do everything: run our family practices, deliver babies, cover the emergency room, look after hospitalized patients, and make visits to palliative patients in the community. We had no specialty training, so we learned through trial by fire and relied heavily on our nurses and senior colleagues to mentor us.

The College of Family Physicians of Canada allows family physicians who have logged a certain number of years in the ER, and who are recommended by peers, to bypass an emergency medicine residency program and challenge the certification examination. If successful, dual credentialing in family medicine and emergency medicine is granted. It wasn't the certificate or the EM initials beside my name that I was after—I simply wanted to ensure that I was as well-trained as possible when my community members' lives depended on me. And so, while pulling together our largest mission yet, my dining room was transformed into my study hall and I spent many late nights preparing. Graham always kept a big pot of coffee brewing.

The expansion of our international health team in 2011 was all due to word of mouth. We were our own version of the iconic Faberge Organics commercial of the '80s "…and they told two friends and so on and so on." In 2011, two-thirds of our team had been on at least one previous mission and the newcomers joining our team were our friends and colleagues. Kyle brought along his best friend, Dr. Joe Chong, who is an emergency doctor in Vancouver. Dr. Sarah Barclay brought along her friends Mary Lovatt, Dr. Kirsten Lindner, and Dr. Gillian Brakel. Susan brought along our first pharmacy technician Cathy Wright, her physician colleague Dr. Rob Drury, and his wife Elena who was an experienced nurse. Magdi brought the surgical nurses he worked with in the UK. And so on and so on and so on.

Along with our growing mission came a larger budget and a greater need for fundraising. As our departure date approached, despite all my efforts, we were still $40,000 shy of meeting our target. I started to panic and came up with a desperate idea to cash in our kids' registered education savings plans (RESPs). I wasn't sure how Graham would react to the idea of using the money we had been slowly setting aside towards our kids' post-secondary education since we first became parents. I remembered the lesson I learned during the infamous double diaper change—the importance of good timing when planning a crucial conversation with one's spouse. So, I began to strategize how I would present my bright idea to Graham.

One afternoon I was sitting in my car in Mississauga, Ontario, about to endure a mock test in preparation for my big emergency medicine exam. I was planning on bringing up my RESP idea that night and I was not feeling good about my plan. I'm not sure why it didn't occur to me sooner, but I decided to pray about it. While I was praying to God about our budget shortfall, my phone rang. On the phone was Bert Dekkema from the Jericho Foundation. Unbeknownst to me, my neighbour Richard Muir and his family administered this Christian charitable foundation. They had heard about our work and Bert wondered if we might have any financial needs that the Jericho Foundation could help with.

Barely refraining from looking over my shoulder for the hidden camera, I explained to Bert that I was sitting in my car, praying to God about my $40,000 shortfall, trying to figure out how to persuade my husband to cash in our kids' educational fund when his call came. He laughed, asked a few questions, and promised to get back to me in a few days. I hung up the phone and promptly burst into tears. Next time, perhaps, I would remember to pray before implementing a terrible idea.

I was quite a sight as I walked in late for my mock exam with red eyes and mascara running down my face. My study mate, Dr. Mary Johnston, who flew in from Ottawa, thought I was crumbling under the stress of it all and gave me a reassuring hug. I told her about my phone call and she casually mentioned that she wanted to join me in Ghana one day. I noted that little nugget in my Moleskine journal—I never leave home without it!

Three days later, Bert called me back with the news that the Jericho Foundation wanted to give our team a matching grant of $20,000. For every dollar donated to our team, they would match it up to a total of $40,000, which would cover our deficit. They hoped that a matching grant strategy might help others catch the vision and stay involved in our work. What a bigger and better idea than anything I ever could have imagined or guessed in my wildest dreams.

The weekend of my certification examination finally arrived, and I was as confident in my preparation as any working mom with five kids could be. I entered the Toronto hotel's sizeable lobby for the exam's written portion to find a large group of confident and very youthful looking candidates (most were at least ten years my junior). As I listened to the conversations around me, rising nausea in my gut and a swirling sensation in my mind announced that I was losing my nerve. My confidence began to seep away. Clearly my imposter syndrome was alive and well.

The exam lasted all day and was the most challenging test I had ever written. Returning to my hotel room, devastated and exhausted, I packed my bags and called Graham to announce that I was coming home. There was no point in staying for the oral exam, as I was convinced that I had failed the written portion. It was over.

Graham, not surprisingly, had something to say about that. His objection wasn't based on the past year of his life that he'd spent doing far more than his fair share of our household duties, and it wasn't the cost of the exam or the hotel room that I was about to bail on. His utmost belief in my abilities and his intimate knowledge of his wife after seventeen years of marriage undergirded his response. He lovingly suggested I should defer any big decisions at such a late hour, go to sleep, and see how I felt in the morning. If I still wanted to come home, he would support me. Then he cracked a joke.

Dr. Terry Bryon, my former high school swim coach (who I've now practiced medicine alongside for over twenty years), often quoted Vince Lombardi, reminding us that "Fatigue makes cowards of us all." How true this is, yet how difficult a lesson to learn. Problems and challenges always look different through the lens of exhaustion or in the dark of night. Sure enough, when the morning came, my courage was renewed, my perspective was restored, and I put on my "big girl pants." They took the form of a black pencil skirt, polka dot blouse, chunky necklace, and a touch of lipstick. If I appeared confident in my power outfit as I marched into my oral examination, I was surely faking it. The exam began and, at the sound of the bell, I moved from station to station where the examiners presented emergency clinical scenarios that I had to respond to and manage. It was so much fun. My nerves and insecurities vanished as I did what

I love to do most—decide on optimal care for my patients. My head was clear and I knew my decisions were correct even though the examiners were not allowed to reveal how we performed. In the end, it was a thrilling and memorable experience that I thoroughly enjoyed. Regardless of the final outcome, I had given it my whole-hearted effort and I knew that all my extra studying and training would surely benefit my future patients.

In the summer of 2011, just a few months before our Ghana Health Team was due to depart, a highly unusual and unexpected sequence of events took place.

On July 20, our lead anaesthetist suddenly developed weakness in his arms. Initial tests revealed what looked like a tumour in his neck and he underwent emergency neurosurgery at St. Michael's Hospital in Toronto.

Five days later, I awoke feeling unwell; while preparing for the day I almost fainted in the shower. I considered taking a sick day, but I was one of a small handful of physicians who remained in town that summer weekend to cover our hospital. By noon, after making rounds on half of my patients on the ward, a pain had settled in the right lower quadrant of my abdomen, nausea had set in, and I realized I had appendicitis. Typically, it takes a few days before an appendix will rupture, so I loaded up on acetaminophen and calculated that I had lots of time to finish my rounds. At the end of the day, I decided to go home and get the kids fed, bathed, and tucked into bed before dealing with the operation I knew I required. As I exited through the back door to our ER, on cue, the ambulance alarm beeped three times, indicating an impending emergency. Two seriously injured patients were en route from a head-on motor vehicle crash. After assisting my colleague with these multi-system trauma patients, I made my way home and fell asleep neglecting to mention my problem to Graham. Hours later, my very concerned seven-year-old daughter Jessica, nudged me awake. With her hand on my forehead she said, "Mommy, you are burning up. Daddy needs to take you to a doctor." Much to "Nurse" Jessica's relief, I was in Dr. Angelo Vivona's operating room by midnight, undergoing an emergency appendectomy.

Having never had surgery in the past, I started to panic as my anaesthetist colleague was about to put me to sleep. To my horror, before I could stop myself, I suggested to him that I didn't think the anaesthetic would work on me. He was kind enough not to roll his eyes. As the medications started to take effect, I felt a large, strong hand fold around mine. Certain that it was God himself comforting me in my distress, I saw instead Dr. Vivona, taking the time to stand beside a sick and tired colleague until she drifted into unconsciousness.

Five days later, I received this piece of verse from my lead eye doctor Martin:

As nothing rhymes with appendectomy,
I had a serious lack of sympathy
Why not a fracture, or rickets, or Lyme?
At least with these there is adequate rhyme
But now I have empathy
As my own appendectomy
Is scheduled tomorrow at nine!

He signed off, "I hope you are feeling better and I'm not kidding. What rhymes with coincidence? Shall we start a pool on who's next?"

He was not kidding—he too had an appendectomy the next day. Three of us for the same mission had unexpectedly required emergency surgery! I couldn't think of a stranger coincidence.

Until, that is, Magdi sent me an email, again exactly five days later. Doctors had discovered a suspicious mass on his neck and he was undergoing immediate surgery. The situation was very concerning, and my heart broke for what Magdi and his family appeared to be facing.

Our anaethestist's surgery was a success and no tumour was found. The pressure on his spinal cord was relieved and he quickly recovered the strength in his arms and hands. Martin and I made full recoveries from our back-to-back appendectomies. Magdi's pathology revealed a very rare tumour that was fully resected and had no potential for spread—no chemotherapy or radiation would be required. Although we were all a little leaner than normal, our families and our doctors agreed we could return to Ghana in November to lead our programs. And thankfully, five days later, no one else fell ill. A tidal wave of relief, gratitude, and celebration rose up and rolled from Canada to the UK and then to Ghana.

Even those who do believe in coincidences found it hard not to assign meaning to those events: four of our health team leaders bound for the same mission, struck down every five days by one of two diagnoses. I'm not an expert in probabilities, but I would calculate the odds of that as remote at best. It was very thought-provoking for us all, regardless of our faith background. The church and leaders in Ghana, who had fasted and prayed for the four of us over those fifteen days, shared their interpretation with me. They unequivocally felt that God was preparing each of the programs we represented (anaesthesia, medicine, optometry, and surgery) for a long-lasting involvement in Ghana and that we were being "tuned-up" so we would not be held back from future work. Magdi confided in me that he promised God that he would do even more to serve the poor in Ghana if his outcome was favourable. About a day after his surgery, he emailed David to request that a third operating room be constructed. As health care professionals, we knew that despite all the advances in medicine and surgery, we would continue to witness the deaths of incredible people—including our own friends and family. We felt collectively humbled that we had been spared and determined to make our days count.

With all of our "tune-ups" and preparations complete, and having overshot our fundraising target, my team of friends arrived in Ghana on October 29, 2011. My heart was bursting with expectation. As I stepped off the airplane into the dark Ghanaian night, I prayed that I would be prepared for whatever emergencies my team might face. I would be very glad that I prayed that prayer and that I had passed my brutal EM exam.

I was going to need both.

CHAPTER 14

Until We Can Stand On Our Own

"Justice will not be served until those who are unaffected are as outraged as those who are."

~ Benjamin Franklin

NEA had more surprises for us when our team arrived in Ghana for our 2011 mission. The first one was waiting at the airport. In place of our beloved church buses, NEA had rented a colossal coach bus complete with air-conditioning, reclining seats, and even televisions. That coach was a game-changer; it meant we could sleep comfortably on the long journey to Carpenter and arrive strong and well-rested, with intact knees and backs.

Our reunion with our Ghanaian family was sweet. We were thrilled that the Mensahs' youngest daughter Carole had joined our team as a volunteer, as had a young American man named Justin Bowler. Justin was a "good friend" of the Mensahs' oldest daughter Elizabeth and had travelled to Ghana to meet her family. I'm not sure he realized that "meeting the family" involved volunteering long, hot days with our health team. We all joined hands and formed a massive circle. After we sang familiar songs, Pastor George prayed for our mission to be successful. It was a meaningful moment as we recalled how, just a year ago, Magdi had repaired George's badly injured leg after his motorcycle accident.

A second surprise awaited us as we were escorted to our rooms. A brand-new dormitory, large enough for our entire medical team, stood ready to be christened by us. A massive central gazebo was surrounded by a perimeter of double rooms, each with an armoire and a desk. Washrooms were equipped with flush toilets and showers with water heaters. The dorm even had a tea and snack station, with a refrigerator stocked full of water and soda pop. Our nurses were delighted to have a fridge to store their suppositories (it is rather difficult to administer a melted suppository to a patient). Above the door frames were the names of men and women who had been essential partners in NEA's work over the years. In case anyone was wondering, the harmless but horrid wall spiders did indeed receive our forwarding address.

As if the coach and the new dormitory were not enough, Brenda had one final surprise for us. Seamstresses and tailors were on-site with Ghanaian fabrics and patterns to make us all new outfits for our final celebration.

The mission began with our traditional first-morning devotions. Joining us were an optician and two optometrists from a major Ghanaian city who gave a brief speech thanking NEA for the opportunity to train with Martin and his eye team. Chef Abraham was the keynote speaker that morning, and he shared a Bible passage from chapter four in the book of Romans. He reminded us that our international team was like the various parts of a human body. Each part gets its meaning from the body as a whole, not the other way around. Like different parts of the body, we all serve different functions from head to toe that are united in one purpose. He challenged our ex-pat and Ghanaian team of over 100 to be what we were made to be and to play our role well. "What you are is a gift to you; what you do is a gift to God and mankind," he concluded.

I realized that the pride I felt well up in my heart as I listened to him speak was like a mother's pride. Young Abraham was growing into a very competent leader before our eyes. While he remained in charge of the hospitality department, he was taking on more and more NEA leadership responsibilities. I also noticed him paying extra attention to a beautiful young woman, Kate, who ran the NEA bakery.

After the meeting, Magdi and I made a special presentation to NEA. Baldwin Sales in Uxbridge donated three beautiful plaques to hang on the door of the David Theatre, the Brenda Theatre, and the brand-new operating theatre named in honour of David's father, Moses. These theatres and the hundreds of professionals that would serve in them would spare countless children like David from the pain and subsequent hardship of losing a parent due to an untreated hernia.

As we made the presentation, I was surprised by the emotions that suddenly swelled in me, emotions that I saw reflected on my dear friend Magdi's face. We had had the recent experience of being patients facing surgical emergencies and uncertain outcomes. Now we were standing in the same gazebo where our Ghanaian pastors and friends had offered up fervent prayers for us when we were sick. Our hearts were full of gratitude and purpose as we stood there, strong and healthy again, helping to equip Ghana with the same services that had saved all four of our lives. Through my falling tears I could still see that the significance of that special moment was not lost on anyone.

Off we went to Nyamboi village, and it didn't take long for the first emergency to occur. That year our leaders implemented a new protocol. Whenever an emergency took place, three whistles were blown. This would activate the doctor, nurse, and volunteer who were "on call" while the rest of us kept working. From that day forward I always wore a whistle around my neck in Ghana—just like I had as a young lifeguard.

Three loud whistles sounded as a little boy was carried in unconscious. Although he tested positive for malaria, the mother's account didn't make sense. She described vomiting and pain in his groin for the past few days. A quick examination revealed that this boy had a strangulated hernia and was in shock. After a brief conversation, David and I decided against transporting him to a hospital. Instead, we made plans to take him to our surgeons on the compound. As David carried the limp child to the truck, one of our British nurses, Lynda Lawton, ran beside him while holding up the life-saving bag of IV fluid. Lynda was on her first mission with us, and this was her first day in a Ghanaian village. She jumped in the back seat of the truck as David placed the dying boy on her lap. What Lynda said next, I have never forgotten. Having not been part of our decision to treat the boy in Carpenter, she told me, "Goodbye, Jennifer. I have no idea where we are going, but I'll do my best to get back to Carpenter somehow." The altruism of my teammates continues to inspire me today.

Back on the compound, the surgical team had an operating room ready to receive our little patient. Magdi brought four surgeons with him that year, including one of his former trainees, Mr. Rob Hicks. Rob was a vascular surgeon in the UK, and he was tremendously enthusiastic about being part of our team. He was a born leader, and Magdi confided in me that he hoped Rob would become his successor in Ghana one day. Dr. Ira Bloom put the boy to sleep, and Magdi, Rob, and the nursing team saved his life. The following day when Lynda and I checked on him, he was standing under the surgical tree, his mother at his side, brushing his teeth with the toothbrush that Kyle had given him.

At the end of our two days in Nyamboi, the village presented us with a unique gift. The village elders had carved each of us a wooden spoon from one of the village trees to thank us for our service. Every time we held that spoon in our hands, they asked us to remember the profound gratitude of the people of Nyamboi. It was a deeply meaningful gift. Just as invaluable was the present that one of my team doctors gave the Nyamboi village nurse named Leticia as we departed. I watched as Dr. Carol Hughes, Ira's wife, reached up, removed the earrings from her own earlobes, and placed them in Leticia's open hands.

Yaara village welcomed us with the usual spectacular fanfare. It didn't take long for us to notice that the residents' general health seemed visibly better than in any previous year. David explained that NEA's farming and agricultural programs were thriving in the area. His nephew Joshua came to visit and was growing into a strong and healthy young boy. Still, countless sick children funneled in from far off villages, and I was so grateful for our two team paediatricians (cross that off my Moleskine wish list). Dr. Sean Godfrey from Canada and Dr. Julie Ellison from the UK were instrumental in caring for our paediatric patients and setting the standard for the high level of paediatric care we would build on in the future. Also joining us for the first time was Dr. Linda Dresser, a clinical pharmacist and professor at the University of Toronto with a speciality in infectious disease. She had no shortage of consultations that year.

Before we knew it, another emergency was upon us as a barefoot messenger arrived in Yaara crying "Eleemeoo!"—a call for help in the Deg language. His screams heralded an emergency that forever changed my worldview. "Eleemeoo! Eleemeoo!!" he repeated over and over. In a crowd of over a thousand, everyone heard him coming. We all understood something was very wrong—cries for help are a universal language. As he got closer, the look of panic in his eyes confirmed that this was "a 911 situation." We held our breath as the translator gathered information and explained the nightmare. A woman was delivering a baby in his village and she needed help. Having heard that an international medical team was visiting Yaara, the village had sent him to request our assistance. I activated our emergency response team—Cindy, Ernestina, a duffle bag, and me.

The messenger rode shotgun and guided the NEA driver to his village while Cindy, Ernestina, and I hung on for dear life in the back seat of the truck (a miserable scenario for Cindy and me, who both get extremely car sick). I recalled a day many years prior when Cindy and I had to transport a critically ill patient from Uxbridge to a hospital in downtown Toronto during rush hour. Weaving in and out of traffic for over an hour, we had been in worse shape than our patient when we emerged, vomiting, from the back of the ambulance at St. Michael's Hospital.

The NEA pick-up truck drove for a short time along the main road and then turned off onto a footpath. Instead of weaving around traffic on a busy Canadian highway, our vehicle swerved around trees and termite hills. Cindy and I were green by the time we emerged into a clearing of thatch-roofed huts. The villagers were all gathered outside and frantically directed us towards one of the huts. We rushed inside. Our nostrils filled with a sweet, metallic, pungent smell and we knew what we would see when our eyes adjusted to the darkness—on the floor was an ashen woman, lying limp in a pool of blood.

A traditional birth attendant informed Ernestina that the woman had finally delivered after a complicated labour, but her bleeding would not stop. We dropped to the barely responsive mother's side and discovered, with relief, she still had a pulse. Cindy grabbed the small vial of oxytocin that we had always carried in our emergency bag since Ama Jennifer's birth on our first mission. She injected the oxytocin into the patient's arm and inserted an IV as fast as possible. I reached down to massage her uterus, pleading silently for it to contract down as the oxytocin took effect.

As health professionals, the moments during which we wait for a life-saving intervention to take effect are hard to describe. Having done everything humanly possible to save someone's life, we stand watching on the precipice of life and death for the outcome that we hope will take place. They are sacred moments of waiting—for epinephrine to stop an anaphylactic reaction, for an electric shock to convert a lethal heart rhythm, for blood to halt hemorrhagic shock, or in this case, for oxytocin to arrest a post-partum hemorrhage. When we have done our best with what we have, we wait.

I glanced around this young mother's one-room home. Her pots and pans were stacked neatly in one corner of the dirt floor. Her kids' clothes, folded with care in another. Her cooking utensils decorated the walls. As we stood on guard, the bleeding began to slow down and, thanks be to God, it finally stopped.

Once the mother's life was out of danger, we inquired about the baby. The mother pointed weakly to the mattress on the floor behind where I had been kneeling. Turning around, I was speechless. There wasn't *a* baby lying on the mattress—there were *two* babies. With no prenatal care or skilled birth attendant to assist her, this mother had single-handedly delivered twins on the dirt floor of her hut.

My mind flashed back to the day I delivered my twins. Because I had reached full term and Joshua and Jessica were almost seven pounds each (yes, I was huge), my obstetrical team decided to induce me at Markham Stouffville Hospital. My delivery took place in the sterile operating room in case I needed an emergency caesarian section. There was an audience of at least a dozen people: an obstetrician, paediatrician, anaesthetist (should I need an emergency caesarean section), obstetrical nurses, paediatric nurses, respiratory therapist, trainees, and one very nervous father holding a shaking video camera. It was quite the production, but I didn't care. All those people were there to ensure that my babies and I survived the delivery. It turned out that Jessica wasn't breathing well at birth and needed the neonatal team's help.

As I compared the care that my family received to that given to this precious family of eight (she had four other children), a wave of rage rose in me. I felt shivers roll up my spine, my arms began to tingle, and despite the unbearable heat in an airless hut, I broke out in a cold sweat. It was unfathomable that an unjust inequality of this magnitude was taking place in this village, and countless other villages in Ghana, and all over our world. Something had to be done.

As we emerged into the bright sunlight, the entire village was standing to greet us, having heard that the mother and the baby boys survived. I knew I should make a speech but could not find my voice after what we had just witnessed.

Thankfully, Ernestina could. She spoke with passion and waved her arms to the sky, the hut, and the path. Her voice was powerful, at times almost yelling at the crowd and at other times speaking barely above a whisper. Whatever she was saying, they were on the edges of their seats and nodding their heads in agreement.

I was glad I was rendered mute—it was Ernestina's speech to make, not mine. As we drove back to our clinic in Yaara village, I asked Ernestina, "What did you tell them?"

"I told them that traditional birth attendants do not have the skills or the oxytocin to save mothers' lives. I told them that all of their women should deliver their babies at a clinic where a skilled birth attendant, oxytocin, and counselling for family planning are available. I told them that no woman from their village needs to die in childbirth ever again."

Without thinking, I responded, "By all means, Ernestina. By all means."

Recognizing her own words, Ernestina burst into bashful laughter.

It was precisely what we all needed.

Returning to the village, my heart sank when I saw the endless line of patients still waiting to be seen. I felt completely drained and my brain felt like mush. I wasn't sure I had the mental capacity to see even one more patient. I stepped onto the back porch to eat a handful of almonds, drink a bottle of water, and regroup.

It is always a challenge for physicians and nurses to return to "business as usual" after a complicated case leaves them emotionally and mentally exhausted. Usually, we take a break. Often, we debrief. Sometimes we are even relieved from duty. But Ernestina was at my side, tapping her foot, zero sympathy on her face, reminding me that it was time to get back to work.

I love that woman.

I sat down at my desk at 3:00 pm, willing myself to get back in the game. This was the time of day when a team volunteer would circulate through the clinic, carrying a red tin that said, "Keep Calm and Carry On." The tin contained candy and a quotation for every team member and volunteer prepared by Dr. Sarah. This simple delivery became a highlight of everyone's day, helping us get through the oppressive heat during the final hours of our clinic. As I ate my medicinal Tootsie Roll, I took a moment to read a quotation by Robert Kennedy:

> *Let no one be discouraged by the belief there is nothing one person can do against the enormous array of the world's ills, misery, ignorance, and violence. Few will have the greatness to bend history, but each of us can work to change a small portion of events. And in the total of all those acts will be written the history of a generation.*

After our two days in Yaara village, we spent one day in an obscure, tucked-away village called Baniantwe. As we approached the Chief and elders for the opening ceremony, I was shocked to see Charles, one of our teammates and an NEA pastor, sitting on the chieftaincy chair. We barely recognized him in his Chief's regalia, but we immediately recognized his deep baritone.

We had a delightful day in Charles' village. I could see Kyle's dental station out my classroom window, and at one point, I looked up to see an entire herd of cows grazing around him as he worked. Kyle and his waiting room didn't even bat an eye. A rooster spent the day on my windowsill, and I soon became used to his interruptions.

The eye clinic was a busy hub of activity with many delighted customers despite the sauna-like conditions. Martin developed a full-body heat rash that day, but still insisted that he was having tons of fun. One woman stepped out of the eye clinic, glanced around with her new specs, threw her hands towards the sky, and gave a long speech.

Martin asked one of the translators, "What is she saying?"

"She is saying the same phrase over and over again. She is repeating, 'God bless each and every one of you for the care you have given me.'"

As we gathered to say goodbye to Baniantwe, the children arrived, one by one, each carrying a huge yam. It was the most enormous pile of thank-you yams we had seen during our time in Ghana. Charles wanted us to know that the children's gifts to us represented something of great importance. He explained that more girls in the region were now attending school because of our example. Seeing so many women serving in professional roles, supported by spouses and families back home, had inspired his people to seriously promote and prioritize education amongst the girls.

I was astounded by Charles' acknowledgment. I knew that for many girls and young women in Ghana and around the world, going to school is merely a wish. I understood the importance of education for girls and what gender equality holds for their lives, their families, their country, and the world. Educating girls leads to tremendous ripple effects, including improved health, fewer maternal deaths, improved nutrition, less poverty and hunger, fewer infectious diseases such as HIV/AIDS, increased economic growth, and more sustainable communities.

As I looked at all of the little girls and boys of Baniantwe village, I was humbled and astounded by this unexpected impact of our work—of us simply using our gifts to serve others.

Our blessed day off arrived and after a sleep-in and breakfast it was time to head to church. Our team had grown too large for the Bamboi church building, so the service was held under the NEA kapok tree, and the Carpenter village congregation joined us.

Ernestina surprised us by asking if she could give a testimony during the service. She stood at the front and thanked God for all the tremendous wisdom, insight, gentleness, love, and compassion that she had learned from our team over the past five years. She wanted us to know that the Ghana government had recognized her exemplary care and was putting her in charge of a large clinic with thirty staff, six emergency room beds, and eight maternity beds. There would be no doctor in this facility, but she would be in charge and on-call twenty-four hours a day, seven days a week. She thanked God for the teaching and training we had given her and for the honour and privilege of caring for her people. She prayed that God would continue to grant all of us many more tomorrows in Ghana.

After her powerful testimony, Charles preached a sermon about the poor widow in the Bible who handed over a bit of oil as an offering to save her impoverished family. God multiplied it over and over, filling every empty jar in the village until she had enough to cover their debts.

Charles reminded us that whatever we hold in our hand—the most familiar things to us— are often the things that God will multiply and use to serve humanity. I thought of my team and what they each held in their hands. I thought of our supporters back home and what they had in their hands—supporters like the Jericho Foundation. I thought of the group of women in my hometown who wanted to assist our mission. They didn't have medical training, but they could knit and wondered if they could send some knitted dolls for the children in our clinics. The hundreds of little dolls they lovingly crafted brought so much joy and solace to the sick children of Ghana. One little girl returned the next day to thank us for the doll that was strapped on her back—just as a Ghanaian woman would strap on her baby.

After the service, NEA packed us all up and announced we were heading for an overnight stay at the Mole ("Moh-lay") Game Park for an extra day off. We were beyond excited. David, recognizing that his health professionals were suddenly acting like giddy kindergarten kids going on a field trip, sat us down and explained that this was no posh game park with hidden electric fences and semi-domesticated animals. This was the real deal, and we must "listen to the man with the gun at all times." Our nurses ran off to the training room to get our trauma bag and some antibiotics that might be suitable for run-ins with wild animals. We had faced so many emergencies of late that I prayed that the next one would not involve *lions and tigers and bears, oh my!*

When we arrived at the game park we were divided into small

groups and we set off on a two-hour guided foot safari. We walked across open fields, through heavy bush, and across streams as we watched the animals of Ghana in their natural habitat. We saw antelope, baboons, buffalo, and many species of birds. The highlight for me was when a herd of elephants made an appearance. Hiding in the tall grass, we watched them interacting with one another for a long time—they were so majestic.

Thankfully, everyone listened to the man with the gun and, much to David's great relief, we returned home intact with our trauma bag unopened despite a close call with a hungry monkey who decided he was entitled to my teammate's lunch.

I was quick to note in my journal that two days off were exponentially more refreshing than one. From that day forward, we always took a two-day break mid-mission. On one level, it seemed wasteful when the need was so great and time was of the essence; however, our entire team's health and productivity during our second week drastically improved. Our NEA teammates also appreciated this break, as they were still expected to keep up with their usual duties when they were not serving alongside us.

Our reprieve from emergencies lasted until our lead nurse Joan fell ill. It should have been a straightforward case of DWD, but despite our best efforts, her condition began to deteriorate rapidly. When it became apparent that her life was in danger, we started making arrangements to evacuate her out of Carpenter by helicopter. Meanwhile, the pastors took matters into their own hands and asked Joan if they could pray for her. They gathered around her bed and began to pray—really pray—all at once. One of our team members, who had stopped by to check on her, described approaching Joan's closed door and immediately recognizing that something powerful was happening. The next thing he knew, he had fallen to his knees in the sacredness of the moment. And he was not a man given to drama.

As Brenda and I worked on Joan's evacuation logistics back at the Mensah home, the front door suddenly opened. There was Joan, on her feet and smiling. Now don't get me wrong, she was not ready to run a marathon or do the waltz, but she was upright, asking for some rice—just like our malaria children. She told us to call off the chopper. The relief that flooded over our entire team was indescribable. There was no fanfare or attempt to put into words what had just taken place. The pastors slipped away, and I never heard them speak of that day again. To them, this wasn't unusual—they were used to relying on God as their only option during medical emergencies. Describing her experience later, Joan said the pastors prayed so hard that beads of sweat ran down their faces.

Our final days on the NEA compound were full of memorable moments, but a visit from a woman with Albinism tops them all.

Albinism is a genetic condition where people are born without the usual melanin pigment that protects them from the sun's harmful rays. They have very pale skin, hair, and eyes, and often do not live long lives on the African continent because of their lack of protection from the sun. This Albino woman had come to our clinic in 2007 with various ailments, and Susan, our lead pharmacist, felt compassion for her. Unknown to me, every year since, Susan had brought her a large supply of sunscreen, lip balm, moisturizer, and sun gear. That year, this woman walked three miles in the hot sun to bring Susan a gift.

She presented her with two tiny yam tubers. We were used to seeing tubers that were two or three feet long and too thick to wrap your hands around, but these were tiny. David explained that due to her condition, she could only spend short amounts of time tending her farm before needing to take refuge from the sun. As a result, her yams were stunted. She gave up two of her precious yams (which were her only source of income) to thank Susan for helping her stay in the sun a little longer to tend to her crops. Susan's most memorable moment of the mission had nothing to do with prescription pharmaceuticals.

On our final day in Ghana, while organizing our leftover supplies and medicines for distribution to the local clinics and hospitals, we had a visit from the District Director of Medical Services for the Northern Region of Ghana. He wanted us to hear first-hand the context into which we were offering our free medical services. He informed us that ninety-eight per cent of Northern Ghana's population could not afford health insurance. The entire region had only seventeen doctors serving 2.5 million people (while we had fifteen doctors on our team). Many of their hospitals did not have a doctor on duty. They had one semi-retired ophthalmologist, too few obstetricians, and no dentists. Then he told us that ninety women had died in childbirth in the Northern Region that year, and he thanked us for preventing the ninety-first death. He concluded by telling us that they were doing their best with limited resources, but welcomed our support in providing care, teaching, and transferring skills "until we can stand on our own."

When he said those seven words, I had one of the most significant "ah-ha" moments of my time in Ghana. All of my senses were immediately on high alert and it was as if a light was suddenly cast upon my path.

As a parent and an educator, I understood that my role was to support, equip, guide, cheer on, and give increasing levels of independence to my children and my trainees until they were ready to launch out on their own. Launching before they were prepared was fraught with risk. Launching too late caused dependence. "Until we can stand on our own" was unquestionably the goal we were all working towards, and this resonated with me on a personal, professional, and global health level. What I now recognized as colonialism's culpability for knocking down Ghanaians in the first place was something this gracious director never referred to, but "until we can stand on our own" became our collective battle-cry.

Oh, how we celebrated that night. We donned our new Ghanaian clothes, threw on a little make-up (even though it would soon melt off), and dined on grilled tilapia, roast beef, tomato soup, vegetables, and Kate's fresh bread. Abraham and his team outdid themselves. While we were eating, there was a sudden commotion under the gazebo where the kids had gathered, and I thought we had one final emergency on our hands. I jumped up and ran over to help, only to realize that the loud commotion was due to Abraham passing out a special treat to the compound kids, who were swarming him with screams of delight. With the funds our team donated towards the party, he had purchased a rarely seen delicacy—a juice box for each child.

The "juice box emergency" was such a beautiful end to a beautiful mission. As Charles had so poignantly said, we had used what was familiar to us—what was in our hands—to serve humanity with a scalpel, a hernia mesh, a vial of oxytocin, a pair of eyeglasses, a toothbrush, a medication, a wound dressing, some sunscreen, a knitted doll, and even a tiny juice box. And when what was in our hands was not enough, we were reminded in dramatic and powerful ways, that we can always use our hands to pray. In return, David, Brenda, and the people of Ghana handed us countless gifts, lessons, and blessings that changed our lives forever.

CHAPTER 15
An Interlude

"The music is not in the notes, but in the silence between."
~ Wolfgang Amadeus Mozart

Plans for our sixth mission to Ghana came to an abrupt and disappointing halt when a presidential election was called for December 2012. Elections in Ghana can be a time of instability and unrest as in many parts of the world, and David and Brenda felt it was unwise for us to be in the country in the month leading up to voting day. Although the Mensahs were people of deep faith, they combined their faith with reason and took no chances when it came to our safety.

My teammates and I were heartbroken. Having borne witness to the significant needs that existed, we dreaded hitting the pause button for two long years. The data analysis from our 2011 mission confirmed the urgency of the situation and added to our feeling of helplessness:

- 450 out of every 100,000 women were dying in childbirth in Ghana (8.3 out of 100,000 in Canada)
- 40-50 out of every 1,000 neonates were dying at birth (as compared to only 3.3 out of every 1,000 in Canada)
- 48 out of every 1,000 infants were dying before their first birthday (in Canada, the number was only 4.7 out of 1,000)
- 57 out of every 1,000 children were dying before their fifth birthday (4.9 out of 1,000 in Canada)

It wasn't the numbers that kept me up at night. It was the faces of the women—the 880 mothers we surveyed—as they looked into my eyes and recounted the number, names, and ages of each child they had lost. Their pain lingered with me, a constant companion never far from my thoughts or my emotions as I cared for my own kids and the children of Uxbridge.

These mothers, and their kids' deaths, weighed heavily on me, and an appropriate response to this injustice seemed nebulous—especially when now we were being prevented from returning to Ghana. I continued to carry a sense of personal responsibility to help end this tragedy while I went about my work in Canada.

I remember being surprised when my Ghanaian friends weren't as disappointed as I expected when our mission was cancelled. David and Brenda tried to explain to me that the concept of time was viewed differently in their culture. They would say things like, "Jennifer, our people have been waiting generations for health care to come. Waiting for one year or two years is inconsequential."

The people of Ghana themselves would also be outstanding teachers on this matter. Each year, when we shut down our last clinic, there was always that "next person in line" who would have to wait an entire year to receive care, have their surgery, get eyeglasses, or have a painful tooth pulled. We dreaded facing them.

One year, that "next person in line" approached me as we began to pack up our clinic. My heart sank. But instead of protesting, she lifted her hands to the sky and thanked me for helping so many of her people. She said that she would pray for God to take us home safely and then bring us back again so that she could be seen in next year's clinic. She left me speechless and deeply moved.

I often think this story would be a good one to post in our nation's emergency rooms that are open 24/7 yet don't seem to satisfy many people's wait-time expectations.

More than that, the people of Ghana have a perspective on life that differs fundamentally from ours. Their perspective can be illustrated by two small but very significant words that they, like many cultures, attach to the beginning or end of their sentences. Two little words—"God willing"—are often added when speaking about doing something in the future. For example, they will say, "See you in the morning, God willing," or "God willing, I will be travelling to Accra on Sunday." It is an acknowledgement that yes, we can make plans, but ultimately, future events are not wholly within our control, and may not come to pass.

Our return to Ghana in 2012 was always dependent on God willing it to happen, so when it was cancelled, they accepted it.

Ghanaians also add three little words—"by God's grace"—to the beginning or end of a sentence that explains something excellent, wonderful, or important that has taken place. For example, "My wife delivered a healthy baby girl, by God's grace," or "By God's grace, my farm is doing very well." These words are extremely important to Ghanaians. It is their way of acknowledging that every good gift comes from above, and they genuinely want to give credit where credit is due. I've noticed that an interesting side effect of these three words is humility. It is hard to become proud (and fall into the traps of pride) when you give credit to a higher power for the blessings in your life.

My favourite Ghanaian phrase for goodnight, *"Korowii te ya kere,"* translated "May God grant us tomorrow," is another linguistic example demonstrating their worldview. Nothing is taken for granted or expected—not your next meal, not waking up tomorrow, and certainly not an event like our yearly mission.

And so, while we were devastated that we would need to wait two years to return to Ghana, our friends in Carpenter took it all in stride—believing a bigger and better plan was unfolding.

Sure enough, with the door to our mission barely closed, taller and wider doors began to open. And they did not open slowly or tentatively—they were blown off the hinges.

At the end of 2011, the Department of Foreign Affairs, Trade and Development of the Government of Canada (DFATD), formerly known as CIDA, made the announcement that GRID and NEA were one of a handful of successful applicants to the Muskoka Initiative. Our proposal, the "Leyaata Project," was accepted to reduce mother and infant mortality in eighty-two marginalized villages in Northern Ghana over three years. Its budget would be $845,000, and the Canadian government would contribute seventy-five per cent of that amount. Our fellow successful applicants were organizations such as the Canadian Red Cross, World Vision, Oxfam, and a number of Canadian universities.

Leyaata means "rescue us" in the Deg language. David Mensah chose that name for a program that was expected to rescue over 10,000 beneficiaries, primarily mothers and infants. We were beside ourselves. Canadians and Ghanaians mobilized with lightning speed, program staff were hired, and the Leyaata "Rescue Us" Project began in January of 2012.

As this landmark project unfolded, it became increasingly apparent to me that I needed more training in global health and international medicine. I was getting by with my basic medical training and the experience I was rapidly gaining in the field, but now we were moving into more sophisticated global health planning, programming, and leadership. I needed more knowledge and skills in the discipline of global health.

Since our mission was cancelled, I took advantage of some "spare time" to pursue a professional diploma program in International Medicine and Public Health. Run by an American organization called the Institute for International Medicine (INMED), I began an intensive combination of on-line and in-person learning on diseases of poverty, HIV medicine, international public health, cross-cultural competency, disaster mitigation and response, and health leadership in low-resource settings. The program also required a one-month field placement in a hospital overseas. I was in my glory—it was a perfect opportunity with perfect timing. My colleague Susan Fockler, who ran our pharmacy program, participated in a parallel program in international pharmacy.

In the fall of 2012, when traditionally I would have been heading to Ghana, I spent a week in Kansas City for in-person training. As part of my diploma, I enrolled in a newborn resuscitation program for low-resource settings. This program, called Helping Babies Breathe (HBB), was developed by the American Academy of Pediatrics (AAP) in collaboration with the World Health Organization (WHO). The HBB curriculum is specifically designed to save babies' lives in environments where human and technical resources are limited. Importantly, the HBB program utilizes a unique mentorship and quality improvement component to adequately equip North American trainers with the skills and knowledge necessary to successfully teach HBB abroad and transfer skills to local trainers.

The paediatrician conducting the training stood at the front of the classroom and began to speak passionately. He explained that this program teaches village midwives and nurses (who typically receive no education on newborn resuscitation) how to resuscitate babies struggling to breathe at birth. As a result, newborn mortality was plummeting all over the world in countries where this simple, cost-effective program was introduced. What he said next, however, would ultimately have a seismic effect in all of Northern Ghana.

He choked up as he continued, explaining that many countries in the Majority World were reporting very high stillborn rates that did not make sense. Midwives and mothers reported active babies with heartbeats during the delivery, yet the baby was inexplicably born dead.

The global paediatric community was starting to recognize that many of these "stillborns" were, in fact, very much alive. The room fell silent as he paused to collect himself.

A newborn baby's cry is the greatest joy for parents to hear and a relief for us as health care professionals, because a crying baby is a breathing baby. About ten per cent of babies, to everyone's horror, are silent when they are born. Most of these babies need simple manoeuvres such as drying, suctioning, and stimulating to kick-start their breathing, and soon they begin to cry. However, other babies are born with what is called secondary apnea. These babies are not breathing or moving, and they are blue and limp. Without education, one would think that they are dead, as no amount of back-slapping and heel-flicking will cause them to start breathing.

But the majority of these babies in secondary apnea are very much alive. Their hearts are beating—they simply need oxygen blown into their mouth under a small amount of pressure (positive pressure ventilation) for them to begin breathing. However, if they do not receive immediate oxygen to their lungs, they will die.

The WHO and the AAP hypothesized that babies born in secondary apnea (blue, limp, and lifeless) are assumed to be stillborn in many cultures, and in those countries, it is considered inappropriate to even touch them. These babies are declared stillborn when all they need is a little help to take that first breath. Neonatal resuscitation education is not available in many places in the majority world, so birth attendants lack both the education to recognize that these babies are alive, and the training and equipment to intervene.

My spine started to tingle, my heart started to race, and I could feel a lump forming in my throat. Before the speaker even finished his remarks, I knew with absolute clarity that this was precisely what was happening in Ghana. It was the missing piece of the puzzle to explain why so many women and birth attendants reported stillborns, and what's more, it was my strong suspicion that in Ghana, those deaths were not even being counted in the already high newborn death rate of 40-50 out of 1,000 births. I started texting Lynnita and Brenda, cursing my keyboard ineptitude. My adrenaline was pumping in a way I had rarely experienced before.

Two days later, I completed the HBB Provider course followed by the HBB Master Trainer course. I didn't need to say much to Lynnita and Brenda—we immediately discerned that this training must be part of the Leyaata Project.

To add to the excitement, on the final day of the course, our group went out to celebrate and enjoy some Kansas City BBQ with our instructors. We were discussing where everyone was hoping to go for their one-month practical field placement when the program director looked up from his ribs and said, "You are working in Ghana, right? We've just added another INMED training site in Ghana!" I was stunned to learn that I could complete my training in the very country I was seeking to assist.

So much for hitting the pause button on 2012. In fact, the traction we got in 2012 towards sustainable health care was more catalyzing and impactful than any previous year, without us even stepping foot in Ghana.

As 2012 drew to a close, I was invited to the convocation ceremony for my degree in Emergency Medicine on November 17th, 2012. It was the only November 17th that I would be in Canada for an entire decade of my life, and I was not going to miss it. This was such a milestone moment for me and such a hard-earned accomplishment that I decided I would invite my family to join me in Toronto to watch me graduate. I was confident that it would be a fantastic opportunity to instill in my kids the importance of life-long learning.

Convocation day arrived, and I was buzzing with excitement. The seven of us dressed up and entered the Metro Toronto Convention Centre, where a banner with the theme for the evening welcomed us—"In Study Lies Our Strength." I made them all memorize and recite those words. Excited about the impact this event could have on my kids, I ran off to get my cap and gown while they took their seats in the audience.

I'm not sure what I was thinking. The room was dim and warm, the speeches were many, and the list of graduates long. Many hours later, we finally reached the W's and I rose excitedly from my chair for my big moment. I turned around to make eye contact with my family only to find all five of the kids—and their father—fast asleep in their comfy chairs. I was certain that I could hear Graham snoring. So much for inspiring them!

That would not be the last convocation of mine that I would drag my poor children to and, despite the uninspiring experience, there would soon be many a convocation that their proud mother and father would have the honour of attending.

Our interlude year gave me no shortage of matters to contemplate. It ended up providing the time and space we all needed to step back and let more critical things unfold that would better equip us for the work. A musical interlude can be defined as "an opportunity to recalibrate and refocus our ears on the bigger picture." That was precisely what the year 2012 felt like to me—a melodious pause, strengthened by study, before the rest of this composition could crescendo towards an exciting finale.

By the completion of 2012, fifty trained Leyaata volunteers were working in fifty villages and the results were jaw-dropping: 1,836 pregnant women had received antenatal visits, 3,671 long-lasting insecticidal malaria nets were installed, and—insert drum roll please—sixty-five per cent fewer infants were dying in the first thirty days of life.

To our absolute delight, David and Brenda decided not to wait two full years for our next mission. They invited us to return in eighteen months—in April of 2013. They also agreed it was time for my children to start joining me in Ghana and extended an invitation for my oldest daughter, Olivia, to come as NEA's guest.

Springtime in Ghana, here we come! God willing, of course.

Luxury transporation!

>
The flag of the United Kingdom added to the collection

<
New dining hall and kitchen

New team dormitory "Nim House"

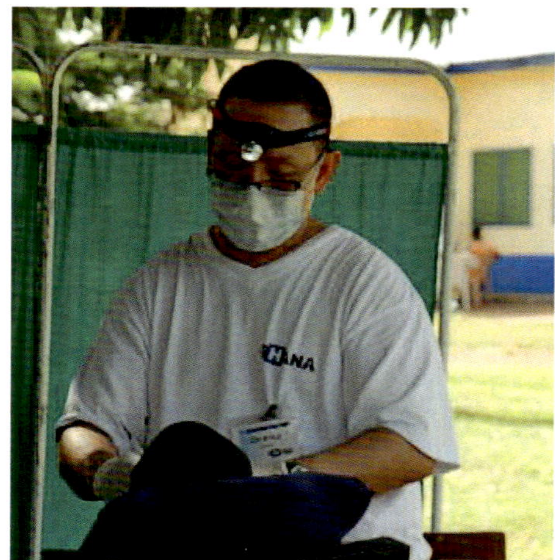

Dr. Kyle Chin on his first mission

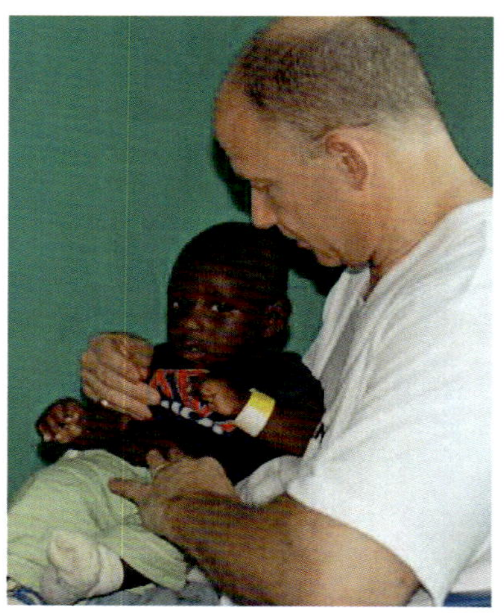

Dr. Charlie Peniston, cardiac surgeon joining our team for the first time

<
Marion Hurlburt (who attended every mission but one) running her reading glasses program prior to expansion of the eye team

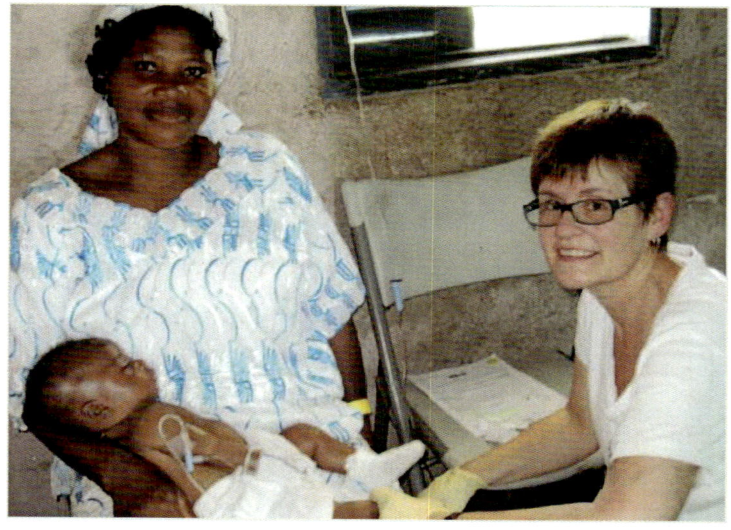

>
Joan Maguire with baby Joshua who is receiving intravenous antibiotics for pneumonia

>
Dr. John Simpson and I making a palliative house call

Dance of gratitude for the house call John and I made to her mother

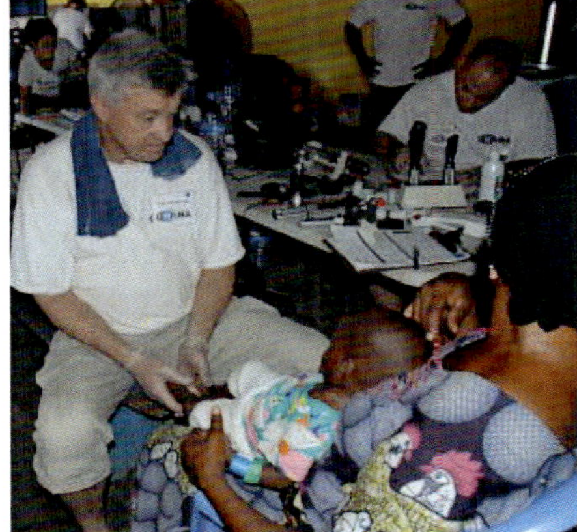

Dr. Martin McDowell, our first team optometrist

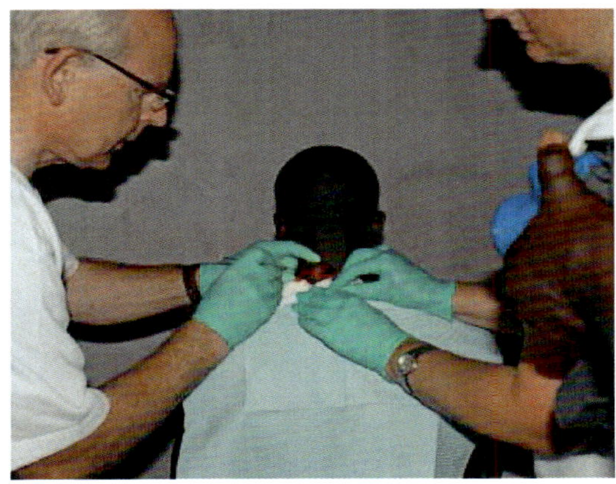

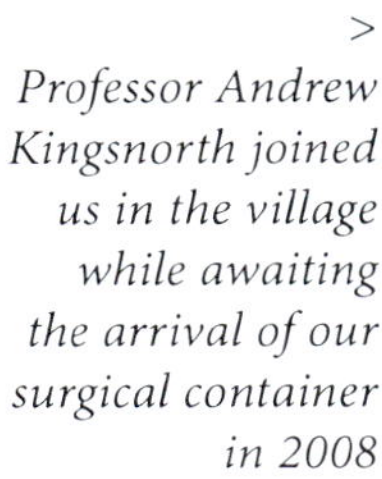

>
Professor Andrew Kingsnorth joined us in the village while awaiting the arrival of our surgical container in 2008

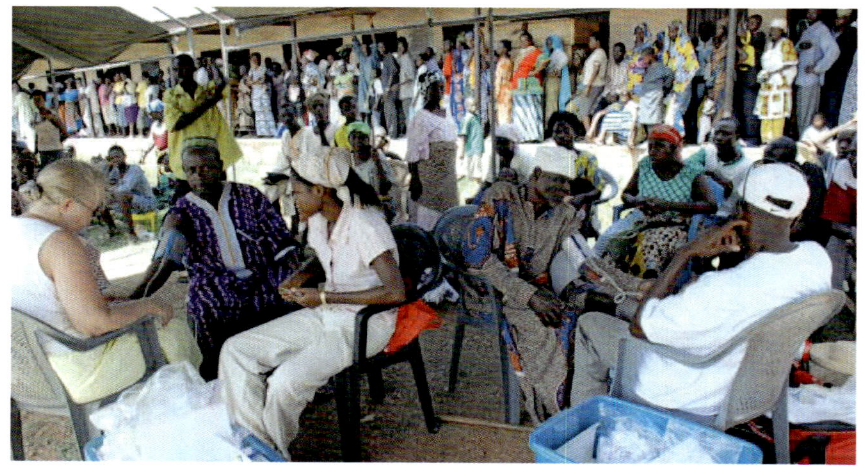

David and Brenda helping process the massive crowds

<
An inspirational quotation and treat were delivered to every team member at 3 p.m. (pictured here is Mary Lovatt)

>
Yaws ulcer

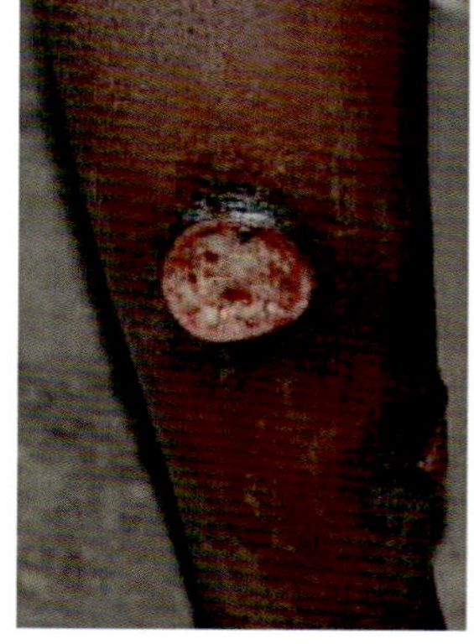

Official medical records played an important role in data collection and reporting of diseases like Yaws to local health officials

The surgical tree

A critically ill boy being rushed from a remote village to Magdi's theatre with a strangulated hernia. Nurse Lynda Lawton accompanies him

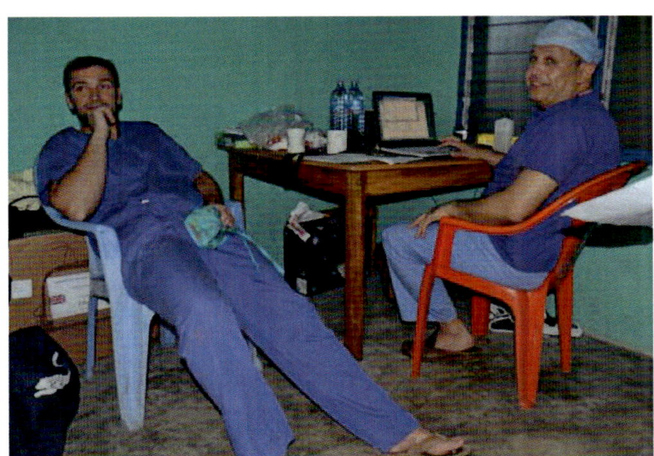

<
Mr. Magdi Hanafy (right) and Mr. Robert Hicks (left) after an exhausting day in theatre (in the UK, surgeons are referred to as Mr. not Dr.)

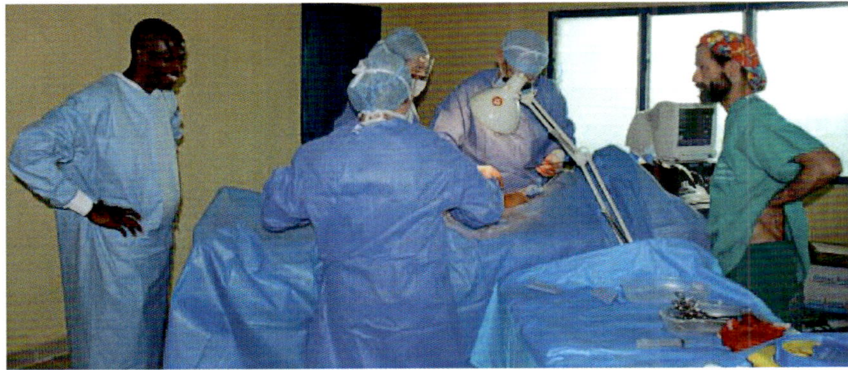

Dr. David Mensah observing the very first hernia surgery in Carpenter

^
Formality forgotten, Chief Joseph jumped up to give me a hug

>
A little boy offered to babysit my chicken while I worked

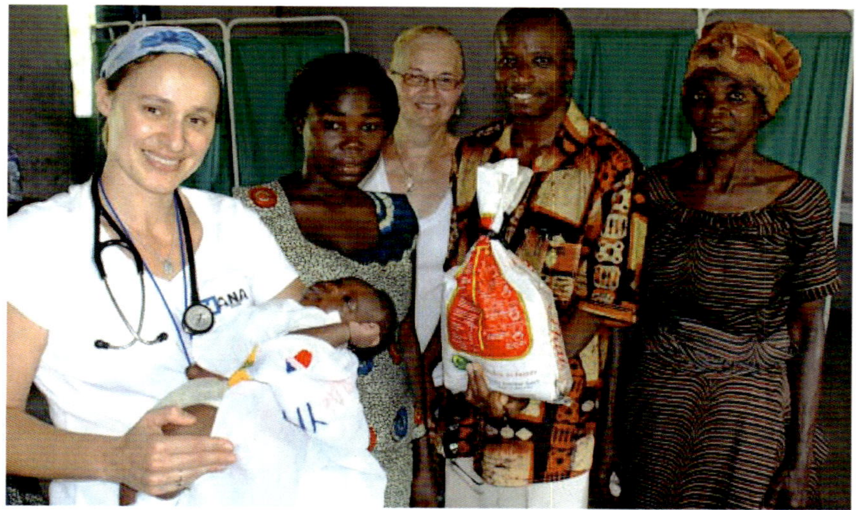

A grateful patient from our first mission in 2007 returned in 2008 to present me with a bag of peanuts and introduce me to her newborn son

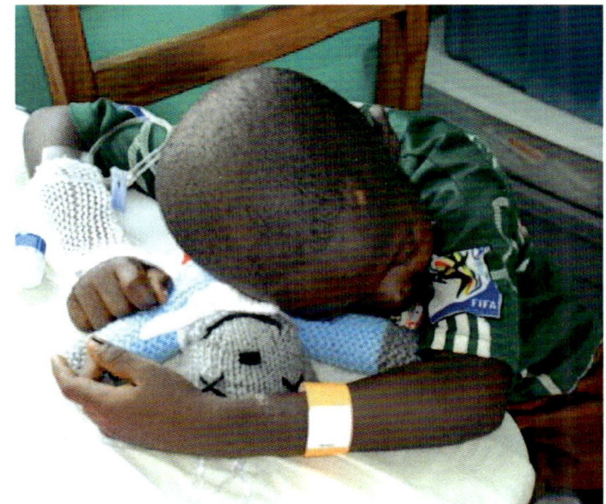

<
Women in Ontario knit and sent hundreds of these little dolls for our paediatric patients

Ernestina and I— side by side
v

<
My Emergency Medicine Convocation (through which my entire family slept)

2008 Ghana Health Team

2009 Ghana Health Team

2010 Ghana Health Team

2011 Ghana Health Team

CHAPTER 16

For Such a Time as This

"It's the action, not the fruit of the action, that's important. You have to do the right thing. It may not be in your power and may not be in your time that there'll be any fruit. But that doesn't mean you stop doing the right thing. You may never know what results come from your action. But if you do nothing, there will be no result."

~ Mahatma Gandhi

Eighteen months after our last visit, the 2013 Ghana Health Team of sixty faithful friends from Canada, the UK, and Germany joyfully set off for our sixth mission.

In April, everything in Ghana looked different. Bright green grass carpeted the NEA compound, trees were aflame with red blossoms, and baby animals (including baby spiders) were running around everywhere. Spectacular, ripe fruit dripped from the branches of the mango trees—a tempting snack for the NEA staff kids.

Springtime in Ghana felt different too. To this day, David and Brenda claim they told us that Ghana in April might be "a little warmer" than November, but none of us remember that warning. As we stepped off the bus, a thick wall of heat and the scorching afternoon sun greeted us. The hottest days of a Ghanaian November paled in comparison.

As I introduced my eldest daughter, Olivia, to my Ghanaian family—the Mensahs, Ernestina, Abraham, and all of the cheering NEA staff—I felt a tad emotional.

Olivia was fourteen years old and in her first year of secondary school. Her teachers were in full support of her trip, so she left behind her French immersion studies, her friends, and her competitive skating to come with us. This was a big adventure for her. With five kids, international travel was not in the Wilson family budget. Our family holidays usually consisted of twenty-four-hour March Break road trips in Graham's beloved fifteen-passenger van to a rental condo in Florida. It wasn't exactly luxurious, but the memories we created were worth more than any all-inclusive Caribbean holiday (or so we told the kids).

Olivia was excited to visit Ghana and experience all she'd been hearing about since she was a little girl. She knew she would be well cared for under the watchful eyes of her protective mother, doctor (Carlye), dentist (Kyle), eye doctor (Martin), and pastor (Dale). I was thrilled that my daughter had the opportunity to be influenced by my teammates and the people of Ghana. I suspected that the worldview and future of this young teenager from a small rural town would be deeply impacted by the next fourteen days.

To be available as a mom to Olivia, I knew that I needed to delegate more responsibilities to my leadership team and they rose to the occasion. With our team's expanding size and scope, I also recruited a new team member to relieve me of the growing burden of administrative fieldwork. Kim Lawson, a local businesswoman who went to my church, had impressed me over the years with her leadership and executive gifts. I knew she could be trusted to keep our team, medical records, and data collection organized in Ghana.

Also joining me for the first time was my good friend and colleague, Dr. Carlye Jensen. Carlye and I work closely together in our family medicine clinic and in the emergency room in Uxbridge. We love critical care and, since we both live minutes from our hospital in Uxbridge, we have found ourselves working side by side during some of the most stressful medical emergencies of our careers. Having Carlye on the team was another weight off my shoulders. I trusted her completely; she's a dynamic woman with courage and a great sense of humour who doesn't shirk responsibility.

Olivia's presence in Ghana was a big deal to the Mo Tribe and they welcomed her with open arms. The children were delighted and called her "O-leeeeeeee-via"—hanging on to the long "ee" for many seconds. The first thing the kids wanted to do was touch the braces on her teeth—they had never seen such a thing. It was priceless watching her continually guide their fingers away from her mouth while trying to explain the purpose of orthodontics.

Our team and all the NEA staff overflowed the gazebo on Monday morning for the devotions which officially kicked off our mission. A shy, young woman named Akosua (one of the new Leyaata Program staff) stepped to the front as the keynote speaker.

Akosua shared with us the story of Queen Esther in the Bible. A lot was at stake for Queen Esther. The fate of her life, her family, and her race was in her hands. Her uncle Mordecai challenged her to use her position as queen wisely "for such a time as this." Despite significant personal risk, Esther stepped up to save her people.

With passion, Akosua reminded us that, like Esther's people, the fate of the people of Northern Ghana was in our collective hands. She believed that God had brought us together in Ghana "for such a time as this." She concluded by reminding us that accomplishing our task would require great courage. She told us to go with joy and bravery and rise to overcome the obstacles we were about to face.

In the collective silence that followed her words, I wondered how many besides me felt that Akosua was foreshadowing something big. My mind replayed some of the mission-defining moments that had required great courage thus far: the mangled motorcycle on the dark Ghanaian road, the woman with a strangulated hernia arriving in a wheelbarrow the night before our surgical container miraculously appeared, baby Joshua gasping for breath with severe pneumonia, David Mensah placing the dying boy on Lynda's lap so we could rush him from Yaara to Magdi's operating theatre, and the mother of twins almost bleeding to death on the floor of her hut.

Would we be ready for what we would encounter this year? How many times would we hear the whistle blow? Would we be brave enough, skilled enough? Would we have the right equipment and medicine? Would my extra training in emergency medicine and global health help me lead and practice more effectively? I looked around at my teammates. Some had their heads bowed, others wiped away tears, others looked at me—some with fear, some with determination. Ernestina had a massive smile on her face, one hand raised in the air, head bobbing in enthusiastic agreement as she looked at me and mouthed the words "BY ALL MEANS" in response to Akosua. There was no question—we all believed we were in Ghana "for such a time as this." Whatever we were about to face, we would face it together. And on that note, we began our work caring for the entire NEA staff and their families. By the end of that same day, Magdi's team had completed twenty-six surgeries.

Kyle was one happy dentist for several reasons. His dental clinic was always held under the mango tree, but we had never seen a mango on its branches. Now, hundreds of them provided stunning ornaments for his patients to enjoy while they gazed up from their dental chair. Kyle brought two other dentists with him that year, allowing him to triple his team's capacity, and he also had a new "toy"—a portable, hand-held X-ray machine. This addition allowed him to offer restorative work, fillings, and more complicated dentistry for the very grateful NEA staff. He also had a surplus of toothbrushes collected during a "toothbrush drive" by the Roxy Kids of Uxbridge.

After the NEA clinic, our mobile team spent two eventful days in Nyamboi village, tending impressive crowds. We were so grateful to have expanded all of our teams—especially our eye team. Martin had recruited a second optometrist, and they were stocked with state-of-the-art eye medications, thanks to donations by Canadian companies. I had no idea how costly the medicines for glaucoma were until I saw the receipts: $12,279.95 worth of drops from TEVA and $139,918.40 from Alcon. Incredible generosity—but definitely not a sustainable solution to the problem.

Along with a growing group of Ghanaian health care professionals who joined our team every year, the first-ever Ghanaian physician joined us in 2013. Dr. Nina, a young doctor, had been assigned to work alongside me for the entire two weeks. I was so honoured. This was an opportunity we had been waiting for since 2007, and I hoped that it represented an open door for increased teaching, transfer of skills, and capacity building by our team.

One of the most significant challenges that Ghana threw at us that year was the heat. By midday, with temperatures into the mid-40s°C, it was hard to stay conscious, let alone practice our best medicine, nursing, pharmacy, optometry, and dentistry. Even the Ghanaians found it unbearably hot. We all found ways of coping, and NEA did everything they could to support us. One day, Brigitte made homemade lemon squares that added zest to the afternoon. Another day, hot coffee was delivered to our desks around 3:00 p.m., which was surprisingly effective at rousing us from our heat-induced stupor. Team members tried to cool off with spritzer water bottles and wet cloths around their neck, but nothing really worked for long. For me, there was only one thing that would temporarily cool me off when my head felt like it was going to explode—Lysol Spring Waterfall Disinfecting Wipes. On the hottest day of 2013 in Ghana, I pulled out a Lysol wipe with my gloved hands to clean the examination bed. The scent of the spring waterfall overcame me, and despite the "avoid contact with eyes" and "may cause skin irritation" warnings, I found myself rubbing it all over my face, neck, and arms, to the dismay of Dr. Nina. It was no waterfall, but for about thirty seconds, while I fanned myself with a piece of paper, I had a slight reprieve.

The nights were not much easier. Ushering in restful sleep required strategy—last-minute cold showers, ceiling fans on full-speed, and mosquito nets sprayed with water. When the heat and the unfamiliar sounds of the African night refused to let sleep come, which often happened, many of us resorted to taking a small sleeping pill—something we reluctantly prescribe at home under normal circumstances.

At about 4:00 a.m., the temperature would dip down just enough that one might reach to the foot of the bed to draw up a top sheet. By morning, the air was cool and our skin, for a few moments, was free of perspiration. On the occasional morning, if the temperature dipped below twenty-five degrees Celsius, we would be greeted by the NEA security guards dressed in their winter jackets and hats.

Yaara village was waiting for us, and the welcome drums could be heard from afar as we approached it the next day. In front of Chief Joseph sat a colourful display of eggs, fruit, yams, vegetables, and a lively ram to help feed us while in Ghana. Joseph called my daughter Olivia out from the crowd and presented her with a small pile of yams and her very own chicken. Olivia does not like being the centre of attention, and she bravely held the bird but not her tears. Joseph thanked her for allowing her mother to come to Ghana every year and spoke of the honour her presence bestowed upon them. Joshua, our little miracle patient, was playing by my side, one year older and one year stronger. His parents, Peter and Lydia, introduced him to

Olivia as "her brother," explaining that I was now considered Joshua's mother since I saved his life.

I didn't see much of Olivia in Yaara, where my team saw 1,100 patients over our two days. The nurses kept her busy weighing babies, conducting malaria tests, and helping run our paediatric rehydration station. One afternoon, Olivia came through the back door of my classroom and hopped towards me. She was hopping on one foot, missing a Birkenstock sandal, and appeared to be laughing and crying all at the same time. She explained between sobs that while she was in the latrine, trying to stand up (from the squatting position one must assume while aiming for the hole), her long skirt caught the back of her sandal, knocking it straight into the pit. Dr. Nina, Ernestina, and I burst into uncontrollable laughter, much to our patients' delight and Olivia's mortification. Someone went looking for an extra pair of shoes.

After Yaara, we had two fun-filled days off as our enthusiastic social convenor, Gillian, planned games, sporting events, and a euchre tournament.

I love to remind my opponents that I come from a long line of excellent euchre players. My Nana taught us to play at the cottage when my siblings and I were very young, and she was one serious instructor. "Never send a boy out to do a man's job!" was her favourite way of telling you that you should have led with a bower. She kept playing until she was well into her nineties despite her failing vision from glaucoma, albeit with king-sized playing cards. I think of my Nana and our many euchre games at the cottage every time I look at my wedding band. The day that Graham and I told her we were engaged to be married, she yanked off the ring that had adorned her finger for fifty-seven years and handed it to me without ceremony.

David and Brenda invited the team to their home on Saturday evening, where we heard story upon story of their early years in Ghana. Brenda shared how, every morning, her three little girls would go to their desks in their classroom/bedroom, stand at attention, and sing "O Canada" before their homeschooling lessons began. We were in awe of Brenda. It was all we could do to survive two short weeks in Ghana, let alone even think about raising a young family there—especially in the days before running water, reliable communication, and electricity. When I look at the extraordinary work the accomplished Mensah women are doing today, I picture their younger selves and their teacher standing there, singing the national anthem every morning.

The following day, NEA held a church service on the compound that lasted a mere three hours. After church, David called a few of our leaders to his home for an impromptu meeting. He wanted our input on an idea he'd had since the 1970s. He had a dream to run a hospital to serve the Northern Region of Ghana and wanted to know what we thought. We were speechless. I'm sure it was partly due to our heat exhaustion after the church service. I also think we were so consumed by the overwhelming leadership needs of our mission that we had no extra headspace for brainstorming around a vision like that.

While many of us worked in hospitals, we hadn't planned them, and we most certainly didn't run them. All I knew was that they were expensive and required resources that did not seem to exist in Ghana. Although no one said it out loud, we didn't think that NEA, without any expertise in hospital administration, could possibly run a hospital in a place with so few medical personnel—they would be in way over their heads.

Let's just say it was a short chat. I felt bad for David, as I could see that our response was a disappointment for him. As always, he was gracious, thanked us for our time, and testified that, "God's timing is the best timing" in all things. Years later, when I asked him about that "I have a dream" meeting in his living room, he said, "I knew you were just not ready."

On Monday, NEA surprised us with a field trip to the Kintampo waterfall. Abraham packed a picnic lunch for all sixty of us—fried chicken and watermelon—after which we spent the afternoon frolicking like little kids in the majestic waterfall. The authentic experience was delightful and far more refreshing than the Lysol version.

Our last three clinic days were spent on the NEA compound. Patients arrived from all over Ghana and neighbouring countries. The Regional Director of Medical Services and a representative from the Medical and Dental Council of Ghana came and toured our clinic, then committed to post more physicians to train with our team the following year. I was thrilled by the impressive reputation NEA was building amongst the health care leaders in their country and the doors that were beginning to open.

We began the final day of our mission by taking our team picture underneath the tree with the flaming red blossoms. It is my second favourite team picture—our first and only springtime in Ghana. We were drained, but the finish line was in sight, with one day left to go.

If we thought we could cruise-control through our final day, we were sorely mistaken. That day, our surgical, medical, dental, and eye teams faced some of the biggest "three-whistle challenges" of our mission.

A thirty-five-year-old father (who I will call Thomas) was found at the compound's gate, near death with a strangulated hernia. His young family was gathered around him. When our surgeons performed emergency surgery, they discovered a catastrophe—dead, gangrenous bowel. Magdi and our anaesthetist, Dr. Tony Brown, had a tough decision to make. The only thing that would save this man was an emergency laparotomy (opening up his entire abdomen) and a bowel resection (removing the dead bowel and reattaching it). This is not a surgery we would typically do in Carpenter, but it was a surgery that Magdi performed regularly in the UK. With NEA's support, we made the call to try and save him. This was a particularly delicate decision as we were constantly aware of the need to maintain trust among the population we served. A death in our operating room threatened to break that trust.

As Tony did everything possible to keep the man alive by protecting and supporting his oxygenation and blood pressure, Magdi removed sixty centimetres of dead bowel and reattached the two healthy ends. The sight and smell of those blackened, dead loops of bowel discarded into the stainless-steel bowl was unforgettable.

By God's grace, Thomas survived the surgery and spent the night in our "Carpenter ICU." When we departed a day later, he was sitting up smiling, sipping water, with his wife by his side. We left him in the care of Ernestina, who nursed him back to a complete recovery. Magdi, Tony, and the surgical team were, indeed, in Ghana "for such a time as this." Together, they completed this and 271 other successful surgeries, with no complications and no deaths.

Meanwhile, a limp and barely responsive toddler was brought to the physician station. Her lips were ulcerated and she was near death from profound dehydration. Our physicians and translators were having difficulty getting the story from the mother, as she came from Coté d'Ivoire and only spoke French. I called for Olivia.

The child was too dehydrated and in shock for Joan to obtain an intravenous line so one of our ER doctors inserted an interosseous (IO) needle into her leg. This is a life-saving technique used when we cannot get an IV on a critical patient. It is a large needle that is bored into the patient's lower leg bone to allow direct access to the bone marrow. Through it, lifesaving fluid and medications can be provided. While they were resuscitating this baby, Olivia, together with one of our French-speaking nurses Margaret Salem-Matthew, helped translate the mother's story for our team.

When Olivia and her siblings began school, Graham and I enrolled them in the French Immersion stream. We thought it would be a great way to provide some academic enrichment in our small rural community. Whenever the kids complained (and they did a lot) that it was "too hard" or that they received no help from their non-French-speaking parents, we would opt for the tried-and-true line, "One day you will thank us." Today was that day. Olivia's knowledge of Canada's second official language helped save that little girl's life. It turns out that the traditional village healer had tried to treat the child's malaria with a caustic tonic that had burned her lips and esophagus. The team that resuscitated her, including my daughter Olivia, were in Ghana for such a time as this.

Back in the dental tent, Kyle, too, was being faced with a terrifying emergency. A young man with a massive dental abscess came to the clinic. It was so big that it was blocking off his airway, and he was about to suffocate. I can still see the man's eyes, bulging in panic, as his airway was slowly closing off. There was no time to waste. Our surgical team was busy with the man with the gangrenous bowel in the theatre, so Kyle called for Charlie, knowing his skills in cardiac surgery might be helpful. Together, they sedated the man under the mango tree, drained the abscess, which was pushing on his windpipe, and averted a disaster. They, too, were in Ghana for such a time as this.

Meanwhile, Martin dealt with an exceptional case in his eye clinic, right when I happened to wander in to take a few pictures. As I approached his station, he was sitting face to face with a mother who had a toddler in her lap. Martin was holding the baby's feet in his hands and appeared to be deep in thought as he studied the child. The toddler was blind. Congenital cataracts, a rare scenario, were robbing her of her vision. With the funds raised in memory of one of my patients (a cousin to Carlye), arrangements were made to send this toddler to Accra, where both cataracts were removed and new artificial lenses were inserted to restore her vision. Martin's presence in Ghana and the memorial gifts donated by the family and friends of James Crane were "for such a time as this."

We had much to celebrate that night, and Abraham's team prepared a feast of goat, beef, fufu, pancake soup, fresh avocado, and pineapple. For dessert, to the sheer delight of the crowd, he served us homemade vanilla ice cream. It was the first cold food we had eaten in two weeks and it was utterly delectable. David's mother gave yet another memorable speech thanking us for "bringing life to their doorstep." Dr. Nina also thanked our team for our service and for all the training she had received. She told us that she was already recruiting her colleagues to join us the following year. When we thought the festivities were over, a local drumming group arrived. Our fatigue was forgotten, and we danced under the stars late into the night.

Someone special once told me that difficult goodbyes are a sign that you had something good in your life. We were so sad to say goodbye to our friends very early the following day. Our relationships with the NEA staff were becoming so deep and meaningful, and our shared purpose so compelling that it was hard to see it come to an end. April in Ghana had proved far too vicious for us Canadians and Europeans, and so the decision was made to change our mission date back to November. That meant it would be eighteen months before we would all be together again. Tears began to flow, and Abraham suggested it might be easier to say "See you soon" instead of "Goodbye." The pastors led us in the traditional closing song "Great Things He Has Done," and, with the arms of every NEA staff member raised to the sky, our bus pulled out of the front gate and onto the long road to Accra.

Olivia and I spent the entire bus ride mulling over all she had experienced. Ghana had presented her with a once-in-a-lifetime opportunity and she had fully embraced every moment of it. Along with her duties on the nursing team, she had watched Magdi operate, helped Kyle pull a tooth, spent time in the eye clinic, and sat with me while I consulted with patients. She had received a personalized tour of the NEA compound with David on his ATV and an in-depth tutorial on the science of fish production from Mr. Soale Gbeadese (known to us as "Soale"), the new sector head for the Aquaculture program. She had developed special relationships with the NEA kids who, many years later, still ask me how "Oleeeeevia" is doing. Aside from the sandal donation she made to the pit latrine and some minor health issues, she'd had the time of her life. She hadn't done much schoolwork, but she had received an education that secondary school in rural Ontario could never teach. I was so proud of the contribution my daughter made to our mission and I cherished our shared experience. Only time would tell how this trip to Ghana would impact her growth, development, and future life choices.

I had trouble sleeping on the flight home. I couldn't stop thinking about Akosua's inspired "Queen Esther Challenge." There was no question that the past two weeks (and, in fact, the past six years) were "our time" to be in Ghana, but I knew that a bigger picture was yet to unfold. The road to sustainability was more arduous than I had ever expected, and the solutions still seemed nebulous. Rather than focusing on an unclear future, I tried to focus on what our journey had clarified.

We now had an incredible team of committed allies from around the world. Our experience and data gave us a much better understanding of the enemies that NEA was up against: malaria, diarrhea, hernia, and blindness, to name a few. It was clear that visiting the sick was, in and of itself, the right thing to do. Stephen Lewis was bang on when he issued the challenge that "even a little help would bring solace and hope to so many." Of all of these things, I was sure.

I also tried to focus on the many miracles that had taken place. I remembered meeting Professor Kingsnorth on the plane and the arrival of his highjacked surgical container at "just the right time." I remembered the woman cured of infertility presenting me with her baby and her gift of peanuts. I remembered the phone call from the Jericho Foundation offering significant funding while I was praying in my car about our financial shortfall. I remembered the endless lines of hernia patients now cured. I remembered the cases of Yaws, now en route to eradication. I remembered the mothers recounting the deaths of their children and, in response to their plight, the emergence of the Leyaata program—now saving moms and babies throughout the region. I remembered the lives of all the men, women, and children whose lives had been rescued—those individual starfish stranded on the beach—lives that matter.

The journey thus far had undoubtedly been full of obstacles. Still, my Moleskine journals were filled to overflowing with the incredible lessons we were learning together, lessons that would ultimately inform and direct our next steps.

As I tried to sleep, my mind was suddenly filled with a prayer that David Mensah had prayed as we sat in the three sacred chairs at the inception of our partnership. He asked God to direct our collective steps and bless the work of our hands so that justice would flow to his people. I knew that it might not be in our power, or even our lifetimes, that sustainable health care would come to Northern Ghana. But I also knew that I would continue to pray that prayer, whistle around my neck, and stand in solidarity with the Ghanaian people for such a time as this.

CHAPTER 17

Pushed Out of the Nest

"Courage, dear heart."
~ C.S. Lewis.

When I returned from Ghana at the end of April 2013, an email was waiting in my inbox requesting that I participate in the Uxbridge Prayer Breakfast. The keynote speaker was Dr. Jane Philpott, who, at the time, was a family doctor in Markham, Ontario and an Associate Professor in the University of Toronto's Department of Family and Community Medicine. Jane gave an inspirational address and concluded with a passage from Matthew 5:14–16:

> *You are the light of the world. A town built on a hill cannot be hidden. Neither do people light a lamp and put it under a bowl. Instead they put it on its stand, and it gives light to everyone in the house. In the same way, let your light shine before others, that they may see your good deeds and glorify your Father in heaven.*

After breakfast, Jane and I had an opportunity to speak together. I told her all about our mission and the Ghanaian health professionals, like Dr. Nina, who trained with us. Her eyes lit up and she suggested I get in touch with the University of Toronto (U of T). They were looking for international training sites for family medicine residents to receive training in global health. She wondered if a future partnership might be possible between U of T, our Ghana Health Team, and NEA. She connected me with a woman named Dr. Katherine Rouleau. How exciting would it be if one day, Ghanaian and Canadian residents could train side by side?

Shortly after that, a conversation began between our Ghana Health Team pharmacists and the Faculty of Pharmacy at U of T. Dr. Linda Dresser, one of our Ghana Health Team pharmacists, was a professor in the department. The university was interested in placing pharmacy students and residents with our future health teams, under Linda's supervision. They, too, were looking for opportunities and partnerships to safely and effectively train future pharmacists in global health.

These two conversations caused me to reflect on a discussion I had had with my translator, Dr Nina, as I left Ghana, concerning the lack of quality training opportunities for Ghanaian medical students and residents.

It was hard to miss it. Three conversations with similar themes: medical education, partnerships, and NEA. Here we go! I could feel myself being drawn into an emerging vision. Unable to sleep, I penned this email to David and Brenda in Ghana, and our GRID Board Chair in Canada, at 1:44 a.m. on May 20, 2013. I include excerpts below:

> *Dear David, Brenda, and Jacques,*
>
> *I want to pass along something that is circling in my head since returning from Ghana.*
>
> *I had a long chat with Dr. Nina before we left. She commented on what a wonderful training ground the Carpenter area would be for Ghanaian medical students and residents. Many of the diseases she saw with us, she had never seen during her training. "If only there was a hospital here!" she said over and over.*
>
> *Then, I bumped into Dr. Jane Philpott. She wondered if U of T could begin to brainstorm with us about training opportunities for family medicine residents to join our medical team one day.*
>
> *U of T also wants to place pharmacy doctorate students with us as well.*
>
> *I keep coming back to David's dream for a hospital in Carpenter.*
>
> *Finally, over the past couple of years, I have been pursuing opportunities in medical education—my Emergency Medicine certification and an International Medicine and Public Health Diploma*

(which, by the way, requires me to spend four weeks at a Ghanaian Hospital). I have also recently been appointed to the faculty at the University of Toronto.

I just can't help but wonder about the timing of all of this. Is it time for us to seriously consider your dream of a hospital?

By 9:02 a.m. that morning, Jacques responded. He had just completed an article for a GRID newsletter entitled "God's Perfect Time." In it, he said, "Our thoughts are turning to what can be done to improve the year-round sustainability of health care in Northern Ghana. The roadblocks that prevented any serious consideration of these matters are slowly being removed. I have absolutely no doubt that in God's perfect time, the right people, facilities, equipment, communication capabilities, and funding will come together to fulfill this next step in His perfect plan…"

Two days later, an email arrived from Ghana. Several events had taken place that were leading David and Brenda to also conclude that it was time to seriously explore a hospital in Carpenter. Brenda signed off her email by saying, "As you both mentioned, God is positioning things again to push us out of the nest as He reminds us that HE can do exceedingly more than we can ask or think! You are such special partners and friends."

And that was all it took—three emails between three people over three days—to create unstoppable momentum. In June, the GRID board commissioned a one-year feasibility study. A few weeks later, David, Brenda, Jacques and I excitedly sketched our vision of the NEA hospital onto the whiteboard of the Uxbridge Hospital Board Room. In July, a task force was formed to determine if NEA could build and run their own hospital. In November, I was back on a plane to Ghana.

Brenda was absolutely correct. I was, indeed, being pushed—if not shoved—out of my cosy, warm, and very safe nest in Uxbridge, Ontario, Canada. I'm so glad that no one told this little birdie how horrific my first solo flight would be.

CHAPTER 18

Who Am I?

"If you have come here to help me, you are wasting your time. But if you have come because your liberation is bound up with mine, then let us work together."

~ Lilla Watson,
Indigenous artist, writer, educator, and researcher

At the end of life, I'm sure that many people can look back and recount the single most challenging experience they have ever faced. Like an unwelcome guest, sooner or later hardship and tragedy arrive unannounced on our doorsteps. Worst nightmares can come to life in an instant, changing who we are and how we live.

An extended professional nightmare began in November of 2013, as I reported for duty in a large hospital in west-central Ghana.

My return to Ghana that year had happened ahead of schedule. After I became a Master Trainer in the "Helping Babies Breathe" (HBB) program, our team at GRID submitted a proposal to the Canadian Government to incorporate HBB into the Leyaata Project. Oh, how we celebrated when the program to save newborn babies in Ghana was approved and funded! Finally, we could take action to combat the unspeakably high newborn mortality rate that our statistics continued to record. NEA asked me to return as soon as possible to conduct the training for thirty-three health professionals in the Northern Region.

Meanwhile, to graduate with my International Medicine and Global Health Diploma, I was required to complete an international field placement. A post was available at a hospital in Ghana, just a few hours away from the NEA project site. David, Brenda, Graham, and I decided that I would return to Ghana in the fall of 2013 to complete my placement, followed by the HBB training. Now that the hospital feasibility study was underway, this was a well-timed opportunity for me to see a Ghanaian hospital first-hand and gather research that would assist our task force.

Being away from home for almost a month was no small decision. The kids were fifteen, thirteen, eleven, nine, and nine, and our household was a swarm of activity. We added a second piano to accommodate five practice schedules and, on most days, could have used a second washing machine as well. Graham ran a full-time chauffeur service between home, school, dance studios, and hockey arenas all over Southern Ontario. His fifteen-passenger van was often full of neighbourhood friends and teammates. The contrast between the opportunities our children enjoyed in Canada compared to those available to the children in Ghana also motivated me to return.

Thankfully, I did not have to travel alone. My team pharmacist, Susan Fockler, joined me to complete her clinical placement in international pharmacy at the same hospital. She graciously offered to accompany me to Carpenter afterwards to assist with the running of the HBB program.

While I had Susan to support me in Ghana, Graham had no shortage of assistance back at home. A father left to care for five children for a month garnered quite a bit of attention in our little town. Laura Boire, the administrator of our local public school, made it her personal mission to ensure Graham stayed organized with school deadlines and gave the kids free passes when they were late. In turn, he gave her banana bread. The church ladies, oozing with sympathy for my "poor husband," sent meals and offers of help. And of course, Graham's mom, my parents, and our siblings provided never-ending help as chefs, extra drivers, babysitters, and errand runners. Although I knew how capable he was of managing solo, I was very grateful for the "home team" who showed love and support to my family when I was in Ghana. Graham also speaks of that time with gratitude, but was uncomfortable with the idea that he was made out to be a "hero" or "super-dad" because he was willing and able to cook, clean (well, sort of), and buy groceries with five kids in tow. It didn't seem fair to him that the same expectations are often placed on women without fanfare, accolades, or support.

Susan and I landed in Accra and were transported to a sprawling hospital in west-central Ghana. This facility served as a referral centre for over twenty public and private health clinics, and was a bustling obstetrical centre. All ailments were cared for, but the most common conditions were malaria, malnutrition, pneumonia, hepatitis, tropical ulcers, typhoid fever, pregnancy complications, schistosomiasis, hypertension, HIV, and anaemia. Although I had studied these conditions, I rarely saw them in Canada and I was excited about all that I was about to learn and experience.

We were escorted to a small apartment a short walk from the hospital that was built for visiting international specialists. It was clean and bright with a furnished living room, dining room, two bedrooms, a flush toilet, and a shower containing two large green buckets. Electricity and running water were unreliable, so we had to keep those buckets full of water for use whenever the taps ran dry. The kitchen held a tiny fridge, a kettle, a propane burner, and an abundance of ants. Uncertain of our cooking facilities or access to groceries, Susan came prepared with most of our food. Breakfasts were porridge and bright yellow bananas purchased at the market. Lunches were tuna, crackers, protein bars, nuts, and dried fruit. Susan pulled out all the stops for dinner with freeze-dried gourmet camping meals, like plates of beef bourguignon, always served on a placemat. The apartment felt safe and had everything we needed.

After a quick rest, our work began. My role was to look after patients alongside the two hospital doctors and engage in a mutual exchange of learning. Susan would do the same with the team of hospital pharmacists. Meanwhile, I would gather as many answers as possible to the list of research questions that my hospital feasibility task force had given me.

I was excited and nervous as I arrived for my first day in the hospital. The emergency "department" was a single, cramped, noisy room jammed with stretchers. Linens for the stained mattresses were absent, as was any privacy for the patients lying on them or on the floor. The air was hot and thick with the smell of blood and other bodily fluids. I heard someone yell, "We need more anti-snake venom STAT!" as a snake-bite victim cried in agony from two bleeding puncture wounds on his swollen foot. As I walked around to get my bearings, I noticed a cupboard labelled "emergency medicines." The door was falling off its hinge. I carefully opened it to peek at what was available. Inside were scattered plastic containers bearing handwritten labels on dirty masking tape. Most of the containers that should have been full of critical medications, such as epinephrine or nitroglycerin, were empty. Before I could receive any orientation, a child having a seizure was carried in. I asked the nurse where the doctors were. "They are unavailable," she said. One was travelling and the other was in the middle of a caesarean section. I asked her what they usually do when the doctor is unavailable, to which she replied, "We do our best." She gently nudged me towards the bedside. *Seriously?*

With no time to say, "I'm supposed to be working with the doctors here!" I found myself in charge of this seizing child. Managing a paediatric seizure is a bread-and-butter scenario for every emergency physician. My training kicked in and I asked the nurse to check the child's temperature and sugar level, insert an intravenous, and draw up a medication called Lorazepam. The seizure continued and the nurse announced, "We have run out of Lorazepam."

"Midazolam or Diazepam will be just fine then," I said.

"We have run out of those as well."

Trying hard to disguise the rising panic in my voice, the bare cupboard of "emergency medicines" in my peripheral vision, I moved down the list to my fourth and then my fifth choices of medication. She shook her head again and again.

Another patient arrived short of breath, with low oxygen levels. I ordered oxygen. "Sorry, Doctor, our tank of oxygen is being used at the present time." *Tank? As in, you only have one of them?*

Then, a young woman arrived with severe abdominal pain and vaginal bleeding. Concerned about an ectopic (tubal) pregnancy, I ordered a stat ultrasound. Again, the shake of the head. "The ultrasound machine has had a "small-small" problem for a month or so."

Thus far in Ghana, the strength of my Ghana Health Team had made me brave. Whenever three whistles sounded, a team of skilled nurses and doctors and a fully stocked duffle bag were by my side. Now—flying solo—I was having trouble locating my courage. My worst professional nightmare, until that day, was that I would lack the required knowledge or skill when faced with an emergency situation on my watch. It never occurred to me that I could be alone in an emergency room, knowing exactly what to do, but lacking the resources to do it.

As I was considering this new reality, a young nurse anesthesiologist named Eric Boatang arrived in the ER asking if he could assist me. Together, we finally stopped the seizure with a milky white medication usually reserved to put people to sleep during painful procedures or surgeries. We converted air into oxygen for the patient who was short of breath using a rusty old concentrator that was in the corner of a dirty storage room. As for the bleeding pregnant woman, her pain escalated as her blood pressure plummeted. Eric and I rushed her to the second operating room and stabilized her with blood products and TXA while we waited for the doctor to complete the caesarian section. He arrived just in time—a two-month pregnancy, the size of a raspberry, had broken through the narrow fallopian tube and was now filling her pelvis with blood.

For the first time in hours, I exhaled and felt my heart rate finally begin to fall. Losing a patient for want of medications and equipment that are so inexpensive, and so readily available at home, was not a reality I had ever considered.

Soon, I would be officially introduced to both hospital doctors on staff, and for the next two weeks, I would work alongside them in every area of the hospital. The respect I gained for them quickly grew deep and wide. They were on duty twenty-four hours a day, seven days a week, covering the endless line-ups of patients in the emergency room, wards, surgery, the HIV/AIDS clinic, and the maternity program. They were expected to do it all, including emergency operations such as caesarian sections, ectopic pregnancies, appendectomies, hernias, and trauma.

I got to know one of the physicians, Dr. Benjamin Asubiojo, well, and I was privileged to witness first-hand the challenges he faced every day. He helped me understand all aspects of the Ghanaian health care system and I filled more than one Moleskine journal with insights that he provided.

Dr. Ben was a great teacher. One day, he asked me to assist him on an operation involving a young boy with typhoid fever. Typhoid fever, which resembles malaria in its initial presentation, has the most unusual complication in that the bacteria, called Salmonella typhi, can cause tiny holes in the bowel. He made the diagnosis without an ultrasound or CT scan to help him. In the operating room he taught me how to meticulously inspect every inch of this boy's small intestine (all fifteen or so feet of it) to find these small perforations. Every few feet, we would come across another deadly hole, oozing out foul contents, and threatening to kill this child if not carefully repaired. Halfway through the surgery, the lights flickered, and the hospital lost its power. The theatre nurse strapped a headlamp onto Dr. Ben's head, and he carried on without flinching.

Throughout my placement he taught me to be creative and do my best with what we had. He also modelled how to fight against the fear or paralysis that dwindling resources could cause—lack of staffing, supplies, equipment, and medication were a constant reality in Ghana. As I watched all of the hospital staff do their work while constantly improvising, I realized how much I took for granted my ready access to the tools I needed to care for my patients at home.

What impressed me most about Dr. Ben was his passion to deliver the best care possible to his patients, no matter what the obstacles. He dreamed of pursuing more training and education—especially in obstetrics and gynecology—due to the complicated cases that arrived at his centre. He confided that transferring patients to bigger hospitals was a last resort, as most of them never returned. The look on his face, when he explained that to me, was the exact same look that had been on David Mensah's face when he told us not to transfer his nephew Joshua to hospital.

A few days into my placement, needing a break from the emergency room, I decided to wander over to the labour and delivery ward. I introduced myself to the lead midwife, who suggested I look around.

I walked through the maternity ward which held at least twenty-five women in labour or recovering from childbirth. A breastfeeding class was taking place in the centre of the room. I walked into the delivery area, where the cries of women in the throes of painful contractions filled the air.

As I turned a corner into the delivery hallway, I bumped into a steel cart. That bump set off a landslide of events, unforeseen by any of us in that hospital, at NEA, or at the teaching institution that posted me there.

On the cart was a motionless, blue, newborn baby. I glanced around, but the hallway was empty. I instinctively placed my hand on his head, assuming he was deceased, and was startled to discover that he was still soft and warm to my touch. My heart began to pound in my chest as adrenaline surged throughout my body. I quickly placed my thumb and my first finger on the baby's still wet umbilical cord—the best location to feel for a pulse. Sure enough, between my trembling fingers was a rapid, bounding pulse, begging me to act. This baby was still alive.

In a flash, I recalled what the Helping Babies Breathe instructor in Kansas City had so emotionally explained to us—the hypothesis that many of the "stillborn" deaths in the majority world were not stillborn at all—they were living babies who just needed help to begin to breathe.

Reflexively I yelled out, "CODE PINK, CODE PINK," which is what we announce when a child is in cardiac or respiratory arrest in Canada. I knew it was a ridiculous thing to say, there in that empty hallway in a Ghanaian maternity ward so far from home. I ripped my backpack off and thanked God and my Girl Guide training that I had packed my bag-valve-mask ventilator (BMV) as I was running out the door that morning.

A BMV is an essential tool in the HBB program. You need it to resuscitate a newborn who is alive but not yet breathing. The device is a small, round plastic mask that fits over the baby's mouth and nose which is connected to a hand-held cylindrical bag that delivers air into the baby's lungs when squeezed. This action can kick-start the breathing of a baby who has not, for some reason, taken its first breath.

I opened the baby's mouth, applied the mask, and began to gently squeeze the bag, following the protocol I was about to teach in Carpenter. "One and two and breathe, one and two and breathe." Over and over I repeated this as I watched and hoped and prayed that it wasn't too late. Then, the baby's colour began to change from deep blue to pale and then to pink. Moments later, he sputtered, gasped, and then began to cry. Shock and relief flooded over me and my eyes blurred with tears. I heard a noise behind me and turned to find a group of wide-eyed, open-mouthed maternity nurses staring at me, the baby, and what was known as the "stillborn cart." Later, the lead midwife confided in me that they thought I was a witch.

The next day, the same thing happened. This time, the nurses gathered around me and watched precisely what I did to help the baby start to breathe. I realized that none of them had any training in newborn resuscitation. This was startling to me. I had assumed that lack of education in neonatal resuscitation was a problem in remote village clinics—not in a major hospital.

The day after that, I was drawn back to the maternity ward first thing in the morning and the same pattern repeated itself. Now appreciating that a newborn who was not yet breathing may indeed be alive, the staff did not place the baby on the "stillborn cart." Rather, they placed the baby on our newly created "resuscitation cart" and asked me to teach them what to do. Together, we resuscitated the baby. The joy on the faces of these nurses and midwives when the baby's life was saved was indescribable. As I was leaving the maternity department to head back to the ER, the lead midwife, who had been critically appraising all of these events, asked if I could teach her the entire HBB program—she didn't want to wait for the training in Carpenter.

When I asked her when she wanted to begin, she responded, "Tonight."

It was around this time, that David and Brenda paid me a surprise visit. Their presence unleashed emotions that I had done a superb job of bottling up. As Brenda greeted me with a big hug, I began to weep, and despite all efforts, I could not stop. I tried to discreetly and respectfully explain the horror—the lack of resources and the responsibility I felt to "fix" everything—but I couldn't get a word out.

Brenda simply whispered, "We know. We know."

Well, of course they knew. And they had timed their visit very strategically, knowing what I had gotten myself into. They knew exactly what I would encounter in the dark, unknown waters of a Ghanaian hospital and they also knew that it was not something that could be explained to me. To believe it, I needed to see and feel it for myself, without the safety net of their presence or my team's. I'm sure there was a lot of advice they could have brought with them that day. Instead, they brought supplies: toilet paper, bottled water, salt, fresh limes from their tree, bananas, NEA peanut butter, and ant traps, along with abundant friendship and love.

That evening, after the Mensahs departed, the midwife knocked on the door of our apartment, and for three hours I took her through the first module of the HBB program, which involved preparing for a healthy delivery and providing routine care to a crying newborn. She soaked up every word and was a swift learner. At the end of our teaching session, I suggested that the following day we film a video of her preparing for a normal delivery and providing routine care to a newborn, to be used during the training in Carpenter. She was delighted by that suggestion.

The next day, the midwife and I carefully set up all her equipment, including her BMV, for a planned caesarian section. This was a healthy pregnancy, and no complications were anticipated. Eric was the nurse anaesthetist in the theatre that morning and he agreed to film the procedure. The c-section was uneventful. Dr. Ben handed the baby boy off to the midwife as Eric began to video. The midwife brought the baby to the infant warmer and started her routine care. She carefully dried the baby and then stimulated him. For most healthy newborns, this is all that is required to start respiration, after which the baby is given eye drops, vitamin K, and placed on the mother's chest. However, there was one "small-small" problem—this baby never started to breathe.

The midwife continued to stimulate the baby and moved on to suction the airway, but the baby drew no breath. She looked at me in horror then back at the blue, limp infant. All her equipment was set up, even though we had not expected to need it, so I held out the

BMV and, with shaking hands, she took it from me. She had not yet been trained to properly use the device (that was session #2), but she had watched me do it, so she placed it over the baby's mouth and nose, and tried to help him breathe.

"One and two and breathe, one and two and breathe," I coached.

Air was escaping from the mask, so I helped her adjust it.

"One and two and breathe, one and two and breathe."

Nothing was happening. The camera was rolling. The baby's pulse was dropping; he was going to die.

I took over temporarily. "One and two and breathe, one and two and breathe." I prayed as I squeezed, a crowd gathering on the other side of the observation window. Then, suddenly, I saw the baby's little finger twitch. As I stared intently, his colour began to change. Then he gasped. Then we gasped. I handed the BMV back to the midwife to continue.

Soon the most melodious sound echoed off the walls of the operating theatre; the lusty cries of a newborn baby.

It worked. It really worked. And we had it all on film. At that moment, everyone in the theatre including myself, felt like we had just witnessed a modern-day miracle. We truly appreciated the lives that could be saved through this HBB program. That evening, there wasn't an empty chair around my dining room table. Eric, Dr. Ben, the midwife, and the maternity nurses didn't want to wait another moment to receive their training. They watched the video of the midwife's resuscitation over and over again and she became something of a movie star.

The next day, while Eric and I worked in the ER, a messenger came running. We were needed stat in the maternity ward. A woman from a remote village had arrived after being in obstructed labour for many days. The baby was in distress and needed help breathing.

This baby was in big trouble. She was grunting, her nostrils were flaring, and she was becoming limp. Her black skin was paler than my white hands that reached out to care for her. She needed breathing support and a neonatal intensive care unit (NICU). Our hospital had none of these resources.

Eric, Ben, and I discussed the case together, and I asked if transferring the baby to a NICU in a larger hospital was an option. This was not usually their protocol, as it was a very long journey. However, we had only two choices: watch her die or attempt the transfer. The decision was made that Eric and I would transport the baby to the regional hospital and Ben would alert the NICU that we were coming.

After intubating the baby and stabilizing her with a glucose solution, we were informed that the ambulance was ready. We rolled the baby out to the front courtyard of the hospital, where a vehicle was waiting. It was not what I was expecting. A van had been modified into an ambulance by removing the back seats to make just enough room for an oxygen tank and a body. The oxygen tank didn't properly connect to our ventilation system, so with scissors and duct tape Eric rigged them together and we all squeezed in, unrestrained, and took off for the NICU.

It didn't take long for the first waves of nausea to wash over me as I faced backward in the make-shift Ghanaian ambulance. It was a frantic and wild drive along a dark, windy, pothole-filled road with this newborn clinging to life. We held on for three hours and prayed that we would make it in time.

Halfway there, Eric tapped me on the shoulder while I was vomiting copiously into my little bag.

"Dr. Jenn, the baby's breathing tube has become dislodged due to the road conditions. Please—you must re-intubate the baby. And doctor—we have a "small-small" problem—we have run out of oxygen."

It felt like I was in a horror movie with no escape, professionally vulnerable and personally terrified. I was sweating profusely, buffeted by tidal waves of nausea, vomiting uncontrollably, and we were still hours away from the neonatal ICU. Who was I to be carrying out the highly skilled procedure of intubating a newborn in the back of a so-called "ambulance" that had just run out of oxygen?

I was way out of my comfort zone and my imposter syndrome was screaming in my ear, "You are a small-town family doctor, not a neonatologist!" *There is no way this baby will survive.*

I instructed the driver to pull over. I steadied myself, prayed for courage and favour, and placed the blade with the light into the baby's mouth to search for the tiny vocal cords through which I somehow needed to thread the tiniest of breathing tubes. As the blade slid in, my target—two small vocal cords—popped immediately into view, lit up like the Eiffel tower, clear as day. Then, like the parting of the Red Sea, the cords opened as the baby took a gasp, ushering the life-giving tube straight through. *Did that just happen?* Using only room air instead of oxygen, we were able to continue to support the baby's breathing.

When Eric finally pointed to the distant lights of the massive regional hospital, the relief I experienced was indescribable.

I've felt it in the past, but to a lesser degree. Before we had critical care ORNGE paramedics in Ontario, we as physicians would travel in the ambulance with our sickest patients when transferring to other hospitals. Pulling up to the Hospital for Sick Children or St. Michael's Trauma Centre in Toronto and handing over the care of a severely ill or injured patient to an expert team in a state-of-the-art centre was the best feeling in the world.

Now, I couldn't take my eyes off the lights of that regional centre as it drew closer. I visualized the neonatal team assembling and preparing for our arrival in the "Promised Land." Once I had passed our little newborn into their capable hands, I planned to record as much information about this tertiary care centre as possible for our task force.

When we entered the hospital, however, no one seemed to be expecting us. As I continued to ventilate the baby outside the emergency room, I could hear Eric involved in a heated conversation. His arms were flailing and he was pleading.

Why on earth is he pleading?

He returned and explained apologetically that they were unable to accept the baby. They had no working ventilators in the hospital and the pediatrician was "unavailable." They were directing us to carry on to the teaching hospital in another city which was three to four hours away.

I began to vomit again, and I knew I was about to faint. I also knew that this baby girl could not survive another four hours on the road.

After making sure I was okay, Eric disappeared again and, in my unfocussed, peripheral vision, I could see him talking to the staff and pointing at me, the semi-conscious, dehydrated, ghostly pale woman slumped against the wall. He returned moments later and announced that we were going home—they had accepted the baby after all. A respiratory technician arrived and took over, promising he would ventilate the baby all night if he had to. I had no choice but to believe him.

We left the hospital, my journal pages disappointingly blank, and I lay down in the back of the ambulance, begging sleep to come and end my misery. About an hour later, I awoke to Eric tapping me on the shoulder. "Dr. Jenn, we have a "small-small" problem. Our vehicle has broken down."

Of course our vehicle has broken down. At that moment, I thought I might just die on the roadside. All I could do was muster a weak but sincere prayer: *"Korowii te ya kere."*

Eric laughed at my pronunciation.

Prayers answered, tomorrow was granted to me and to the resilient baby girl whose parents sent word about ten days later that she had made a full recovery and been discharged back to her village.

David Mensah was not pleased with me when, eventually, word got to him that I had made that journey. Travelling on unlit treacherous roads, the risk of becoming a victim of a traffic crash or crime rose exponentially in the dark of night. But how could I not? The life of a baby girl was at stake. To be honest, I just forgot to properly consider my personal safety.

The last day of my placement finally arrived, and I was honoured to be asked to give a teaching session for the entire medical staff. We gathered in the outdoor chapel and worked through a variety of emergency medicine topics and procedures. With a broader and deeper understanding of the limitations of their system, I could tailor my teaching to the Ghanaian setting. Eric asked me to instruct them on how to use an interosseous (IO) needle—something he had only read about. This was the device we had used on our 2013 mission to save the French-speaking little girl who drank the caustic liquid. I didn't bring any IO needles with me (incorrectly assuming they would have them), but I used pictures to explain. I promised to send a box by mail when I got home so Eric could train the emergency room staff how to use them. From that day forward, boxes of IOs travelled from Uxbridge Hospital to Ghana once a year and Eric soon became the regional expert and trainer in IO needle insertion.

On a monthly basis, he would send me a picture of IO patients, always with the same caption, "Another life saved."

When the two-hour teaching session ended, Susan and I bid farewell to our new friends and colleagues. We would see many of them in Carpenter the following week for the HBB training, including Eric and my new physician colleague, Ben.

I exited the chapel and relief flooded over me. I was officially off duty! It is a feeling that every emergency room physician anticipates and celebrates as they walk out the door at the end of a shift—the responsibility of saving lives lifted off our shoulders for just a little while. Not only was I off duty, but I had a couple of days off in Carpenter to refresh and recharge before the Helping Babies Breathe program would begin.

If I'm honest, I felt a bit proud of myself at that moment as I walked back to my room to pack my few belongings. These had been the most difficult two weeks of my life, but I had persevered. Furthermore, I had collected a great deal of information from the countless interviews I conducted with hospital staff and my Moleskine journals were full. I would compile it all into a report for our hospital feasibility group. If I could have properly patted myself on the back, I just might have.

As I made my way back to the apartment humming, I heard someone yelling my name. *Please, no.* I could tell by the tone of the yell that something was very wrong. I wanted to ignore that cry for help and pretend I didn't hear it. I was so done. All I wanted to do was pack and leave. *Keep your eyes down Jenny, and just keep walking. Just keep walking.*

It was Eric. Eric was a national level soccer player, so it didn't take him long to catch up to me. A toddler with diarrhea had arrived with his grandmother during the teaching session and the ER staff hadn't wanted to interrupt me. His veins were too flat from severe dehydration to obtain an IV line and they were losing him. Eric wondered if we could somehow make an IO needle, like the one I had just taught them about.

We sprinted back to the emergency room while I frantically brainstormed what we could possibly use to create an IO. As we pushed our way past the boisterous waiting room crowd and approached the toddler's bed, we stopped short. The little boy's grandmother made eye contact with me—her eyes weary and stricken in her wrinkled face—holding mine for a long moment while she raised her hands and waved us off. *What was she doing? Why did she not want me to help her grandson? Where were the parents?* Then, with those same weathered hands, she took off the long colourful cloth wrapped around her waist. She had used it as a sling to carry her weak grandson on her back a great distance from her village to the hospital. Then, she opened her mouth and began to wail as she wrapped it carefully and lovingly around his lifeless body. I looked to Eric, his protective arm now extended in front of me, preventing me from rushing forward towards the deceased child. *Why wasn't anyone calling a "CODE PINK"? Why wasn't anyone doing anything?*

The emergency staff continued their work, acting as though the death of a child happened every day. And then it finally sunk in—it did. This was their reality. It was the first paediatric emergency room death I would witness in Ghana or in Canada.

I had to get out of there. I needed to escape the wails of this grandmother and the walls of this hospital that had been unable to save her grandchild. I pushed my way through the waiting room crowd and ran back to my residence.

I didn't know what to think or how to feel. While I was teaching and then mentally patting myself on the back for a "job well done," a child had died of dehydration. He was a boy. A son. A brother. A grandson. *If I had not been teaching that session, would we have been able to save him? Why didn't they feel they could interrupt me? If I had thought to pack IO needles, would he now be alive?*

I tried to pretend that it didn't happen. I willed myself to block out those piercing wails and focus on the "good things" we had accomplished. But my intrusive thoughts kept breaking in, uninvited. *After all I had endured over those two weeks—bumping into babies left to die on steel carts, risking my life in "ambulances," learning, teaching, and training—this was how it was going to end? With the death of a child? This was the memory that I would be forced to forever carry with me?*

I arrived back to my room and slid to the floor. A sensation of helplessness, of failure, welled up in me. I began to spiral into a dark place of despair. I dialed Graham's cell phone. All it took was the sound of his voice and the dam collapsed. I wept over this boy and over the injustice upon injustice I had witnessed since arriving in Ghana.

I tried to speak but my constricted vocal cords would only allow me to utter three words: "EVACUATE ME NOW!"

I wondered what Graham was doing when I made that desperate call. I could tell he was busy—probably helping five kids with their homework and piano practices while simultaneously making dinner. *What were they having for dinner? Maybe he was making his famous Shepherd's Pie or perhaps it was "dipping egg night"* (what we fondly call soft boiled eggs in cute egg cups that we dip thin fingers of buttered toast into).

Snapping me back to my Ghanaian reality, he asked me, with deep concern in his voice, what was going on. I told him I was not equipped for this work, that the problems in Ghana were far too massive, that building a hospital in Carpenter was just a dream, that a child died because of me, and that I needed to immediately return home to my family. I wanted back in my nest and I never wanted to leave it again. I needed him to send me help NOW. I needed sympathy and support—for him to rescue me. Instead, my husband said, "Well Jenny…maybe God wanted you to witness all of that for a reason."

I heard the timer go off on his stove—and I hung up on him.

Light-headed and dazed I rose from the floor, still wracked with sobs, and my feet somehow carried me back to that emergency room. The crowd was large and deafening, yet the tiny boy still lay there, silent and motionless on the dirty black stretcher, covered in his grandmother's parting gift. *Why was he still there? Had she gone for help to carry him back to their village? Or would he remain in the morgue until the family could save enough money for a funeral in the months ahead, as is often the custom in Ghana?*

I stood vigil across the room and forced myself to look at him—that small, ashen bundle—swaddled in the lively patterns and vibrant colours of Ghana. His long journey to me and my long journey to him was over. I realized that he likely had no parents. They most certainly had died and he, like so many orphans, had been left in the care of his grandmother—just as Stephen Lewis had said during his keynote address that awoke me from my slumber.

The permanence of a child forever separated from loved ones moved me deeply. I thought of my kids and how separated I was from them—as they delightedly ate their dipping eggs in my mind's eye. I reflected on how Graham and I had come close to losing three of them, on three separate occasions, many years ago. It took three wonderful hospitals and countless health professionals to save them—Olivia from complications of Kawasaki disease at age four, Joshua from meningitis at six weeks of life, and Jessica when she did not draw her first breath at birth. My hand instinctively reached up to clutch my keepsake necklace.

This boy, like five million other children in the majority world every year, had died needlessly of a preventable and treatable condition in a hospital that was ill-equipped to save him.

My global health brain knew these statistics and would quote them to obtain the diploma that would soon hang on my wall—but on that day, these statistics pierced my heart. They now had a face and a name and an indelible memory attached to them, a memory of a grandmother's grief, and her colourful cloth. An unfamiliar mixture of sadness, anger, and longing to hold my own children began to swirl in my soul. The weight of this little boy's death, and the pain that his loved ones would forever endure, pressed down on me. I felt nearly suffocated by my inability to save him or his 4,999,999 future friends.

Oh God. What on earth am I doing here and what am I supposed to do now? Who am I to be considering these things? Suddenly, another power outage plunged the room into darkness.

The answers to my prayer and to my nightmare's many questions would not be forthcoming. The absence of light could not extinguish the image of that boy from my mind. Defeated and diminished, I fumbled my way out from my Ghanaian classroom, the infirmary door creaking shut behind me for the final time.

CHAPTER 19

Empowered by Epiphany

"The size of your dreams must always exceed your current capacity to achieve them. If your dreams do not scare you, they are not big enough."

~ Ellen Johnson Sirleaf
Africa's first female president

The room was full of anticipation as David Mensah walked to the front of the NEA training room. As was often his custom, he began with a story:

The group of villagers had no choice but to cross the Volta River in search of food. It was a risky decision as the river was full of danger, including crocodiles. Facing starvation if they remained, the villagers set across, the water level low enough to cross on foot. The group made it safely to the far bank when suddenly, they heard a cry for help. Somehow, a young boy had been left behind and was caught in the current—struggling to get to shore. The villagers watched in horror as they saw the head of not one but two crocodiles making their way towards him. The oldest man in the tribe, Mr. Gonga, threw himself in the water and frantically splashed towards the child as the crocodiles prepared their attack. Scooping the boy onto his back, Mr. Gonga single-handedly fought off the beasts as he carried the boy to safety.

David took a long pause in order to look directly into the eyes of each of the thirty-three health care workers who had gathered for the inaugural Helping Babies Breathe (HBB) program. He raised both hands in the air and said, "Mr. Gonga was a Leyaata."

David continued to address the wide-eyed crowd. He reminded them that too many of Ghana's children were being lost in the river—snatched by the jaws of poverty, inadequate access to health care, and birth asphyxia. So now, this army of Mr. Gongas would join NEA and the Leyaata "Rescue Us" team to fight the forces that were stealing their children.

Then he looked at me and gave me his famous "now-it's-your-turn-to-give-a-speech" nod. I stepped to the front of the room full of Northern Ghana's midwives, nurses, and physicians and was surprised that my strength and confidence, depleted by my recent hospital placement, had returned in full measure.

On the journey from the hospital in west-central Ghana, where I had completed my global health placement, I slept all the way to the NEA compound. David and Brenda were waiting for Susan and me on their front porch and welcomed us with a luncheon of mushroom soup, salmon sandwiches, and hot tea. That morning, Frank had harvested mushrooms, and Kate had baked bread in honour of our arrival. David slipped out to enjoy his more typically Ghanaian lunch of fufu (boiled cassava, yam, or plantain that is pounded into a dough and served with soup or stew). I've never forgotten that meal shared with Brenda at her dining room table. Three Canadian women sipping tea as if we were in the Château Laurier, so far from home, surrounded by so much poverty and suffering. Flavourful food, rich fellowship, hearty laughter, and therapeutic "girl talk" did wonders to refresh my weary heart.

There is nothing like the presence of family to bolster you up when you are wounded, and that was precisely what my NEA family did for me that day. I spent the afternoon sitting in the shade, visiting with the NEA staff and the compound kids—something that I rarely had time to do during our busy Ghana Health Team missions.

They all wanted to know how "Oleeevia" was doing. Abraham and Kate arrived hand in hand with news that they were engaged to be married! It was the first of a few health team romances that blossomed under the Ghanaian sun, and it was such a delight to celebrate with them.

In the afternoon, Brenda prescribed me a cold shower and a nap in my air-conditioned room—heaven. That evening, Ernestina arrived, and we sat on the Mensahs' living room couch, munching on peanuts from the NEA farms, and talked late into the night. Before falling asleep, I finally got two small bars of cell phone coverage when I leaned far enough out Brenda's kitchen window. Graham was so relieved to hear from me and know that I was safe and sound in Carpenter. I was relieved to apologize for hanging up on him during my epic "evacuate-me-now" SOS call. He updated me on the kids and news from home and that night, I slept in peace for the first time in weeks.

The following day, five highly experienced birth attendants, hand-picked by NEA, arrived to join Ernestina on the compound. To make this training as effective and sustainable in the long term as possible, I spent the first two days teaching these select men and women to become HBB facilitators. They participated in two days of rigorous training to understand the HBB program and learn how to facilitate it. After the two days, they were required to pass a written exam, a skills station exam, and two practice oral exams. All six completed the training.

That evening, the compound sprang to life as twenty-seven local birth attendants, each representing a different health facility, descended onto the project site for the HBB provider training. Eric and Dr. Ben, from the hospital I had just come from, arrived to assist me. I was thrilled to introduce them to the Mensahs. David, Brenda, and Dr. Ben quickly realized that they knew one another—Ben had been the youth drummer in their Tamale church many years earlier.

The following day, we gathered under the gazebo for morning devotions, always the custom with NEA. Everyone was dressed to the nines, wearing their participant ID badges with great pride. They had minimal opportunity for continuing education in Ghana, and most had never set foot on the famous NEA compound. Eric asked if he could share a testimony and he thanked God for bringing this training to his hospital, which had already saved the lives of at least ten newborns. Abraham and Kate cooked a hearty breakfast for us all, after which the training began.

Now, it was time for me to address these eager recruits. David

Mensah's "Mr. Gonga" river story was a hard act to follow. Still, when I stepped to the front of the room after my introduction as the "Canadian expert in neonatal resuscitation" I felt surprisingly confident. I knew the material inside and out, but more importantly, because of all I had witnessed at the Ghanaian hospital, I could now authentically teach this course. Because my eyes had been opened to the nature of the crocodiles that lurked along the rivers in Ghana, my instruction could be relevant and practical.

Armed with this knowledge and insight, I was able to embrace this role and accept my calling to train this group to save the lives of babies. My imposter syndrome was nowhere to be found that day, and I was able to focus on being a bridge between what was and what could be.

I began the day by sharing with them that, according to UNICEF, up to twenty-five per cent of neonatal deaths are caused by birth asphyxia. In addition to this, three million babies (and probably many more) worldwide are termed "stillbirth," when many of them could be saved with simple measures. I reminded them that we believed that newborn death rates in the Northern Region could be as high as 135/1,000 (much higher than the national average of 50/1,000 that we included in all our grant applications). They knew these statistics only too well. I explained that HBB was an evidence-based program endorsed by the World Health Organization, scientifically designed to reduce newborn mortality using simple, inexpensive interventions. Over ninety per cent of at-risk babies in the Leyaata Project catchment area could be saved by what they were about to learn.

Then they watched something more powerful than any words could speak; I showed them the video Eric had filmed of the hospital midwife saving the life of the newborn while I coached her.

The room erupted in singing and dancing when they witnessed our midwife, now an HBB facilitator, bring this "stillborn" to life. They wanted to watch it again and again. I was struck by how much rejoicing there was over this one life saved. It wasn't just the one life, though—they immediately appreciated that this one life-saving incident was about to be multiplied exponentially.

For the next two days, we used an adult model of education to train them. First, I would give a brief lecture, after which they would divide into small groups where their HBB facilitators would teach them the skills, then they would practice. Once skills training was complete, we ran simulations to practice under pressure, over and over again.

I was struck by how wholeheartedly they threw themselves into the training. Often in the evening, I would see groups of them refining their technique late into the night. During breaks, I saw them studying their notes. When examination day arrived, everyone was extremely nervous. They were required to complete both a written exam and a skills-testing station, followed by a simulated scenario run by my facilitators.

All twenty-seven participants passed the course. Because of everyone's diligence, we finished with time to spare, so I added a half-day program called "Helping Mothers Survive"—a brief introduction to emergency obstetrical training which included management of postpartum hemorrhage.

NEA was tasked with arranging the graduation ceremony. The participants gathered in the training room, all in their very best attire. David Mensah gave the opening remarks and explained that it was time to introduce them to some "elephants"—some of the top medical leadership in Northern Ghana. Then, the door opened and in strode a representative from the President's Office, the District Chief Executive, and the District Directors of Health for Bole Region, Kintampo North, Wenchi, and Kintampo South.

The Bole District Director of Medical Services announced that he wanted to start training other health professionals in the northern half of the district the following week. People had been "filling his ears" with the quality and importance of the training they received. He didn't want his other health workers left out.

Then, one by one, the twenty-seven participants were called to the front. Their facilitator and one of the "elephants" presented them with a framed diploma and tracking sheets to monitor the impact of this program. With extra funding from Canada, the leadership team gave everyone a briefcase full of resuscitation equipment. They received a stethoscope engraved with "Leyaata" and a blood pressure cuff. These attendants were now officially part of the Leyaata Program. It was to these men and women that the community-based surveillance volunteers would now be sending pregnant women to deliver. It was a convocation like none other I had ever witnessed—by Ghanaians for Ghanaians. I wish I had thought to recreate the banner that welcomed me to my last convocation: "In Study Lies Our Strength." It would now be Ghanaians that would fan out and multiply the training—adding more HBB soldiers to their army.

After the ceremony, there was a flurry of activity outside the gazebo. Always the entrepreneur, Abraham had set up an NEA grocery store where participants could buy fresh chicken, tilapia, or eggs on their way home. I also noticed a group of nurses in deep discussion with the Leyaata team under the tree, so I made my way over. This group, from remote villages, had no running water or electricity in their nursing clinics, making it extremely difficult to provide a safe and clean environment for deliveries. The Leyaata Program would rectify that problem by upgrading these facilities before my feet would return to Ghanaian soil.

On my final day in Ghana, I woke very early and went for a walk on the compound. It was still dark as I watched the red taillights of the Leyaata field vehicles make their way down the driveway on their way to the villages. My heart was so full. It had been a rich and vital time, and I felt privileged to have been there. As I made my way back to the Mensahs' home, the sun rising over my shoulder, I was stopped in my tracks beside the NEA well.

There have been four times in my life when I'm sure that God spoke directly to me. I didn't hear a voice or see a vision. There were no flashes of light or thunderclaps. It was just a thought—a compelling thought in my head—that didn't feel like my own.

At that moment, beside the well, I most definitely had an encounter.

"WHY DO YOU DOUBT THAT NEA CAN RUN A HOSPITAL?" boomed in my head.

My mind flashed back to the meeting in David's living room when he shared his vision for an NEA hospital, and we brushed him off with our "we know best" attitude. I thought of our hospital feasibility task force and the barriers *against* building a hospital. I thought of the Ghanaian hospitals' experiences that had crushed me, also crushing my hopes that a quality hospital could exist in Ghana.

I scanned the scenery in front of me. To my left, I saw the new oyster mushroom operation—now generating income and protein for the region. Next to that was the new bulldozer and excavator that would soon be digging fishponds stocked with NEA fingerlings for fifty villages. In front of me stood the gazebo under which I'd been given some of the most incredible spiritual and leadership lessons of my life. My gaze travelled to the two-storey dining hall where hundreds of Ghana Health Team members gathered to eat hundreds of meals and tell hundreds of stories of lives saved and skills transferred. To my right was the NEA training centre, where our thirty-three birth attendants had just been commissioned to go out and save lives. In that same building, NEA trained pastors, youth leaders, and Leyaata's eighty-one community-based surveillance volunteers. Then my eyes, which were now welling up with tears of admiration, fell on the entrance to the Leyaata Program Office. Even before the HBB training, that team's leadership had resulted in reducing newborn mortality by sixty-five per cent in fifty villages after only one year.

The voice in my head was back: "IF NEA CAN DO ALL OF THIS, WHY COULDN'T THEY RUN A HOSPITAL TOO?"

That's a very good question.

As my mind flashed back to all I had just experienced in the Ghanaian hospital system, the reality of what currently existed compared to what could be and what should be, dropped me to my knees. Suddenly, a group of compound children who must have been watching me, rushed to my side. "Let us help you, Dr. Jen-i-fa."

It was then that I knew that NEA would open a hospital. I knew my role was to bring this revelation back to the feasibility study group. This epiphany would never be something I could slot into a column on one of the hundreds of our study's spreadsheets, but it had come from a Voice of Truth. All that we learned through our Ghana Health Team missions, my time at the Ghanaian hospital, and the Helping Babies Breathe program had so perfectly equipped and positioned us to consider taking this next step together.

I thought back to the river story from my first day of medical school once again. Without an accessible and excellent downstream hospital, NEA's upstream efforts would always be limited and health for all, unattainable. I knew it was time for my minority world people and me to rise and take our place as participants in the dream of David, Brenda, NEA, Leyaata, and the army of Mr. Gongas. My encounter at the well caused a fundamental change in my perspective and I knew sharing it could do the same for our hospital feasibility group. Although it was still scary, I was ready to embrace this bold vision of the future.

CHAPTER 20

Semper Fidelis

"Never give in. Never give in. Never, never, never, never—
in nothing, great or small, large or petty—never give in,
except to convictions of honour and good sense.
Never yield to force. Never yield
to the apparently overwhelming might of the enemy.."
~ Winston Churchill

Even before my feet touched down on Canadian soil and my arms wrapped tightly around Graham and our five kids, David and Brenda were receiving exultant reports from the Ghanaian villages. Lives were already being saved by the Helping Babies Breathe and Helping Mothers Survive training. Its immediate impact was profound, and our African instructors wasted no time in scaling up their program.

As we rang in the year 2014, there was much work to be done. The hospital feasibility study was well underway, and I shared my research (and the promptings of my heart) from my placement at the Ghanaian hospital with our task force. At the same time, preparations began in earnest for our next Ghana Health Team to return to Ghana in November. To balance these activities with my family and medical responsibilities in Canada, I expanded my leadership team once again. How grateful I was for the incredible friends and colleagues who stepped up to help. The momentum surrounding our next mission and the future Carpenter Hospital felt unstoppable.

Then, tragedy struck.

Peter, an NEA staff member, and his wife Cecelia were expecting their first baby. When Cecelia arrived at the local clinic in labour, no midwife was available. Cecelia delivered a healthy baby girl, but soon after began to bleed. The attendant, not trained to administer oxytocin for a postpartum hemorrhage, put her in a taxi and sent her to the nearest hospital. She bled to death en route.

Cecelia's death had a profound impact on us all. We had just completed the first year of the Leyaata Project, and maternal and neonatal mortality was plummeting. We had just trained an army of nurses and midwives in Helping Babies Breath and Helping Mothers Survive, and yet, it wasn't enough to help save one of our own—to save Cecelia. Our entire community was devastated.

NEA made two critical decisions after her death. Firstly, they requested an official inquiry so that system issues could be appropriately identified and addressed to prevent this from happening again. Secondly, they committed to helping Peter raise their baby girl, who was given the name Princess. Cecelia's death and the birth of a little princess motivated us to get back to work with even more urgency and seriousness of purpose.

The Carpenter Hospital Task Force, with members in Canada and Ghana, pressed on with the overwhelming assignment of gathering all the necessary data to determine the feasibility of this hospital. One of the biggest challenges we faced was determining the actual construction costs for the facility.

Then, a miracle happened.

No sooner had we acknowledged this roadblock to our study than we were connected with an organization called Engineering Ministries International (EMI). EMI is a non-profit organization made up of architects, engineers, surveyors, and construction managers who use their skills to serve people worldwide through the design of hospitals, schools, water systems, and many other facilities. EMI immediately understood our vision for this model hospital, participated in in-depth meetings with our task force, assembled a large team, and booked their flights to Ghana. At the NEA compound, they spent two intense weeks designing every detail. At the end of their mission, they handed us a Master Plan, architectural drawings, and detailed cost estimates for the hospital. And they did all of this free of charge.

One month later, in June of 2014, our one-year feasibility study was complete. David, Brenda, Rob, Carol, Jacques, Lynnita, and I met together one final time. In my Uxbridge Hospital boardroom, with the master plan spread out on the table before us, we said a prayer and cast our vote. It was unanimous. This hospital was feasible and we eagerly awaited the opportunity to present it to the GRID board in Canada.

This was a massive decision for GRID. It was by far the most ambitious project that we had ever tackled. The total price tag was ten million US dollars. The business plan included some financial support for the hospital for three years, after which it would be self-sustaining and no longer reliant on any external sources of funding.

On June 20, 2014, the GRID board unanimously approved our study and commissioned the beginning of a model hospital for Northern Ghana. It would be built in Carpenter, right beside the NEA compound, and the facility would be given the name "Leyaata Hospital." As its name translates, it would be a place of rescue and sanctuary for all who enter its doors.

Our GRID board paused to take a group picture, marking the historic decision. I was so full of joy. I knew without a shadow of a doubt that it was the right thing to do. Our faith was backed up by high-level research, and our high-level study was backed up by faith—a divine-human cooperative that nothing could thwart. Everything was falling into place.

Then, a deadly virus interrupted our plans.

On March 13, 2014, the Ministry of Health in Guinea issued an alert for an unidentified illness. Shortly after, the Pasteur Institute in France confirmed the illness as Ebola Virus Disease (EVD). On March 23, 2014, with forty-nine confirmed cases and twenty-nine deaths, the WHO officially declared an outbreak of EVD.

Poor public health infrastructure and weak surveillance systems contributed to the difficulty surrounding the containment of the outbreak. It quickly spread to Guinea's bordering countries, Liberia and Sierra Leone. By July 2014, the outbreak had spread to the capitals of all three countries, providing an unprecedented opportunity for transmission. Now, only Côte d'Ivoire stood between the epidemic and Ghana.

On August 8, 2014, WHO declared the deteriorating situation in West Africa a Public Health Emergency of International Concern (PHEIC), which is designated only for events with a risk of international spread or that require a coordinated global response. Over the duration of the epidemic, EVD would spread to Italy, Mali, Nigeria,

Senegal, Spain, the United Kingdom, and the United States.

On August 12, 2014, I penned the following letter to my Ghana Health Team:

> *Dear Team,*
>
> *With tears in my eyes, I am writing to inform you that a decision has been made by NEA and the leadership of this team, to cancel our Ghana Health Team Mission for 2014.*
>
> *Based on the scientific information we have right now about the Ebola outbreak, we are confident that this is the wisest and most responsible decision to make. Today, five probable cases of Ebola were reported in Ghana, and the universities have closed down. Canada has issued a travel advisory for West Africa.*
>
> *The safety of this team is, and will continue to be, our top priority, and we are not willing to put you in harm's way...*
>
> *Although this is heartbreaking, it is not as heartbreaking as the situation West Africa is facing as I write. We are discussing how we can help equip our colleagues in Northern Ghana during this crisis and will keep you posted on our efforts...*
>
> *In conclusion, I just want to thank you all. Thanks for hanging in there and trusting us with this decision. The Mensahs and I cannot believe that not one of you withdrew over this Ebola crisis. That speaks volumes of your commitment to this work and to the poor in Ghana. And so, my hope is that this is not the end for most of us, but rather a pause until such a time as it is safe for us to serve together in Ghana once again.*
>
> *Fondly and with a deep appreciation of each one of you,*
>
> *Jennifer*

In September, our Ghana Health Team had one final team meeting planned in Uxbridge, and I decided not to cancel it. Even though our mission was called off, I invited everyone to gather as scheduled for a meal together. Graham, as he so often did, got stuck executing my hospitality plans. David and Brenda happened to be in Canada at the time, so I asked them to join us.

Everyone came. Many were wearing their team t-shirts. I expected the mood to be sombre and full of disappointment, but I was entirely wrong. As this team without a mission gathered around tables and ate Graham's wonderful cooking, the room began to fill with animated voices and laughter. I had spoken of "cancelling" our mission. They spoke only of "postponing" it. We spent the evening adjusting our plans, strategizing communication with our donors, and looking ahead to our return the following year. Martin announced he wanted to procure a laser to offer permanent treatment for the glaucoma epidemic in Northern Ghana. Our pharmacist Linda announced she had been approved to bring along a Doctor of Pharmacy student from the University of Toronto on our next mission. A group of us physicians excitedly made plans to travel to Philadelphia for a three-day Tropical Medicine conference to better equip us to care for our Ghanaian patients and teach our Ghanaian colleagues.

After dinner and this planning time, David Mensah walked to the front of the room and addressed our team. He was visibly emotional. He began with two words: *"Semper Fidelis."* I didn't understand what he was saying—this term was unfamiliar to me, and it did not sound Ghanaian. When he continued to repeat it, over and over, I discreetly asked Google for a translation."Semper Fidelis" is a Latin phrase that means "always faithful" or "always loyal" and it is the motto of the United States Marines. David's audiences are inevitably impressed by his broad knowledge and application of concepts and cultures.

And so, it was. We had become NEA's supporting troops. David and Brenda were not alone in their struggle. They were surrounded by faithful and loyal soldiers who refused to yield and whose fighting spirit would carry us towards the objectives we agreed upon in 2007. All epidemics and pandemics eventually end, so we would continue to plan and learn and fundraise to make 2015 the best mission yet. The seriousness of purpose shared by those in the room as well as our colleagues in the UK moved David, Brenda, and me deeply.

As Canadian autumn arrived and the leaves began to turn their spectacular shades of red and orange, Ebola raged on in Africa and questions about the future began to consume me. *Would Ebola spread to Ghana? How many friends and colleagues would we lose? Would Ebola also kill the momentum of our Ghana Health Team? How on earth can we launch a capital campaign for an African hospital while an epidemic threatens to become a worldwide pandemic? Would an effective vaccine be developed?* These musings kept me awake at night.

In October, I set off to San Francisco for some therapy. I like to call it "educational therapy," which for me is even better than "retail therapy" (although that has its place too). I attended a large Emergency Medicine conference that usually conflicts with our annual mission. After a jam-packed day of education in trauma, resuscitation, and procedural skills, I went for a walk to the Yerba Buena Gardens in the heart of San Francisco. There, I came across the Martin Luther King, Jr. Memorial, which features a majestic waterfall and shimmering glass panels inscribed with his inspiring words, poems, and images. I stood in front of one particular panel, listening to the sound of water falling over the monument, and read these words:

> *No. No. We are not satisfied, and we will not be satisfied until justice rolls down like water and righteousness like a mighty stream.*

I began to weep. I thought of Cecelia and Princess. All of the injustices I had witnessed in Ghana rolled through my mind in full colour—one by one. *No. No. I am not satisfied.*

It was a sacred moment as I realized that, just as the water rolled down over the monument above me, so too was justice rolling down towards Northern Ghana through our collective efforts. I returned home with even greater resolve. *Thank you, Dr. King, for your inspiration. Thank you, Essentials of Emergency Medicine, for the wonderful therapy.*

On November 21, when David Mensah and I should have been giving a speech in front of a village prior to our clinic, we found ourselves side by side on a stage in Stouffville, Ontario. The event was entitled "One Step Closer," where we launched the Leyaata Hospital capital campaign. The auditorium was packed full of GRID supporters, past donors, health team members, family, and friends. I opened the night with the river story told to me on my first day of medical school. I described the "perilous river" claiming the lives of men, women, and children in Ghana. I spoke about how NEA had a proven track record of building fences along that river to save people from ill-health—fences like clean water, food security, education, and peace-building. I explained that despite these numerous fences and all efforts, people like Cecelia, and like the little boy who died in his grandmother's arms, still fell into the river of ill-health and needed a hospital. I asked them how many of their loved ones had needed a hospital in their lifetime.

I explained how the vision of sustainable health care had been percolating over the past seven years. As we witnessed the needs in Ghana and responded to them, the vision began to crystallize. I showed them, step by step, how this had miraculously happened: the need for medical care—the Ghana Health Team; the need for hernia surgery—our partnership with Operation Hernia; the need for eye and dental care—our expanding vision and dental program; the need to save moms and babies during childbirth—our Leyaata Program and Helping Babies Breathe training; the need to design a model hospital—our partnership with EMI. Each step we took led us to the present need—a model hospital called "Leyaata."

Jacques explained the budget and business model, Lynnita explained the staffing and equipment requirements, and David Mensah closed the night with Ghana's perspective on the Leyaata Hospital. He powerfully communicated what it would mean to his people, the entire region, the country of Ghana, and perhaps even to all of West Africa.

The response was unbelievable. Cheque books flew open, new connections were made, and that night was the beginning of a capital campaign that would see US$1.2 million raised by the end of the year.

As the next six weeks raced by, an announcement was made that filled us with joy: NEA had chosen the future administrator for the Leyaata Hospital. GRID had secured funding for this candidate to begin a two-year Master's Degree in Hospital Administration abroad. Accepting this position was none other than our friend, our brother, our chef with the kind heart and big smile—Abraham. Abraham would soon be packing his bag, saying goodbye to Kate and his newborn daughter for a little while, and boarding a plane for England. He was leaving Ghana for the first time in his life.

With a tumultuous 2014 drawing to a close, Ghana was declared Ebola-free and we thanked God for His grace and mercy. The momentum towards our next mission and the Leyaata Hospital was picking up in magnitude and speed while we happily hung on, enjoying every moment of the ride.

CHAPTER 21
I Dreamed a Dream

"Cherish your visions and your dreams,
as they are the children of your soul;
the blueprints of your ultimate achievements."
~ Napoleon Hill

On his deathbed, the father of So-Naba Mahami Nantogmah related a vision to his son. As long as anyone could remember, 2,000 acres of communal land in Northern Ghana had remained unsettled, and the time had come to tell So-Naba why.

It all began with a dream. One night, his great-great grandfather dreamt that the land should only be given to its rightful inheritors—one of whom would be white. The conditions of the deed were that the land should not be used for private gain, but for humanitarian purposes.

Years later, in the summer of 1981, his father's vision was fulfilled as David Mensah, two friends, and his future Canadian father-in-law Eugene Paisley, met with So-Naba. They told him about their desire to begin a sustainable development organization in Northern Ghana. They asked if they could purchase a small amount of this land. None of them knew about the prophecy. The chief did not hesitate and offered the entire 2,000 acres to them as a gift. The deed was signed, sealed, and the work of NEA began.

I love a good dream. I can often remember my dreams in the first moments of a new day, but inevitably, their details begin to disintegrate despite my attempts to cling to them. Before our seventh mission to Ghana, I had three very unusual dreams, the details of which remain with me to this day.

My first dream took place in early 2015 after I attended a job interview. The position involved co-directing a family medicine residency program with a focus on global health. It seemed like a perfect opportunity to combine my love of family medicine, global health, and teaching. I was offered the job and given one week to decide whether or not to accept a five-year term.

The night before the deadline, I dreamed that God was giving me advice about this job offer. I awoke and somehow knew that I needed to look up a very particular Bible verse. For the first time, I read the words of King David from Psalm 16:5-7:

Lord, you alone are my portion and my cup;
you make my lot secure.
The boundary lines have fallen for me in pleasant places;
surely I have a delightful inheritance.
I will praise the Lord, who counsels me;
even at night my heart instructs me.

I sat down at my desk and got out my journal. On a blank page, I wrote down, "The boundary lines have fallen for me in pleasant places." I glanced up at my office wall, knowing exactly what my eyes would see.

Back in 2006, before any of this story began, I attended a weekend conference for women called "NextLEVEL Leadership." At the end of the conference, we were sent into a room with a large piece of blank paper and told that we had thirty minutes to draw a picture of our personal mission statement.

This was a horrifying exercise for me. I cannot draw to save my life. At the end of the exercise, my page remained blank, the lids never coming off my magic markers. One of the instructors,

Lynn Smith, noticed my blank page and kindly encouraged me to stick with this important exercise for as long as it took. Time passed and all the other participants went home. When I finally emerged with my "artwork," Lynn and the other leaders were waiting patiently for me. On my page were three large intersecting circles. One circle represented my family and contained six stick figures. One circle represented my vocation and held a big blue hospital "H". One circle represented God's work on this earth and contained a red cross. An oddly shaped stick figure (me) was standing in the middle where the three circles intersected. Lynn looked at it and her team prayed a prayer over me that God would help me to fully discover and live out my mission. That drawing, created before my work in Ghana even began, hangs on my office wall to this day.

Back at my desk in 2015, staring at this drawing and the colourful "boundary lines" around my family, my practice of medicine, and my work in Ghana, I understood my dream and the sentence scrawled across the page of my journal. With great clarity, I could see that I was right where I needed to be—living and serving within my boundaries at the intersection of three essential places.

I was overwhelmed with this revelation, the counsel of that particular verse, and how meaningful my "artwork" had become. As a result, I turned down the job. I realized that many critical events would be happening in those three circles in the next five years—launching our kids off to university, building a new medical clinic in Uxbridge, expanding our Ghana Health Team services, and building the Leyaata Hospital in Ghana. As "perfect" as the job offer seemed to be, it would pull me away from the three circles to which I felt called to give my wholehearted attention.

The second dream involved a big party. I can still recall every detail in full and living colour. It took place in a fancy banquet hall and all my Ghana Health Team friends and supporters were there, dressed in formal attire. The Mensahs, Ernestina, and team members from all over the world gathered and brought their friends to try and raise funds for the Leyaata Hospital. Graham was the emcee, and he ran a live auction. It was a reunion and a party to remember—full of joy and celebration.

This dream was so vivid and beautiful that I shared it with a small group of women I had been meeting with every month. We were participating in a one-year leadership development program run by an organization called Arrow Leadership. My sister-in-law Sharon Simmonds, the Director of Programs at Arrow, facilitated our sessions, which included my good friend Lynnita, and new friends Julie Fotheringham and Jenn Michel. Upon hearing about my dream, these four women decided that this dream should become a reality. They began planning the first Leyaata Hospital Fundraising Gala.

The final dream was the most significant one of them all.

It occurred after our Leyaata Project had come to a close. Newborn mortality was reduced by two-thirds, and the Helping Babies Breathe team had resuscitated 570 out of 575 babies to date. The program was so successful that GRID decided to apply to the Government of Canada for an extension to scale up all the Leyaata activities in another eighty villages.

The night before the proposal was due, Lynnita asked me to review it. This was an unusual request. She knows very well that grant applications are not my area of expertise and spreadsheets might as well be a foreign language. Nevertheless, I reviewed the proposal and was thrilled to see it contained a special focus to strengthen maternal care. We were still grieving the loss of Cecilia and determined to prevent other children like Princess from needlessly losing their moms. The proposal also included a scholarship for a Ghanaian physician to complete a four-year specialty fellowship in Obstetrics and Gynecology (OB/GYN). It was fantastic and I had nothing to add.

That night I had the third dream. In Canada, the Society of Obstetricians and Gynecologists (SOGC) have an emergency obstetrical course called ALARM: Advances in Labor and Risk Management. This is a course that all doctors and nurses who deliver babies are required to take. In my dream, we ran an ALARM course in Ghana. I could see it all—the Helping Babies Breathe participants were in the NEA training room, practicing their emergency obstetrical procedures and skills.

I awoke from my dream in the middle of the night, went straight to my computer, and googled the ALARM course. Unknown to me, the SOGC had developed an ALARM International Program designed for health professionals who provide Emergency Obstetric and Neonatal Care in middle and low resource countries. It was a five-day training tool delivered in more than thirty countries worldwide based on the latest research and evidence in obstetric and neonatal care.

My heart began to race, and a warm, tingling sensation spread throughout my body. I'd had no previous knowledge of the international component of this program that had been the subject of my dream. I sent a manic email to Lynnita and Brenda. At the eleventh hour, Lynnita (who NEVER does anything at the last minute) added the five-day ALARM training program into the Leyaata Ane proposal.

In July of 2015, the announcement arrived. The Department of Foreign Affairs, Trade and Development (now Global Affairs Canada) approved a four-year extension to Leyaata to which they would contribute $1.9 million. It would be called Leyaata Ane (Ane means "second") and was projected to impact 40,000 mothers, pregnant women, newborns, and children from 162 communities. The ALARM program was approved in full, as was the scholarship for a Ghanaian physician to pursue further training in Obstetrics and Gynecology.

That scholarship—once an unreachable dream—was now a reality for a young physician that NEA and I had come to know very well; a physician who had taught me and mentored me during the most difficult weeks of my life. He had then come to Carpenter for the Helping Babies Breath program and it was there that he and the Mensahs realized that they knew one another. Now, he would be given the opportunity to pursue the training he so desperately desired to better serve his people and save the lives of women and children. NEA awarded the scholarship to Dr. Benjamin Asubiojo.

So many dreams—of the past, present, and future—were being masterfully woven together before our eyes. This tapestry was the landscape that our 2015 Ghana Health Team stepped into after two and a half long years and a horrific epidemic. As the African drums welcomed us back to Carpenter, we were embraced by our Ghanaian family as if we had never left.

CHAPTER 22

Through Eyes Cleansed by Tears

"It is only with the heart that one can see rightly; what is essential is invisible to the eye."

~ Antoine de Saint-Exupéry

Le Petit Prince

Our reunion in Ghana in November of 2015 was extremely emotional for us all. We were so delighted and relieved to finally be back together again after a two-and-a-half-year separation caused by a deadly, submicroscopic RNA virus. We thanked God that our dear friends were spared from Ebola and that a global pandemic had been averted.

The talking drums had much to declare as we bounded off the bus onto Carpenter soil—by now a second home to so many of us. David Mensah, usually dressed in shorts and a t-shirt, stood before us in a robe of white and gold, his fingers and wrists adorned with traditional tribal jewellery. After we greeted the Mensahs and all of the NEA families, we held hands and formed a massive circle. Canadians, Ghanaians, Britons, and Germans stood shoulder to shoulder, commissioned and supported by so many friends and families at home, bound together in service to humanity. Then David stepped into the middle of our circle and began to dance. The talking drums instructed his movements and, with his gestures, he spoke of the past, marked the present, and declared the tribe's hope for the future. Our collective expectations for this mission were higher than the kapok tree which presided over our reunion.

Two people were noticeably absent from our gathering. Abraham, trying to stay warm and dry in England, was studying to become the Leyaata Hospital administrator. Sandra, our nurse practitioner, diagnosed with breast cancer, remained home to fight a battle that affects one in eight Canadian women. This disease would strike five of my teammates.

We would miss Abraham and Sandra dearly, but were delighted to welcome new friends into the celebration. Brenda's father, Eugene Paisley, the white man who fulfilled the chief's prophecy thirty-four years earlier, sat grinning on his electric scooter with both canes lifted high in the air. At eighty-nine years of age, mourning the loss of his wife Laura, he returned to the work that his presence had helped to establish. We were also introduced to Dr. David Aduwia, who was the first NEA scholar to graduate from medical school. He would be joining our team for the next two weeks.

We dove into the familiar rhythms of our mission, arriving in Nyamboi village, who welcomed us by bringing out the rarely seen talking drums. As each team member approached the chief, the village linguist asked for our first name after which the talking drum would personally "introduce" us. During his speech, the chief thanked us "elephantly" for all we had done, and he and the elders presented me with a stool. The Ghanaian stool is used as a symbol of chieftaincy and used on special and private occasions. It is seen as a symbol of royalty, custom, and tradition. Queen mothers (women leaders in Ghanaian communities and tribes), sit on the traditional stool during public gatherings as a seat of authority. When a chief or queen mother is raised to power, the popular term "enstoolment" is used. The stool is so integrally connected to a leader's personality that the expression "a stool has fallen" defines their death. My stool was elegantly carved with a pedestal base that rose into a traditional Gye Nyame symbol, which means "Except God." It is one of my most treasured gifts. In presenting me with this stool, the village of Nyamboi was granting me the title of honorary queen mother—the highest honour a Ghanaian community can give—for my service to their community.

We were happily setting up our clinic in Asantakwa when, from across the room, I saw her being carried towards Dr. Tom Filosa's station. She was a very young woman—and too weak to stand on her own. I watched Ernestina pull down her lower eyelid and examine the undersurface where the eyeball meets the lid. Then, Ernestina looked at her palm and shook her head as her eyes searched the room for mine.

Tom, our doctor on duty for emergencies that day, took one look at this patient and helped carry her straight to our nursing station. Surprisingly, her temperature, malaria test, HIV test, pregnancy test, and glucose were normal, and the cause of her profound weakness remained unclear. Neither she nor her family were able—or willing—to provide us with any helpful history to lead us to a proper diagnosis.

Moments later, a volunteer came running to my desk. "Dr. Jenn, you are needed in the nursing station stat." I ran into the room.

"ONE AND TWO AND THREE AND FOUR AND FIVE!" our nurse counted as she pressed hard and fast on the young woman's breastbone.

Tom was attaching a defibrillator to her chest as his eyes locked on mine. His patient was in cardiac arrest. "Clear!" he shouted, but no shock was administered—a flat line inched across the monitor.

"Please administer a litre of fluid as fast as possible!" I called moving to the head of the bed. "Continue CPR. Epi, one amp," I ordered as I forced air into the lifeless woman's lungs with our BMV.

"ONE AND TWO AND THREE AND FOUR AND TEN! ONE AND TWO AND THREE AND FOUR AND FIFTEEN!" continued the breathless nurse.

Ernestina looked on, wide-eyed at the foot of the bed as we intubated our patient and continued the cycles of CPR and epinephrine—willing a miracle to take place.

She never regained a heartbeat. She never took another breath. There was nothing we could have done.

I looked at Brenda who stood off to the side and shook my head. "Time of death—10:05 a.m."

The room fell silent as the young woman's mother approached the bed. Her wail rose up into the thick, hot air and travelled throughout the clinic and into the village. The tears of my teammates began to fall onto the dirty classroom floor and a sob escaped from my lips as the village women arrived to wrap her body in a colourful Ghanaian cloth.

As the village men picked the young woman up off the bed to

carry her towards the NEA pickup truck, I noticed something unusual. There was a small pool of blood two-thirds of the way down on the stretcher.

Ernestina, who by then had surmised her cause of death, sat down to speak to her wailing mother. When she was finished, she beckoned me over to join them and I listened to a tale that still haunts me today. Our patient lived in poverty. To pay for her school books, she sold herself into prostitution.

Illegal, small-scale mining called "Galamsey"—a word derived from the phrase "gather them and sell"—had come to the region. Between 20,000 and 500,000 migrant workers, including thousands from China, were on a quest, seeking gold by day and women by night—young women lured by promises of food and wealth. As a result, teenage pregnancy, syphilis, and HIV were skyrocketing.

When this young woman became pregnant, she knew her fate would be banishment from school and her village. So, she turned to the only option she thought she had to literally save herself—illegal abortion.

She had been bleeding for weeks since the procedure. Her family had spent all of their money seeking a cure for her at three different hospitals, and yet she continued to bleed. I'm still not clear why she never received the proper care or the blood transfusion she needed. Ashamed by the circumstances, but desperate to save their daughter, whose life was draining away, the family brought her to us praying for a last-minute miracle. The miracle she needed was a blood transfusion—a service we could not provide.

Ernestina explained that this was not a unique scenario—Galamsey was destroying the environment and teenage girls in its wake. This was the first I had heard of it. I ran to the bush and vomited.

Back at my desk, all I could envision was one of my four daughters, who were eleven, thirteen, fifteen, and seventeen years of age, living and dying through that nightmare. I had much to process about why this young woman had died. There were so many complex and intersecting issues that led to the cause of her death.

My translator, Soale, seeing my distress, put his hand on my shoulder and simply said, "This is a war zone."

I appreciated Soale so much. He was an outstanding translator and had an excellent understanding of the human body and disease. He learned to anticipate the questions I would ask, which made our consultations more efficient. He memorized my counselling instructions for most conditions and when I would ask him to counsel a patient, for example, on ways they could lower their blood pressure, he would smile and say, "It is done." Most of all, he had a compassionate heart. He loved his people and wanted to be part of building a better future for them.

Soale's statement was even more poignant to me when I recalled what date it was—Remembrance Day, Nov. 11th.

And so, at the eleventh hour on that eleventh day of that eleventh month, we paused and stood in honour of the fallen—and of the young woman. Without fully understanding our act of remembrance, hundreds of patients in our clinic rose to their feet with us, and for one minute, there was silence in Asantekwa. And then we returned to our work.

November 11, 2015 was a day to remember for another reason. That day, the first six patients received Selective Laser Trabeculoplasty (SLT) to treat glaucoma. Martin had brought a brand new and costly laser, along with four eye doctors, to serve in his ever-expanding eye program that year. It was a momentous day for him after months of fundraising and special training to prepare for this mission.

Martin was ecstatic as he gave his report at dinner that night. He reminded us that glaucoma, nicknamed the "silent thief of sight," is the most frequent cause of irreversible blindness worldwide. Ghana has the highest incidence of glaucoma in Africa and the second highest incidence in the entire world, with 8.5 per cent of persons above forty years of age having the disease. One treatment with this laser would cure a patient of their glaucoma and avoid the need for lifelong, expensive medications.

As the sun set on November 11th, our team gathered under our residence gazebo. A guitar began to strum Beatles' tunes, the pieces of a puzzle were laid out on a table, and someone pulled out shoestring licorice. We didn't talk about what happened that day, and we didn't debrief. We just sang and laughed and ate candy and visited until our eyelids began to droop.

Joy and sorrow, sorrow and joy—I noted with surprise the coexistence of such powerful emotions as I tried to fall asleep that night.

We spent the next two days back in Yaara village, after which I completed my blog. It had become my practice to write almost every night while in Ghana. Perhaps it was my desire to ensure the memories of each day were recorded. Perhaps I wanted the families and friends of my team members to know what their loved ones were part of. Perhaps it was a belief that future days and future missions would be informed by the lessons learned in each crowded day. The following blog went home to our family and friends that day:

The Twelve Tribes

"Code Pink Nursing Station! Code Pink Nursing Station!" Our clinic in Yaara had barely begun as these words rang out over the walkie-talkies. Something else was ringing out too. It was wailing—the wailing of a mother whose child was dying.

Iddrisu, a five-year-old child from the Fulani tribe, was our first patient in the nursing station. Somehow Leslie spotted her in a crowd of about 500 people (she saw her foot hanging at a funny angle from behind a tree) and carried her to the nursing station.

Lynda's bedside malaria test was positive. Dr. Norman Musewe and our incredible nurses Joan, Inessa, Ang, and Kim had already started an IV, given Tylenol for a fever of 40.5, and injected her with antimalarials. Now, this tiny child was having a grand mal seizure, and we were running a code pink.

One of the things the local nurses have taught us here is that a child's glucose level will drop precipitously during treatment for severe malaria. Iddrisu's sugar level was 0.8, which is incompatible with life. As concentrated sugar was pushed through the IV and Valium administered, Ernestina began to sponge down the child with water. The seizure stopped, and so did the wailing. Joan wouldn't leave her side. By day's end, the child was eating rice, walking around, and ready to return to her home in the bush. Can you imagine? My translator told me that the mother was going around the village saying, "These people bring our children back from the dead." We thank God that we were in that village at that moment of that day to save this little life.

I don't tell this story to pat ourselves on the back. We just did what we would have done in an emergency room back home. Instead, I tell it to remind us and remind our supporters that this region needs a hospital. We must help.

That was the beginning of the most significant day we had ever had with our mobile team. Twelve tribes gathered for this clinic, travelling long distances to get to Yaara. Carol, who leads our logistics and operations, shared with the team that today's clinic was like a symphony. Everyone did their part so well that a beautiful harmony was created. This symphony managed to see all of the twelve tribes that came, 650 people, our preliminary numbers indicate. On top of that, hundreds and hundreds with minor complaints were treated and released by our triage nurses.

Martin and the team had an extraordinary case in the eye clinic today. David requested drops for a patient with recurrent eye ulcers. Martin said he had better see the patient. The "patient" came to the clinic but ran away in fear when he saw Martin. He was retrieved, and he finally sat quietly on Moses' lap while Martin examined him and provided the medicine he needed to heal this eye ulcer. David was so happy that his dog wouldn't suffer any longer.

Yup… even the dogs need care!

Martin said the look on the face of the patient waiting to be seen after the dog was just priceless.

Tony reported that the surgical team had their biggest day ever. Due to some accidental "double bookings," the team didn't get to dinner until 9:00 p.m. The patients had come from so far that they just decided to keep operating. They were "knackered" and "gutted,"— two new favourite words I've learned from our British friends— which describe an exceptional level of exhaustion. Nevertheless, we are thankful that all the surgeries, including those performed on two children, went well with no complications. Tony is our star anaesthetist, and adjusts and adapts to the many challenges that a

Ghanaian OR presents.

I was going to close with one of the inspirational quotes handed to each team member and volunteer at 3:00 p.m. every day. However, Kyle and his dental team received their own inspirational message from a patient which trumps any famous person's quote. A woman from one of the twelve tribes approached Kyle with a dozen tiny quail eggs and these words: "I pray you will have a safe journey home and that God will protect your family. I thank God that He has given you a good life so that you can come to Ghana. And I hope you will come back."

Two days off for rest and recovery were critical to sustaining our high performance and maintaining our mental and physical health. A field trip to the massive Bui Hydroelectric dam, an excursion to the local market, and a party at David's and Brenda's home were therapeutic—and just so much fun. On Sunday at church, Ernestina stepped to the front of the crowd and gave the sweetest testimony. First, she thanked God for all his blessings. Second, she thanked Dr. David and Brenda Mensah on behalf of the Ghana Health Service for their work in Northern Ghana. Finally, she thanked our team. She went on to explain how the local health professionals were deeply impacted by our response to the woman who died in our clinic. They were surprised by our compassion—that we had even shed tears—over someone we did not know. They realized the depth of our genuine care and concern for the people of Ghana.

After church, we had a very important event to attend. Just a few weeks before our arrival in Ghana, Magdi and I received an unexpected and tragic email from Brenda that one of the NEA volunteers in our surgical program, who we knew well, had passed away. He was a young man. Adding to the tragedy, his wife succumbed to the same illness two weeks later, leaving three young orphans. Magdi and I were devastated. Two and half years ago, he and his wife were strong, robust young parents. How could they possibly be gone? I already knew the answer when I asked Brenda what illness claimed their lives. "They died of AIDS," she said.

Human Immunodeficiency Virus (HIV), another submicroscopic virus causing another epidemic (some experts refer to it as a pandemic), is a retrovirus that targets the immune system and can lead to acquired immunodeficiency syndrome (AIDS) without treatment. According to the WHO, 37.6 million people worldwide were living with HIV, two-thirds of whom were in the WHO African Region in 2020. Unfortunately, young women in sub-Saharan Africa continue to be left behind by the HIV/AIDS epidemic. According to UNAIDS, six out of seven new HIV infections among adolescents aged fifteen to nineteen years in the region are among girls, and AIDS-related illnesses remain the leading cause of death among women aged fifteen to forty-nine years in sub-Saharan Africa.

The global AIDS community and UNAIDS have used an inequalities lens to develop an ambitious and achievable strategy with new targets to reach in the HIV/AIDS epidemic by 2025. If achieved, the targets will bring HIV services to ninety-five per cent of the people who need them, reduce annual HIV infections to fewer than 370,000 and AIDS-related deaths to fewer than 250,000 by 2025. In June of 2021, Winnie Byanyima, the Executive Director of UNAIDS, before the United Nations General Assembly High-Level Meeting on AIDS, announced, "The world cannot afford to underinvest in pandemic preparedness and responses."

Protocol dictated that our entire team visit the grieving family on Sunday to pay our respects. Our team of sixty arrived in the village of Teselima and David guided us through the huts to a place where an older woman sat on a chair under a tree. Three small children cowered behind her. One by one, our team members bent before this grieving mother and shook her hand. She cried quietly the entire time. David Mensah gave a speech. I was so grateful that he did not give me "the nod"—recognizing I had no words worthy of this occasion. Then, Magdi presented a photo album of our deceased teammate, his wife, and his children. It was apparent that the grandmother had never seen an album like this before. As she turned each glossy page over with her weathered hands, her wide eyes studying each photo of her lost son, her shoulders began to shake, and she wept. We wept too, until she finished visiting every image on every page, closed the cover, and drew the book into her chest, cradling it like an infant.

Regret burned in my chest. Had we not been kept away from

Ghana for over two years, we would have noticed our friend and his wife becoming ill. With access to treatment and care, their HIV infections could have become manageable chronic health conditions, and they both could have lived long and healthy lives.

My thoughts turned once again to the speech Stephen Lewis gave in 2006. He talked about the grandmothers left to care for their grandchildren, as an entire generation was lost to HIV/AIDS. This exact scenario motivated him to create the Stephen Lewis Foundation, which champions health and human rights to respond to the AIDS pandemic in sub-Saharan Africa.

The following day, the grandmother brought the three young orphans to my consultation desk. I was filled with dread as we tested the children for the same virus that took the lives of their parents. The look on the nurse's face who conducted the rapid HIV tests said it all. Ernestina, with a hand on my shoulder, offered to break the news to the grandmother that the youngest of her three grandchildren—the baby—tested positive for HIV.

The barriers to access care for children living with HIV in sub-Saharan Africa are far-reaching. Stigma, geography, lack of medicines, and the complexity of treatment and monitoring meant that this baby would likely not live to see his second birthday. The grandmother stood under the mango tree with her orphaned grandson in her arms as Ernestina explained the diagnosis. Brenda stood with them—in her yellow skirt—eyes brimming with tears of compassion. I knew NEA would do everything in their power to support this grandmother and these three orphans, but I feared we would be attending another funeral—with this same grieving grandmother—before too long. I watched from afar—those three women under that mango tree—and I wondered how many pieces a grandmother's heart could break into before it stopped beating altogether.

The next day we carried our grief with us to a new village called Banda Ahenkro. After our long journey we were excited to find a brand-new latrine complex in the back field, however, there was a barricade in front of it. We were told that it had not yet been "commissioned" so no one could use it. Despite the massive crowds waiting for medical treatment, the village held a prolonged welcoming ceremony with many speeches and we were joined by a camera crew from a Ghanaian news station.

When the formalities were finally complete, we set up the clinic in record time and began our work. About an hour later, I happened to look out my classroom window to see Brenda and a small crowd gathered in front of the new latrine building. She had found someone to act as an "inspector," and once the facility passed the "inspection," she raised her arms in the air, blessed that bathroom as if she was the Queen, removed the barricade with her own two hands, and declared the latrine open for business.

That woman!

At the end of the day, we brought one of my patients back to the compound with us. This teenager had arrived wearing a cloth over her face. She had been suffering from pain, foul discharge, and bleeding from her nose for two years. As a result, she was an outcast and unable to attend school. When I looked in her nose, there was something lodged in it—a mass or a growth of some kind. I tried to remove it, but it was fixed down. The putrid odour was almost unbearable to everyone in the room. We brought her back to Carpenter, where our surgeons delayed their dinner yet again to remove the growth. It turned out to be a rock that had been there for years. Her mother remembered the witch doctor "putting something in there" to cure a runny nose when she was a toddler.

At dinner, David took a moment to be certain we understood the impact of our care for this one patient. He explained that this girl's family was destitute because they had spent years—and all their money—travelling around Ghana trying to find someone to help her. Her siblings were forced to withdraw from school so the family could afford these hospital visits. The life of this family was forever changed as a result of this most basic of procedures.

Banda and the surrounding region were so grateful for our care, and a fifth ram was added to the collection. NEA also received a truckload of yams on behalf of the General Secretary of the ruling Party of Ghana, the Paramount Chief of the Banda Traditional Area, two Queen Mothers, and the local Member of Parliament. So, the name of NEA and the name of our team continued to travel far and wide.

My last blog summed up our final days in Carpenter:

The Catalyst

I am so happy to report that our team has arrived safely at the Accra Airport after an exciting journey that began at dawn. But first, let me rewind a little.

Yesterday, our packing and inventory day was interrupted by an envoy that arrived at the compound. David called us all together under the gazebo, where the District Chief Executive of the Bole-Bamboi District came to thank us on behalf of the President of Ghana. Speeches were exchanged, and a photo of our entire team with the government representatives was taken. The gift he brought was a gift we have never received on any of our missions. The President of Ghana gave us a bull. That's right, a bull. And according to Brenda's dad, Gene, it is one fine animal! David was so happy to add this bull to his collection. The bull didn't look at all pleased.

While we were meeting with Honorable James Janga, an artisan arrived and filled the gazebo with local crafts, fabric, and jewellery, so we spent the afternoon shopping.

The kids on the compound decided to have a football (soccer) match, and they were thrilled when Dr. Martin and Dr. Anthony joined in. With sticks as goalposts and a brand-new football (given to the boys by the surgical team), we witnessed the incredible skill of these young players. As I sat with David and Ernestina watching the match, the intensity of these two weeks seemed to dissipate. We didn't talk about disease and death. We didn't talk about the future of health care delivery to this region. We just sat there—three friends genuinely enjoying a great game of football. I will cherish that moment.

And the party—I must tell you about the party. Decked out in our Ghanaian outfits, we all arrived at an outdoor dinner party where every NEA staff member and volunteer had gathered under the stars. I'm guessing there were 250 to 300 people there. We enjoyed fufu and mushroom soup as an appetizer, followed by a roast beef dinner, and custard for dessert. It was incredible, and Abraham, so far away in England, would have been proud of the hospitality team he had trained. David and Brenda took the time to honour each of our team members with a token of thanks, and three team members received their five-year anniversary gift. This was the fifth mission for Dr. Kyle, Joan, and Dr. Magdi.

The best part of the night for me was when David's mother, Abena Fulamuso, addressed our team. She spoke in a soft voice that we could barely hear. As David translated, I was astounded by her words. This woman, who had witnessed so much suffering in her lifetime, told us that she never dreamed that one of her children would be the catalyst to bring health care to this region. She told us that she had ten children and had lost most of them to preventable diseases. Then she said, "Tonight, it does not feel like my children are dead because now you are all my children." These words speak for themselves.

And so, we wait to board our various airplanes to return to our various countries. It is hard to say goodbye to our dear friends. Our time has been rich, and we have all been impacted in different ways. We will all return a little different from when we arrived. We have completed our mission with excellence. We have served thousands of patients wholeheartedly and are now ready to return to our loved ones and our places of work.

JanJam (thank you) to each person who has been involved directly or indirectly to make this mission possible. So many individuals contributed in so many ways. Thank you all for helping NEA be the catalyst—"an agent that provokes or speeds significant change or action"—to bring sustainable health care to Northern Ghana! Let's continue to link hands with our brothers and sisters in Ghana until this dream becomes a reality.

Adjoa Jennifer
(born on a Monday)

Upon returning home, I was asked to report to Uxbridge Baptist Church about the mission, and I struggled with what to share.

My eyes had been opened to upsetting and complex issues—some, previously invisible to me—facing the people of Ghana. These were sensitive topics to speak about during a Sunday morning worship celebration when what I really wanted to do was simply thank our faithful supporters and celebrate the mission that they helped make possible.

As I pondered what to include in my report, I was corresponding with David in Ghana and Abraham in England and noticed that they both signed off their email with the term "Shalom." This really got me thinking, and I decided to research the deeper meaning of the word. The biblical concept of Shalom can be described as the webbing together of God, humans, and all creation in justice, fulfillment, and delight. The idea that Shalom is "the way things ought to be" really resonated with me. I decided to speak to the church about Shalom.

David's mom, losing most of her children, is not Shalom. Our friend and his wife dying of HIV/AIDS when stigma prevented them from accessing effective and free treatment is not Shalom. A grieving grandmother being told that one of her orphaned grandchildren is HIV positive is not Shalom. Shalom is not a young woman being forced by poverty into prostitution. Shalom is not illegal miners robbing Ghana of its natural resources and young women of their innocence. Going blind from glaucoma when a simple laser surgery offers a permanent cure is not Shalom. Neither is a young woman being stripped of education and her family of all their resources when a simple, inexpensive surgery to remove a pebble from her nose could save them all. None of these situations is "the way things ought to be."

I shifted gears, stood up a little straighter, and asked the church, "What then, is Shalom?" I paused for a moment, feeling entirely unqualified to answer this question. My voice began to crack as I spoke.

"Shalom is 250 people who will not die because their hernias were repaired. Shalom is 100 people receiving laser eye surgery so they will not lose their sight from glaucoma. Shalom is NEA helping to raise three AIDS orphans." I paused to collect myself and then began to speak more rapidly, in a louder and stronger voice. "Shalom is strengthening communities because 12,000 individuals received health care—communities with clean water, schools, food security, peace, and fishponds. Shalom is Ghanaian health professionals receiving the training and resources to care for their own people. And, one day soon, Shalom will be a model hospital offering excellent and accessible care—run by Ghanaians for Ghanaians—and supported by people like us who have so much to share."

I concluded my remarks to the church by saying, "That, my dear brothers and sisters, is what I know of Shalom. I was going to thank you 'elephantly' for all of your support, but I've decided that I will reserve that for the day you help NEA get their hospital."

Many in the audience, including myself, were in tears when I finished. I sat down in my pew, bowed my head, and prayed that none of us would turn a blind eye to injustice again. I also prayed that, together, each in our circles of influence, we would rise up and become agents of Shalom.

CHAPTER 23

Our Elephant

"Pray as though everything depended on God.
Work as though everything depended on you."
~ St. Augustine

In Ghana, the fabric of a woman's dress can send a message that is as bold as a newspaper headline. The dress that NEA gave me in 2016 is a vibrant emerald green, covered in flourishing groves of red trees and little red birds. When you look carefully, a single broken tree lies on the ground between healthy groves of trees. The proverb given to my dress translates, "When a single tree receives a storm, it breaks." Everything about the year 2016 solidified the truth of this proverb in my heart and mind.

The year began with the news that David and Brenda Mensah had received one of the most prestigious distinctions in Ghana. They were awarded Ghana's 2016 Millennium Excellence Award as Laureates of Peace. This was a remarkable honour for the Mensahs and the entire NEA organization, whose collaborative work was gaining national and international recognition.

This fantastic news was soon dampened by reports that an outbreak of meningitis had struck Northern Ghana. Fifty children had already died from the villages we visited every year, and many hospitals ran out of antibiotics. Our pharmacy team always left behind a supply of medication for emergencies, so Brenda emptied the cupboards and donated our stockpile to the outbreak.

A few months later, I was back on a plane to Ghana with a team of three to teach Helping Babies Breathe (HBB) to another sixty-five participants. I was delighted that my two dear friends—Carlye and Lynnita—were joining me. Carlye would help me co-teach the course and Lynnita, who was the Canadian Senior Program Director for Leyaata, would spend her time planning and evaluating with the Leyaata team.

It was Ernestina who provided the opening remarks to the sixty-five Ghanaian health professionals gathered in the NEA training room, and she had quite the speech prepared: "We thought they were dead." She paused, and then a slight smile tugged at the corners of her mouth as she raised her voice and repeated, "We thought they were dead." Then she raised her arms to the sky, jumped up and down, and exclaimed triumphantly, "We thought they were dead!" She went on to describe the now thousands of babies—thought to be stillborn—who had been saved by the HBB training that this group was about to receive. Then she spoke of the mothers of Northern Ghana whose tears had turned to joy. This training was so important to Ernestina that she had turned down a very special invitation in order to be with us. For the exceptional leadership she provided in her new health centre, Ernestina had received the "Best Health Facility Award" from the National Health Insurance Authority in Ghana. She had been invited to fly to Accra, all expenses paid, to accept her award. That would have been Ernestina's first time flying on an airplane. Instead, she sent the clinic midwife in her place so she could be with us in Carpenter. An intense but fun-filled week followed, and by the end, fifty participants were trained in the program, and fifteen were certified as HBB coaches.

That workshop would mark the last time we would provide this training—Northern Ghana now had enough instructors to continue scaling up, monitoring, and providing refresher courses without our help. We prayed that the impact would be exponential.

Carlye, Lynnita, and I had a free half-day to relax at the end of the week before heading back to Canada. The Leyaata staff had raised several critical issues during our week-long stay, so we decided to hold a "symposium."

Under the NEA gazebo, with a flip-chart and a pack of magic markers, we gathered with Brenda, the Leyaata Program team, and local health leaders. We listened intently, documenting the barriers and challenges they were facing. I was moved by how seriously the Ghanaians took this "symposium," arriving in their Sunday best and engaging wholeheartedly with so much intensity and enthusiasm. Together, we discussed these issues, attempted to discern their root causes, and brainstormed ways that we could begin to address them.

Adolescent health rose to the top of the list of problems. Teenage pregnancy, unsafe abortions, and HIV were climbing exponentially. Sadly, the tragic death of the young woman on our last mission from an unsafe abortion represented a growing number of adolescent girls losing their lives to this practice in Ghana and worldwide. NEA decided that adolescent-focused interventions needed to become a top priority.

I was, and continue to be, amazed at how much can be accomplished when stakeholders gather together, identify issues, write them down, brainstorm solutions, and decide upon measurable actions. Within weeks, our little "symposium" gave birth to the NEA Adolescent Health Club pilot.

Within a month of my return to Canada, my dream from the previous year—about a big formal event involving all our health team friends—literally came true and we held our first Leyaata Hospital Fundraising Gala in Uxbridge. Magdi and his wife Sue flew in from England the week before to stay with our family, and they quickly became like grandparents to our kids.

We still talk about Sue and her Egyptian cooking, and Magdi and his long-division math lessons with Jessica. They still talk about Graham's tea "cakes" (tea biscuits) and how much fun Magdi had cutting our grass on our lawn tractor. Magdi spoke for hours about future plans in Ghana, and he informed me that he had decided to bring on the next generation of surgical leadership for our team. Although he would remain involved as a surgeon, he wanted to hand over the leadership reins of the surgical program to Dr. Rob Hicks.

The night of the gala arrived and Ghana Health Team members from past, present, and future (dressed in our finest Ghanaian clothes) gathered with the GRID board, donors, friends, and family who came from far and wide. It was a sold-out crowd, and Graham was the emcee—just like in my dream. The planning team—my girlfriends Lynnita, Julie, Jen, and my sister-in-law Sharon from the leadership development group—planned a night that will remain etched in all of our memories forever.

My favourite moment of the night occurred during my opening remarks when I thanked the man whose company had funded our hernia program for the past four years. When Magdi heard my words, he stood up, crossed the ballroom, and embraced Paul Minshull. My speech was put on pause as we watched these two men, unacquainted partners in transforming Northern Ghana, meet and embrace for the first and only time.

Soon, our GRID chairman, Jacques, would proceed to make the most important announcement of our campaign—the Jim Pattison Foundation in Canada was donating a $2.5-million matching fund towards the Leyaata Hospital! The ballroom came alive with excitement. At the end of the night, Sharon issued a bold call for everyone in the room to join us in helping create a preferable future for the people of Ghana by making a yearly pledge for three years. Pledge cards containing Ernestina's photograph in her Ghana Health Team shirt and hat sat on everyone's table. We smashed our fundraising target, and a half-million dollars was raised (before the matching fund was applied). I will never forget that night planned in its entirety by a small group of brilliant women leaders who had become my dear friends. And I will always remember the meaning of my emerald green dress and the way my team members and their friends, families, and colleagues formed a metaphorical grove of trees around the people of Northern Ghana.

On Remembrance Day of 2016, our eighth Ghana Health Team pinned on our poppies and departed for Carpenter to bring our largest team yet to Ghana—sixty-five of us and 10,000 pounds of equipment and medicine. All of my leaders were back—even Carlye returned, making her second trip to Ghana that year.

Also joining me that year was my sixteen-year-old daughter, Claudia, who had been patiently waiting for her invitation to come. Of all the children, Claudia's personality is the most similar to mine. We think and act alike. We are both very task-oriented, driven, and "don't-let-the-grass-grow-under-your-feet" type of women. We get things done, but our approach differs from the more laid-back members of our family who inherited my husband's "chill" approach to life.

Claudia was blessed with more of my mother's Macedonian genes than the rest of her siblings, who are all much fairer. Her dark hair and olive skin stand out so much that, on more than one occasion, she's been asked if she is adopted. She fits right in at any of our Micheff family funerals or weddings and is the spitting image of many of my Macedonian cousins. When she—my prima ballerina turned rugby player—ruptured her MCL ligament in her knee just months before our departure, I was sure she would need to withdraw from the team. However, she was determined not to miss this mission and boarded the plane with her mechanized knee brace.

Our arrival in Ghana that year was completely different. Just before the mission, David and Brenda faced a family emergency that required them to remain in Canada. My first response was that of disbelief. In my wildest dreams, I had never thought I would be in Ghana without the safety, security, and wisdom of their presence. I was overwhelmed and scared when they shared this news with me. However, the Mensahs quickly assured me that they had selected a leadership team, "The Wonderful Five," who were ready and prepared to run the mission: Abraham, having completed his Master of Hospital Administration, would be in charge; Soale, my translator and head of the Aquaculture program, would be Chief of Operations; Mumuni, the Leyaata Ane Program Leader, would be in charge of the hernia program; Stephen, David's personal driver, would be responsible for transportation; and a young accountant named Ernestina would look after the finances and book-keeping. They had every confidence in this team and their staff, and felt the mission should proceed as planned. If I'm honest, I wasn't as sure.

When I informed our leaders that the Mensahs would not be in Ghana with us, to my surprise, they barely batted an eye. Similarly, when we announced to our entire team that the Mensahs would not be joining us—wondering if some might withdraw— there was next to no reaction. Of course, everyone was disappointed. We would miss David's friendship, inspirational leadership, and famous stories, and we would really miss Brenda's love, care, shortbread cookies, and attention to our "minority-world" needs. Still, everyone understood the values and objectives we had committed to, and knew what was at stake if we cancelled. My team was confident in the leadership that the Mensahs had put in place and remained focused and ready to serve despite this news. For me, the mantle of leadership under these unexpected circumstances felt very, very heavy. Still, I knew that GRID and NEA were all about sustainability, and it was indeed time to "walk the talk" and allow the next generation of NEA to rise up and lead this mission.

When we pulled into the NEA gates, the compound looked spectacular. The grounds were absolutely immaculate. The trunks on the trees lining the driveway were all painted a bright white. While this had been done to protect the trees, it provided a decorative appearance and celebratory atmosphere to the compound. "The Wonderful Five" and the NEA staff stood ready and waiting to greet us. Abraham looked so much like David Mensah in his big straw hat that many of us thought for a moment that David had made the trip after all. When he opened his mouth to speak, he even sounded like David.

We didn't waste a moment as our massive team and all of the NEA staff and families set about unpacking and organizing our 10,000 pounds of equipment and preparing the operating theatres. Our NEA health professionals and scholars were by our side: Ernestina helping our nurses, Eric setting up the anaesthesia equipment in the theatre, Moses (an NEA medical student) assisting the physician team, and David's and Brenda's nephew Emmanuel (a pharmacy student) assisting Linda's and Sherry's pharmacy team. I was so delighted that Sandra, after her victorious battle with breast cancer, was back co-leading our nursing team with Joan. Sandra was now a professor of global health with York University and planned to conduct a research study on risk factors for heart disease and stroke while we were there. Charlie, our cardiac surgeon with the contagious laugh, was by her side—he and Sandra were engaged to be married.

When we finally gathered in the dining hall for dinner on that first night, drenched in sweat and knackered from our long journey and unpacking, Abraham, our new chief, walked to the front of the room. He had gained confidence and experience after his training in the UK, but his humility remained intact. He told us a story about an elephant:

> *A hunter went hunting for game. He toiled a bit but eventually his efforts paid off when he killed an enormous elephant. He thought of ways to convey it home. While in the bush, he couldn't carry it home all by himself, so he decided to invite other people from his community. When they started moving the elephant, the pace was slow, and his helpers got weary. He wanted to motivate them to increase their pace to get the meat home quickly so that it didn't deteriorate, so he came up with a song which he sang: "...my elephant, my elephant, my elephant...." This song was demotivating enough to cause a complete stop to the elephant conveyance. This disturbed him deeply, causing him to change the lyrics to "...our elephant, our elephant, our elephant...." By this later song, they (he and them) identified teamwork as the key in the hunters' game expedition.*

Abraham issued the challenge: this mission is OUR mission, this Leyaata Ane Program is OUR program, this hospital is OUR hospital. It does not belong to David and Brenda Mensah. It does not belong to Abraham or Jennifer or Magdi or Ernestina. We need one another, standing together, lifting together, walking together, and singing together to carry the load and deliver the prize.

Teamwork was indeed the key. Whenever our energy waned or discouragement set in during the next fortnight, he would hold his arms in the air and say, "Our elephant, our elephant!"

Every evening, "The Wonderful Five" and our team leaders would sit under the gazebo debriefing and adjusting our plans for the next day. It was a mission that embodied collaborative leadership every step of the way. As a result, our productivity soared. My daughter Claudia would sit with the staff kids outside the gazebo's edge during those nightly meetings. I loved the way they pronounced her name, "Clohhhhhh-jia." I could hear them peppering her with questions about living in Canada. I overheard her explaining things like "snow" and "indoor stoves" as they giggled with delight. Always on her lap sat a toddler, often in a pink tutu. Princess, the little girl whose mother's preventable death sparked the need to begin the Leyaata Project, would not leave Claudia's side. Princess was at the age that she was normally terrified of anyone with white skin, but this motherless girl clung to Claudia at every opportunity.

Back in our room every evening, I was surprised by Claudia's observations and the things she wanted to discuss. Whereas Olivia wanted to talk and debrief about biomedical matters, Claudia wanted to discuss team dynamics, organizational issues, and inefficiencies. She noticed things that had eluded me, and I was struck by her understanding of organizational leadership at a young age. She had sensed some interpersonal conflict brewing on the team and had some advice for her mother about how I might intervene. Claudia was never afraid of conflict and wasn't shy to have a "fierce conversation" with anyone—one area where our personalities diverged markedly. It was such a joy for me to watch her growing and developing these skills. Claudia had dyslexia (a fact she insisted on hiding from her teachers) and academics had required a great deal of extra effort her entire life. However, when it came to organizing or leading people or events, it was easy and natural for her. Even the note I left her when I went to Ghana for the very first time reflected her budding leadership and organizational abilities: *"Claudia, you are one of the most organized seven-year-olds I know. I love the way you keep track of everything and how capable you are. Dad might need some help organizing (and cleaning) while I'm away. I love you."*

Our first week on the mission was a resounding success, with thousands upon thousands of patients receiving medical, surgical, dental, and eye care from our incredibly dedicated and resilient team.

Youthful creativity abounded on that mission as we all tried hard to make up for David's and Brenda's absence and do them proud. The kitchen staff added surprise treats to our lunches, such as a heavenly frozen orange drink called "Fandango." Our dental team decided that birthdays required a proper gift and began a tradition of the birthday shoebox—containing precious items such as a teabag, a protein bar, a sticker, dental floss, and maybe even some anti-diarrhea pills. "The Wonderful Five" decided that, when the weekend arrived, we should be granted a sleep-in (until 7:00 a.m.), after which the kitchen staff made us a big pancake breakfast.

That evening our social convenor, Dr. Sue Shepherd, planned a team talent show. With the "parents" away, we crashed the Mensahs' living room for the first annual "Ghana's Got Talent" show. My brother-in-law Bryan Ferguson, who was part of our logistics team, was the emcee and he opened the night by leading a choir of team members singing the national anthems of their birth countries. It was powerful to hear the anthems of Egypt, Canada, Spain, Germany, Romania, France, England, Wales, and Ghana sung simultaneously. We laughed hard over low-budget skits, parodies, fashion shows, knock-knock jokes, and lip sync battles. Martin read a touching "Ode to Living Friends" followed by Abraham's a cappella song entitled "Make My Heart a Home for You." The evening closed when Sue sang a parody entitled "Hey Jenn" to the tune of the Beatles' "Hey Jude." It was incredibly moving—I keep a copy of the lyrics on my desk—with one line in particular that continues to comfort me to this day. She changed the Beatles' lyrics and sang: "And anytime you feel the pain, hey Jenn, refrain. We will take any weight off of your shoulders." I would continue to hear this melody in my head whenever the challenges of our mission threatened to overwhelm me.

Despite appearing to have a fabulous time, I was surprised that our UK friends didn't participate in our talent night. After the show, I asked Magdi and Rob why their team didn't sign up for any acts, to which they replied, "We just don't do that sort of thing in the UK!" However, after experiencing the event, my proper British friends promised to join in the following year.

As the super-fun weekend drew to a close, Ernestina rose from her place at Sunday night dinner and asked to say a few words. "It is going to be a very big week ahead. I strongly recommend you all go to bed early and add more 'grease to your elbows' my friends!" And so, we did just that. As we walked back to our residence, my dear friend Dave Norton (who was assisting Kim with logistics and operations) said to me, "Jenny, being here changes you." I could not have agreed more.

The second week of our mission began in the village of Asantekwa. My tech-savvy friend John, back with us again, decided to bring his wireless speaker to add extra energy to our set-up. Suddenly, the air was filled with Josh Groban's "You Raise Me Up" and we all sang along with passion.

It was a fitting prelude to two young patients we were about to meet. The first was a little girl who looked to be only about eleven or twelve years old, when in fact, she was sixteen—the same age as Claudia. She sat in my chair, eyes downcast, clothes covered in filth. The smell of urine was unmistakable. Her mother knelt lovingly beside her and explained that her daughter had a fistula due to a childhood injury. This fistula left her with no control over her urine. The family had spent all their money trying to get her help and were now destitute. She had been banished from school as the other students could not stand her smell.

My heart sank. I had nothing to offer this child. Pleasantries, vitamins, or prayers for the future seemed too hollow even to consider, and I found myself speechless. I did the only thing I could think of and called for Ernestina. It didn't take her long to fully comprehend the situation. She and I both knew that this child's problem required expertise that did not exist anywhere in Ghana. She gently took the broken child by the arm and they walked out, leaving behind a puddle of urine on the seat next to me. How could I not reflect on this girl's life compared to the life Claudia was living—never having to think twice about the limits imposed on her by hygiene or poverty?

At the end of that exhausting day, I left my station, and while I was walking to the gazebo to check on one final patient, I saw Ernestina walking across the field towards me, holding the hand of a teenager in a lovely floral dress. The teenager saw me, dropped Ernestina's hand, and ran towards me smiling. I had no idea who she was until her jubilant mother arrived to stand beside her. It was the girl with the fistula. And she was wearing Ernestina's dress. Ernestina had taken the girl back to her room, removed her dirty clothes, bathed her, cut her hair, and presented her with a new dress. It was the only dress Ernestina owned. She then went to the nursing station, where the nurses put together a care package of products to help the child manage her condition.

The hope and the joy on that girl's face, feeling clean and beautiful—the recipient of such authentic compassion—caused a sob to travel from my heart to my throat. That night I told my teammates about what Ernestina had done. Without any discussion, a collection was taken to purchase a new dress for our dear friend.

The next day, one of my most experienced and energetic nurses, Leslie Feddery, approached my consulting desk holding the hand of a little boy who hopped along by her side. He was grinning from ear to ear as he pointed to his left leg, which was a tiny stump. He was about six or seven and his name was Evan. Leslie, close to tears, said to me, "Dr. Jenn, I know there is nothing you can do for Evan, but I couldn't turn him away from triage. Could you visit with him and his parents for a bit?"

Evan and I had a wonderful visit. He showed me how fast he could hop and climb on one leg—he was so agile! I brought Claudia in to see this remarkable child and she was able to show him that she too had a problem with her leg. After that, his parents told us that he was no longer able to attend school. The few kilometres from his village were too far for him to hop and it had become too difficult for his mom to carry her growing son on her back.

I turned to my translator Soale and said, "There must be something we can do." He replied, "Mum, give me a minute," as he pulled out his cell phone. About half an hour later, he returned smiling. He had found an orthopaedic technician in Accra who made prosthetics for children that could be adjusted as they grew. Our team provided travel funds for the family to go and obtain a quote for a prosthetic limb that could change Evan's life.

Seven days later, on the last day of our mission, I was busy seeing patients inside the NEA training room. Out of the corner of my eye, I saw the front door swing open as a young boy in a white collared shirt and a pair of yellow jeans came bolting towards me with a slight limp. It was Evan— wearing a prosthetic limb. No one could believe it. His parents said that the moment the prosthetic went on, he began to run and had refused to remove it since. No rehabilitation was required. For the next twenty minutes, this boy did laps around our clinic and played soccer on the field. Joy rose up and blanketed the entire NEA compound as we witnessed again how one compassionate nurse could trigger a series of events that would change reality for one precious child.

As our mission came to a close, we put on our new Ghanaian outfits (Soale's wife, Esther, had made thirty-five new dresses), and we gathered for our traditional party under the stars. That year, we even had a DJ! Prosper, one of the Leyaata Project staff, was behind the microphone, and once dinner was over, DJ Prosper hosted a dance competition. He called out different groups of people—the nurses, the drivers, the pastors, and the doctors—selected a song and asked us to dance. We laughed and cheered so hard that our voices disappeared. The night ended with a conga line made up of our entire team and all of the NEA families "conga-ing" around our outdoor banquet hall until we were too hot and sweaty to dance another step. Oh, how I wished David and Brenda had been there to see it!

At 5:00 a.m. the following day, after only a few hours of sleep, we prepared to board our bus for Accra after what had been a great mission, devoid of any serious challenges or obstacles. Then, we realized we had a "small-small" problem on our hands—the coach bus was nowhere to be found. Our team, eager to begin our long journey home, waited patiently. Twenty minutes passed, then forty, and an hour later, there was still no bus. If we didn't leave soon, we would miss our domestic flight from Kumasi to Accra.

I looked for Abraham, Soale, and "The Wonderful Five," but no one was in sight. *Where are they? Why aren't they "doing" anything?* Panic began to rise. We needed a Plan B. My leadership team and I began to brainstorm. We quickly decided that all twenty-one veterans plus Claudia would remain behind, while the rest of the team would go on ahead in the smaller church bus to catch the flight from Kumasi to Accra. The rest of us had fifteen hours to find our way to the capital. As I rounded the back of the training centre looking for Abraham and our driver Stephen, I stopped dead in my tracks. In front of the vehicle depot stood the entire NEA staff, pastors, and four of "The Wonderful Five," holding hands and praying about our dilemma. They prayed earnestly, knowing full well that there was no good Plan B.

A few minutes later, the fifth "Wonderful Five" member, Stephen, roared through the front gates in the honking NEA pickup truck with our coach on his heels. We said a quick, teary goodbye to our friends and set off for the four-hour journey to Kumasi. Our plane was due to take off in four and half hours. We didn't think we were going to make it until our driver decided to take a "short-cut" which resulted in us arriving just in the nick of time. Somewhere during that tumultuous short-cut, either right before or right after I vomited in my barf bag, I made an almost illegible note in my Moleskine journal: NEED BETTER PLAN B FOR FUTURE TRANSPORTATION FAILURES!

As we travelled home, my brave Claudia with her swollen knee by my side, I listened to "You Raise Me Up" over and over. Claudia would roll her eyes every time I double-fist-pumped the air on the powerful key change at the end—I just couldn't help it.

The truth of these lyrics, the proverb of my green dress, and Abraham's elephant story coalesced into a beautiful truth for me: Abraham, Soale, and "The Wonderful Five" stood on the shoulders of the Mensahs, who had spent years preparing them for that moment in time; a little girl with a burdened heart was raised up by Ernestina's compassionate heart and her only dress; a one-legged boy unable to attend school could now climb mountains; a motherless Princess was loved by my daughter who came and sat with her a while; an army of Helping Babies Breathe professionals were now independent and no longer needed my shoulders to stand on; and a generation of adolescent girls and boys were being detoured around stormy seas by the powerful rudder of education.

I glanced at Claudia, now fast asleep, and my tears began to fall. I was so grateful that Graham and I had been given the privilege of helping to raise up our five incredible children. They, too, would stand on our shoulders for a little while until they were ready to impact the world in their own way with their remarkable gifts and skills.

My social-convenor/song-writing friend Sue was correct; I didn't need to carry the weight of the world on my shoulders. The world's ills and the storms of life are meant to be shared—shared by all citizens of the world as we live our lives and raise our children in communities that support, protect, cheer us on, and give us birthday shoeboxes with dental floss and anti-diarrhea pills. After all, our shoulders were never meant to be weighed down with a difficult yolk or a heavy burden. When the yolk is easy and the load is light, our shoulders can be used for others to stand on.

About a month after I returned home, I received a message from Abraham. A visiting international surgeon who specialized in paediatric fistula was in the country. NEA contacted our little girl, and with funds left over from the mission, she received a surgical procedure that cured her. She was already attending school—the only teenager in kindergarten. Abraham reported that she was a bright and diligent student who would soon catch up to and surpass her peers.

Then I received a message from Eric that he was accepted into a Masters of Anaesthesia training program. NEA awarded him a scholarship to pursue this opportunity. I thought of the two of us in the back of that makeshift "ambulance" years ago with the dying baby. I thought of him helping me train Leyaata's HBB army. Now, thanks to NEA, he had a chance to rise to the top of his profession. He would return every year to work with the surgical team that Magdi would ask Rob to take over and lead into the future.

There were so many of us now, from all over the world, carrying OUR elephant. We had further to go on this long and challenging road of bringing sustainable health care to Ghana. Still, the people of Ghana continued to raise us up to more than we had thought we could be.

CHAPTER 24

Angels of the Mo Tribe

"Compassion is not a relationship between the healer and the wounded. It's a relationship between equals. Only when we know our own darkness well, can we be present with the darkness of others. Compassion becomes real when we recognize our shared humanity."

~ Pema Chodron

I've noticed an interesting pattern in my global health work. Anytime I become proud or content with the accomplishments of our Ghana Health Team, I receive a stark reminder that humbles me and reminds me that there is much more work to be done. One hundred days before our 2017 team departed for Ghana, it happened yet again.

Ernestina sent me an urgent message and photograph regarding a critically ill child. We discussed my recommendations, and I signed off saying, "My heart breaks to see the picture of this girl."

She responded, "Don't let your heart 'brake' Doctor, I will support her for sure."

I am certain these moments are God's way of preventing me, a health care provider who carries power and privilege, from becoming complacent and forgetting the moral obligation human beings hold towards one another—regardless of where we were born or live. In fact, looking back, these devastating reminders always become yet another catalyst for something deep within me. For change. For perspective. For stepping outside my comfort zone. For daring to dream big as a leader. For not allowing my heart to "brake," but rather, to accelerate towards helping co-create a future that is better than what we have today. "Brake" was definitely not a typo or auto-correct—it was a well-timed and much-needed reminder.

When the message from Ernestina arrived, I was in our nation's capital, Ottawa, taking a course in emergency department ultrasound. This tool would change my daily practice of emergency medicine and become a life-saving instrument in low-resource settings like Ghana where X-rays and CT scans can be impossible to obtain. Needing to process the haunting image that Ernestina sent me, I went for a walk and found myself at the foot of Canada's Human Rights Monument. This sculpture, standing ten metres high, narrates the struggle for human rights in Canada. It suggests a new approach to power—power based on recognizing rights and empowering the individual and the community. The monument boldly proclaims:

All Human Beings Are Born Free And Equal
In Dignity And Rights.

Tous Les Êtres Humains Naissent Libres Et Égaux
En Dignité Et En Droits.

The words "EQUALITY," "DIGNITY," and "RIGHTS" are etched on red granite plaques in seventy-three languages of Canada's First Nations peoples. When Nelson Mandela visited this monument in 1998, he issued a challenge: "May this monument inspire all who see it to join hands in a partnership for world peace, prosperity and equality."

I began to cry. This sculpture and its symbolism caused my heart to race and the hairs on my arms to stand at attention. It was as if I could physically feel the weight of the world—no, the sins of the world and the injustices against humanity (that my very own country could commit)—pressing down upon me. I had to sit down.

Past and present human rights violations rolled through my mind like a movie. That year, eight million Yemeni citizens were at risk of starvation; a catastrophic war in Syria was continuing to evolve on a global scale; Canada was in the midst of a public inquiry into the murders and disappearances of Indigenous women and girls. The movie in my head kept playing, crushing my spirit further with every scene.

Then, suddenly, I heard my friend Sue's sweet voice in my ear singing her Beatles parody at our Ghana's Got Talent Show: "And anytime you feel the pain, hey Jenn, refrain. We'll take any weight off of your shoulders." I also recalled the advice given to me in the middle of the night a few years prior that I had written down and memorized: "The boundary lines have fallen for me in pleasant places."

I reset my heart and my sense of responsibility to do precisely what this monument and Mandela's exhortation were designed to inspire. I needed to refocus on what I was called and equipped to do in my corner of the world—at home and in Ghana as I led my team to join hands in partnership with our colleagues at Northern Empowerment Association on our march towards peace, prosperity, and equality.

In November of 2017, sixty-seven of us hopped on a KLM plane where the flight attendants presented our team with a signed letter wishing us success on our mission, along with a little bell with the inscription "Together We Have a Great Story to Tell." The bell now sits on my desk with my other inspiring treasures.

That was my mindset when I stepped onto the Carpenter compound in 2017—a decade after our first mission. My leadership team (now over twenty-five in number) and my third daughter, Amelia, were by my side. I was also thrilled that my niece Kathleen Simmonds, a brilliant trauma nurse, was part of our team.

Amelia, fifteen years old at the time, has always been the most adventurous of our children. Even as a toddler, when the "Wilson Five" would walk out our back door and down the walkway to the driveway, Amelia would never stick to the path. She would meander through the grass, mud, or snow, exploring while her siblings waited patiently in Graham's big van. Amelia has always seen the world through a slightly different lens and asked big-picture questions more often than the rest of us.

In the compound, I received a message that all of the NEA staff, Leyaata team, and Helping Babies Breathe instructors were eager to meet Amelia. She was so tall (already towering over me) and so blonde that the Ghanaian people seemed to be drawn to her out of sheer curiosity. Amelia took it all in while Princess climbed into her arms, snuggled into her neck, and reached up to touch the shiny metal things on her teeth.

The following day we all gathered under the NEA gazebo for devotions. After a time of singing, a tiny, elderly woman named Lucy from Carpenter village limped slowly with a cane to the centre of our gathering. Through the translator, she sang a song to express her deep gratitude to God and our team for the kindness extended to her people over the past ten years. She explained that she was a poor woman with nothing to thank us with, so she had worked all year to provide us with a small gift from her farm. Then she presented us with ten massive yams (one for each mission year) and nine guinea hens. I had a hard time keeping my composure while I tried to find words to thank her.

David Mensah then laid down the theme of the mission when he shared the story of Jesus healing a man who had been paralyzed for over thirty years at the pool of Bethesda. He explained that, to his people, our "healing hands" were stirring the waters and Carpenter had become their "pool of Bethesda" and their "house of mercy." As he walked around the gazebo—stopping to grasp the hands of my teammates—he gave examples of the sick, lame, and blind whose health had been restored. On and on he went. All eyes followed David. All tongues were still.

Also adding a spring to our step on those first days were a few special visitors who we'd met the year before. Dorcas was four years old. She had swallowed battery acid and was dying of malnutrition when she was brought to us in 2016. It was a devastating situation, and we could not help her. Leaving her in the trusted hands of NEA with extra funds we had raised, a referral was made to the highest level of care in Ghana. One year later, Dorcas was fully recovered—a happy, robust child ready to begin kindergarten. Her mom and three uncles brought her to Carpenter just to say thank you. Evan, the little boy with the prosthetic leg, returned for a visit too. He was taller and stronger, and his mother could not stop bragging about his soccer skills. Finally, I had a visit from Sarah, the young woman with the disfiguring facial tumour who I had met during our very first mission. She came to see me every year. She never asked me for anything—she just liked to sit and catch up on our lives and hear about my family. She had completed college and was now running a small business.

We were particularly excited to return to Yaara village that year. After a very long and bumpy bus ride, many team members had to rush to the facilities before the opening ceremonies commenced. Suddenly, there were whoops of joy as my team discovered brand new latrines, built by NEA and the Makbraneth Foundation for the Yaara school. These latrines had doors. These latrines had locks on the doors. These latrines had—wait for it—toilets sitting on top of the cement hole. There was such a commotion as team members began to cheer from behind those doors, and nurse Joan's unmistakable voice broke out into the *Hallelujah chorus*. One really cannot appreciate the luxury of a toilet until one does not have a toilet to sit upon. The Mensahs did well to keep those thrones a secret.

The Assemblyman of Yaara welcomed us and spoke eloquently on behalf of the chief and elders. He explained that our annual visits over the course of ten years had become a strong, motivating force for them. Our efforts and our presence year by year had inspired their community to do everything possible to improve their situation. For example, for years they had been advocating for a health centre in their community and finally, approval had been given. Soon a nurse and a midwife would be posted in the newly built NEA Yaara Health Centre to provide year-round care to this remote village that was inaccessible at certain times of the year. He also told us that their health had improved not only because of our medical, surgical, dental, and eye services, but also because of their consistent interaction and socialization with us. "Health and life are returning to Yaara!" he proclaimed as the village presented us with a white ram, more tubers of yams, and heaps of fruits and vegetables that neighbouring villages had contributed to the group gift. The chief then called my daughter Amelia forward, and his wife, Hagar, presented her with a live chicken. Unfortunately, her chicken fell out of the pickup truck on the way home but survived his attempt at the great escape.

Near the end of the day, our dentist, Kyle, in Ghana for the seventh time, walked into my consulting classroom carrying his own chicken. It was a gift from the Fulani woman who he had been caring for since 2009. Every year, when she came with her children for their check-ups, Kyle would take a picture of her family. That year, he presented her with a collection of all those precious family photos. Later that afternoon, this woman, from an extremely poor and nomadic tribe, returned to her family dentist to present him with a chicken.

It had been a very memorable day, and we enjoyed regrouping with our surgical colleagues to tell detailed stories over dinner. Rob proclaimed it had been "a sterling start to the fortnight!" (the British just make things sound so much better). Magdi chimed in, with a smile that enveloped his entire face. "I'm just so happy."

I was happy too—especially when I ended my day with a twenty-point cribbage hand and almost skunked my dear friend Charlie. His contagious laugh was particularly joyful that year—he and Sandra, our team nurse practitioner, had recently been married, and many of our leaders had had the honour of celebrating their beautiful wedding day with them. Instead of wedding gifts, their guests were asked to donate to our next Ghana Health Team.

Amelia found it comical how health care professionals chose to relax in the evening—puzzling, colouring, and extremely competitive "bananogramming." I may have heard her call us "nerds" under her breath after Linda, our lead pharmacist, confessed that her favourite childhood book was the dictionary!

As I was heading to bed, I noticed Carlye speaking with a group of team members in the corner of our gazebo. I wandered by and asked if everything was ok to which she replied, "Nope. I'm running a constipation clinic." She began passing out laxatives like candy. My poor team members and the things they endured in Ghana!

Our first week went by in the blink of an eye. On Friday night we all gathered in the Mensahs' living room where David opened the evening noting, "We have come into agreement with tender hearts that everyone deserves things like clean water, food, education, and health care." He then invited Mumuni, the manager of the Leyaata Ane Project, designed to rescue moms and babies from dying in childbirth, to share a few words.

Mumuni explained that between 2016 and 2017, 3,814 pregnant women had been visited by community-based volunteers and assisted in delivering in a health facility. After the initial visit, he explained, the volunteers visit all of those babies three times in the first week of life to look for danger signs such as fever, poor weight gain, and jaundice. These conditions would trigger an emergency referral to the local health facilities. In addition, since Carlye and I had completed the last neonatal resuscitation training in 2015, our Ghanaian master trainers had scaled up and trained seventy-nine health workers and 105 traditional birth attendants. As a result, 1,145 babies who would have died at birth had been successfully resuscitated since 2016. Our team was speechless.

We also received a detailed update on the expansion of the NEA Adolescent Club Pilot (birthed at our gazebo symposium). Sixty teachers in thirty schools were now trained in the sexual and reproductive health curriculum and 2,276 adolescent girls and boys had joined the Leyaata Adolescent Clubs. Teenage pregnancy was plummeting. I couldn't help but note how wide Amelia's eyes became as she heard about the reality of being a teenager in Ghana.

Dr. Mensah concluded our evening by sharing his vision for the Leyaata Hospital: a fifty-bed model hospital, staffed and run by Ghanaian health workers under the leadership of NEA and supported by people like us. It would be a centre of excellence and it was desperately and immediately needed. We were in the same living room where he had shared this exact vision with us just a few years prior—and we had told him it was impossible. He thanked us all for continuing to stand in the gap and look after his people while we waited for the hospital's doors to open.

As we were leaving, Sandra's daughter Caitlin (who was studying International Development at Dalhousie University) said to me with tears in her eyes, "Everything I have learned about on paper has come to life in this place."

We made the most of our two days off and filled them with recreation, which truly did "re-create" our bodies and minds. When the temperatures dropped a few degrees in the late afternoon, we held our first-ever volleyball game against the NEA staff. David Mensah joined in, and it was so sweet to watch his staff react to their boss (and the high Chief of Mo Land) lacing up his running shoes to become a teammate on the court. Whenever he touched the ball, the crowd went wild.

David has always been an accomplished athlete, having qualified to represent Ghana at the 1980 Olympics in the 800-metre race. Ultimately, however, a boycott prevented him from running.

After volleyball, the teams moved to the football (or "soccer" as it's known here in Canada) pitch, and another great match took place which ended in a "tie"; so, as darkness fell, the game was settled with penalty shots and we emerged as the "grand champions."

Football is the national sport in Ghana, so I must qualify our "tie" and our "grand championship" with a few comments. First, we had twice, if not three times, as many players on the field as our NEA friends. Second, NEA may not have been trying their hardest.

In fact, after the game I asked Soale how much they held back to allow us to win.

He hesitated, then smirked, choosing his words carefully. "Mum, we want you around next week, so we held back—but only by approximately fifty per cent."

The event we had all been waiting for finally arrived after dinner. It was time for the second annual "Ghana's Got Talent." Our team and our Ghanaian colleagues piled into the Mensah living room once again, where we were treated to candy, cookies, coffee, and tea. It was a night that left us with sore faces and bellies from all the laughter.

The show opened with a repeat performance of our team's national anthems. That year, ten countries were represented. What a joyful noise to hear anthems from Northern Ireland (Dave), England (Karin), Wales (Rob), Canada (Leslie), USA (Judy), Egypt (Magdi), France (Francois), Germany (Elke), South Africa (Aaron), and Ghana (David Mensah) all being sung at the same time.

Then the fun really began. When I read on his application that Dan, one of our new surgeons, was a jazz pianist, I had jokingly suggested that his acceptance was conditional upon him bringing a piano to Ghana. Much to my surprise, Dan showed up with a tiny professional keyboard and, playing by ear, accompanied Carlye and I for our opening act. It was a rendition of "Ghana Man" to Billy Joel's "Piano Man." Everyone joined in on the last chorus of "Bring us along, you're the Ghana-man," after which we received a standing ovation! Next, our UK friends, who were "too proper and reserved" for this sort of thing the year before, came up with an incredibly creative rendition of "My Hernia" to Tom Jones' "Delilah." We all joined in on that chorus too: "My, my, my—my hernia. Why, why, why—my hernia?" These two epic songs would continue to be sung at future talent shows, and will go down in our personal history books.

Time with old and new friends, no clinical duties, the absence of distracting technology, a soccer ball, a nap, a talent show, and some candy—it was such a simple weekend, yet so profoundly rejuvenating to all as we bolstered ourselves for the second half of our mission.

On Sunday evening at dinner, as we were about to begin our final week, David Mensah walked to the front of the dining hall and told us a story. The day prior, he went to the village to check on the hernia patients housed in the elementary school. As he was coming back towards the gate, he heard two men arguing. The topic of their argument caught his attention—they were arguing about angels. One man said that these white people, bringing healing to the region, must be endowed by God with the spirit of angels. The other man said that we were just humans who have chosen to develop an angel spirit here on earth. David thought he would insert himself into the conversation.

Just then, Martin popped out of the residence to announce that the power had gone off. The man turned to David and said, "See, there is an angel right there!" (which really went to Martin's head when he heard the story).

David explained that the one man rolled up his pant leg and started banging his leg. He told David that he had been to every hospital in Ghana last year with an infection that was causing his leg to rot. No one could help him and he was facing amputation until he visited our clinic, and now his leg was perfect. He continued to argue with his friend (all the while banging on his leg) that the doctor and nurse who treated him were real human beings, but they had developed the spirit of an angel to such a degree that could finally cure him. He was at the gate because he wanted to be first in line to find his human angels to thank them.

Finally, not knowing they were talking to David Mensah, they said to him, "And we also hear that there is a Ghanaian angel who coordinates all of this help from afar. Are you from around here? Have you heard of him?"

Oh, how David laughed when he told us this story, but he wanted us to appreciate that his people were absolutely confounded by what they were witnessing and experiencing. "You are angels to the people of the Mo tribe. Angels that come to stir the waters at the pool of Bethesda," David proclaimed. He concluded our evening by challenging all of us to continue to develop the spirit of love, compassion, generosity, and service to humanity that brought us to Ghana—to this special place for this very special time of service. "Let's go to Bethesda," he said as he dismissed us into the final week of our mission.

At least once during each mission, I made it a priority to walk around our entire clinic and visit each station. I wanted to see my colleagues in action and place a hand on their shoulder. That day arrived, and I told Soale that he and I were going on a tour. He was thrilled. Soale and many of the NEA staff had started calling me "Mum," which is considered a high honour in Ghana.

It made me think back to the man who, when I announced that I was going to medical school, told me, "You would have made such a great mother." In fact, medical school positioned me to become a mother and grandmother to more people than I could have ever imagined.

Soale, my Ghanaian son, always placed a wrapped gift on my desk whenever I arrived in Ghana. Those gifts are some of my greatest treasures; however, just before that 2017 mission, he gave me a gift that I had never been given before. He and his wife Esther asked me to name their third-born child. I chose Timothy, which means "Honoured by God." The honour was truly mine.

Our first visit was to the triage team where the nurses should have been closing down for the day. Instead, they were in emergency mode. A limp little girl had been pulled out of the crowd. Her temperature was forty degrees, and she had severe malaria. Thank God her mother got the attention of our team, who insisted we add just one more. She was rushed to Dr. Anne Smith, our team pediatrician.

Soale and I continued on to the diagnostics station, which was humming. Led by our lab technician Tracey Barkey, they served a constant stream of patients requiring tests for malaria, HIV, urine, pregnancy, or glucose.

Next up on our "tour" was the physician team—a happy bunch because of the large, air-conditioned training centre they were working in on the NEA compound. We felt so guilty (well...kind of) as we worked comfortably all day long. Our translators, however, were not so happy. It was too cold for them, and many of them had to fetch their sweaters or coats. A few even wore winter hats.

Soale and I then made our way to the big NEA gazebo that had been transformed into our nursing treatment station. It was full of patients. Wounds and ulcers were being cleaned and dressed, IV infusions were hanging from the rafters, and ears were being syringed.

My Amelia was running an oral rehydration station for sick babies. Amelia had always been a very conscientious child and took her responsibilities extremely seriously—sometimes too seriously. (I wonder where she gets that!) Watching this fifteen-year-old manage ten babies, keep track of their oral rehydration solution (ORS), and coach the mothers on what to do amazed Soale and me.

That night at dinner, Sandra and the nursing team gave her a medal of honour. Her medal was a sachet of ORS tied around her neck with a string. She still likes to remind her siblings that she is the only Wilson child who received this distinction, which still hangs on her bedroom wall. She says it is one of her most valuable trophies.

Then we popped into the eye clinic held in the NEA peanut storage facility, affectionately known as the "nuthouse." A thick wall of heat from this windowless dark room assaulted us as we entered. However, inside was a sight to behold as our newest eye team superstars, Dan and Barb Brazier, enthusiastically measured eye pressures, while the optometrists conducted complete eye examinations, and Jane Smith lovingly dispensed prescription eyeglasses. Abba tunes were blaring, and despite the sauna-like conditions, team members and patients were tapping their feet and singing along to "Mamma Mia."

Meanwhile, sight had been restored to thirty-five glaucoma patients in the laser clinic. Dr. Toylin Musewe, our ophthalmology resident, finished her day by performing bilateral ectropion surgery on an elderly man. Ectropion (ek-TROH-pee-on) is a condition in which the eyelid turns outward leaving the inner eyelid surface exposed and prone to irritation.

The pharmacy was in high gear and under a great deal of pressure. I couldn't believe that ample medications were still left after the thousands upon thousands of patients we had cared for on this mission. It felt like the miracle of the loaves and the fishes.

Finally, one of our Ghanaian pharmacy technicians from Wenchi named Daniel ushered me over. With his big smile, he said to me as he looked around at the pharmacy and his team, "This is how NEA will run their pharmacy!" Linda and Sherry, who poured their heart and soul into our pharmacy program, were beaming.

We then made our way over to the dental team, which included a visiting Ghanaian oral maxillofacial surgeon. They had a packed waiting room under the mango tree and were so full of life; the dentists had taken our Ghana Health Team logo and made their own "team uniform"—a t-shirt which said, "I'm GHANA fix your teeth." Just as we arrived, Garrett Bent, a university student volunteering with the dentists, pointed out a man "with an unusually big face" to his dentists. Sure enough, a severe dental abscess that was about to obstruct the man's airway needed to be dealt with ASAP. Garrett must have enjoyed his mission—the following year, he was accepted to dental school supported by three outstanding references from our team dentists Kyle, Francois Bessay, and Neil Martin.

Finally, we made our way over to the surgical centre, where three operating theatres were in full motion. The surgeons had a funny story from the pre-operative clinic to tell Soale and me. When a surgeon is assessing a groin hernia, they place their hands on the patient's groin region, and ask the patient to cough. This manoeuvre, old as time and the subject of many jokes, pushes the intestines down through the hernia opening so the surgeon can determine the size of the hernia and the type of operation required. Because this manoeuvre is repeated so often in the pre-operative clinic, our surgeons quickly learned the word for "cough"—"boa"—to avoid wasting time for the translation. On this day, it was finally pointed out by a translator that for the past two weeks, while examining their patients' groins, the surgeons had inadvertently been adding an "a" to the beginning of the word "boa." So, when they placed their hands on the groin hernia and said "ABOA, ABOA!" instead of "BOA!", they had actually been saying "ANIMAL, ANIMAL!"

David Mensah was on the floor with laughter when he heard about this unfortunate translation mishap.

I poked my head into the third operating room, where one of the surgeons from Ireland, Dr. David Hunter, was operating. He looked up at me and announced, "One more kiss, Jenn, one more kiss."

I blushed, wondering what he could mean and what my teammates must have been thinking. No one reacted, forcing me to finally clue in that an Irishman with a thick accent pronounces "case" precisely like "kiss."

As Soale and I left the operating theatres to get back to work, he appeared deep in thought. Finally, I asked him if everything was okay and he responded, "Mum, there are no cowards in this place."

It was a profound statement. It takes a great deal of clinical courage to do this work. It is one thing to care for patients with all of the resources of our health care systems back home, but working in a low-resource setting with myriad challenges takes a lot of guts. And to do all of that while maintaining composure, professional boundaries, and a sense of humour is something else. I was so grateful that my children's lives were being influenced by my brave friends, who were modelling what it means to serve others, at their own expense, and contribute to a purpose bigger than themselves.

Preparation for our very last clinic began at 2:00 a.m. While we were sleeping, NEA gave out 200 tickets to the elderly, the women, and the children sleeping on the ground outside the gate. In a lovely gesture, they moved this vulnerable group inside the gate to ensure they would be safe and seen before the "big crowds" arrived in the morning.

We were at our workstations by 7:30 a.m. to begin the largest clinic we had ever run in Ghana. Each team cared for a record number of patients, and by dinner time, high-quality health care, surgery, dentistry, and eye care had been provided to over 900 patients. Rob's surgical team finished this mission with 296 procedures performed. The eye team rushed through their dinner in order to run one last "all for one, one for all" after-hours clinic. It truly was a sterling finish.

Our journey home was not so sterling. When we got to Kumasi, our flight was delayed due to severe weather, so we waited two hours only to discover that the flight was cancelled. In fact, the plane had been involved in a "small-small" crash.

Whenever our best-laid plans get thwarted in Ghana, David Mensah always laughs and then says, "Murphy has struck again!" referring to the law which states that, "If anything can go wrong, it will." David often reminds us that Murphy is alive and well in Ghana. This is precisely why we chose resilience as one of our team's core values. So, when Murphy's law struck, the team kicked into action.

We decided to attempt the journey to Accra by road together, keeping the team united. NEA quickly mobilized two buses. Charlie drained the ATM to pay cash for them; one team member bought all the water the airport had to sell; others pooled all the snacks in backpacks to divide up, and finally, bladders were drained as much as humanly possible. There would be no time for pit stops; we had six hours and twenty minutes to make a six-hour drive—in Ghana.

Bus number one arrived, and it could only hold fifty passengers. A quick decision was made that all North Americans would go on this bus as our flight took off thirty minutes before the UK flight. Magdi and a few other British team members joined us. The second bus would be smaller and would make better time, so the rest of the UK team stayed behind to wait.

Murphy struck many times along the way, causing bumper to bumper traffic, torrential rains, malfunctioning windshield wipers, just to name a few. As the minutes ticked by, it was evident that we would miss our 10:00 p.m. flight.

What could have been an extremely tense ride was, in fact, filled with lots of laughter, games, and sharing of food. The UK team spent some of their time practicing a talent show act for 2018. Everyone stepped up and made the best of our nail-biting ride, keeping each other's spirits high, all the while recognizing that we might be staying a little longer in Ghana than planned.

At 7:55 p.m., Murphy struck once again with a text from Rob: "We are all on the side of the road. We have a puncture. Thankfully there is a spare. Standby."

At 8:21p.m.: "The flat tire is stuck on the wheel, and they cannot get it off. Progress is slow. Blimey—it's just like the movies."

At 9:00 p.m., with one hour until our flight to Toronto, our coach arrived safely at the airport. The plan was for Magdi and me to sprint into the airport and beg the staff to allow us to check in late, leaving the team to coordinate the world's fastest offload of our luggage. As I was ready to jump out of the bus, Amelia grabbed my arm and said, "You've got this, Mom!" Those words meant so much to me that, in the years to come, whenever she faced trials of her own, I would simply return the encouragement with a wink, "You've got this, Mels."

The gate was closed, and Magdi and I were told in no uncertain terms that there was no way to process fifty people and all that luggage in an hour. Furthermore, because we didn't cancel our flights in time, we would not be refunded our money, and we would have to pay for another flight the following day. And so, I did what any great leader does in a situation like that—I started to cry. And it worked like a charm.

Suddenly, without any announcement, the airline personnel began processing us all as fast as humanly possible. It felt like a modern-day miracle as we were ushered through and onto the plane. The delayed plane full of people didn't look too happy when we boarded, and I think we made it worse with our happy dances and high-fiving in the aisles.

Meanwhile, Rob's team missed their flight, and just as we were about to take off, I received this text: "Dear Jenn. Have a safe trip, and I hope you all get home safely. It has been a fabulous trip this year. We have just spoken to David—he is clearly tracking all of us. All will be fine—one way or another. Safe travels and all our love to the awesome GHT 2017." Rob had been a fantastic leader to this surgical team, and he and his wife Jo were becoming dear friends and colleagues. These parting words, amid our happy ending and their not-quite-so-happy ending, did not surprise me one bit. Rob's team ended up booking a night at the Holiday Inn, spending the evening lounging around the pool while reminiscing about our extraordinary adventure.

Eventually, we all made it home safe and sound, and as more news of the "small-small" crash emerged, we were thankful that we were not on that plane. We never travelled with that domestic airline again.

The mission in 2017 had been memorable for us all. The people of Ghana had helped us comprehend how our imperfect offering over the past decade had impacted them. If only we could explain how that same offering had transformed our own lives.

As I reflected on my experience at the foot of the Human Rights Memorial in my nation's capital, I found myself looking at our mission through the lens of "EQUALITY," "DIGNITY," and "RIGHTS." I found myself reflecting deeply about power and politics and the type of partnerships that could lead to world peace, prosperity, and equality instead of causing harm. I found myself wanting to share our story.

As the year came to a close, a special prayer by John Baillie found its way into the front cover of my Moleskine journal. It was simple, but it settled me and brought clarity whenever opposition arose or the responsibilities of my work (or of the world) threatened to paralyse me:

Make me a more worthy follower
of the One who cared for the poor and the oppressed.
Let your power, O Christ, be in us all,
to share in the world's suffering and redress its wrongs.

CHAPTER 25

More Than Mere Friendship

"You have been my friend," replied Charlotte to Wilbur.
"That in itself is a tremendous thing."
~ E.B. White,
Charlotte's Web

Our Ghana Health Team leaders often met at a quaint coffee shop in Uxbridge called Nexus. Kim, Lynnita, and I were sipping our lattes and finalizing our 2018 mission itinerary when I glanced up at a sign on the wall. As I read the definition of Nexus, I had an epiphany.

Nexus, from the Latin word *nectere,* means "to bind or tie." It refers to a connection or series of connections linking two or more things. These five letters so beautifully captured the unique relationship between our international Ghana Health Team (GHT), Canada's Ghana Rural Integrated Development (GRID), and Ghana's Northern Empowerment Association (NEA).

Our GHT was about to begin their journey from all over the world to Carpenter, where we would be in a nexus for two weeks: we would be linked to, bonded, and in a relationship with an extraordinary group of people working towards a most critical goal. We often comment that there are zero degrees of separation when it comes to our GHT. That year, joining our faithful veterans, our new team members were all connected to us in one way or another. For example, one of our doctors, Dr. Helen Dempster, and I went to elementary school together and she is the niece of our veteran nurse, Leslie. Our paramedic, Greg Meservia, is a cousin to Carlye. Our anaesthetist, Dr. David Cressey, is the godfather of Rob and Jo Hicks' son.

The year leading up to our 2018 mission was thrilling on so many levels. Our fundraising target of US$10 million for the

Leyaata Hospital had almost been reached, the tendering process for construction was complete, and approval had been granted by all parties to proceed with construction in 2019.

At the same time, construction of another health care facility was about to begin in my hometown of Uxbridge. In 2018, I became the president of my family practice, the Uxbridge Health Centre. At my first meeting in my new role, I thought I would take my colleagues through a SWOT (strengths, weaknesses, opportunities, and threats) analysis of our clinic. We had just completed this exercise with our GHT leaders, and I found it extremely helpful and informative. We spent an afternoon working through this exercise and came to a surprisingly clear and unanimous decision: we wanted to build our own medical clinic. We required more space and we wanted to become part of a more integrated and sustainable hub of health care in our community that would last long after our retirements. It was not at all what I had in mind when I suggested the analysis.

That simple exercise catalysed a series of events that would see my colleagues at the Uxbridge Health Centre partner with Oak Valley Health, under the visionary leadership of President and CEO Jo-anne Marr and Elena Pacheco, who held the poetic title "VP of Planning and Transformation." Together, we decided to build a medical office building on the existing grounds of the Uxbridge Hospital. It was exciting for our community and terrifying for us. Still, the skills I learned during our Leyaata Hospital Project were highly beneficial and relevant to this endeavour.

It was also a big year for our family: Olivia spent the summer studying to take her Medical College Admission Test prior to her third year of university; Claudia attended her senior prom, graduated from secondary school, and began her Bachelor of Commerce in Management at Guelph University; Amelia turned sixteen and started driving; and the twins graduated from grade eight and began secondary school. Graham celebrated his fiftieth birthday and I planned a weekend trip for us in New York City to see our favourite singer in concert—Billy Joel. While people of all ages were there, it seemed like the bulk of us were middle-aged couples, arm in arm, remembering the days of our youth while singing our hearts out to "Piano Man." We were on our feet, arms in the air, for most of the concert.

While we were in New York, we visited the Empire State Building, and I was captivated by the exhibits explaining the building process. In 1931, this 103-storey building was constructed in just thirteen months, ahead of schedule and under budget. On the way through the gift shop, I picked up a tiny, silver replica of the building as a reminder that if that team in New York City could accomplish such a feat in 1931, then surely in this day and age, we could build a hospital in Ghana and a medical office building in Uxbridge. Between Billy Joel's music, that inspirational piece of architecture, and a fun-filled getaway with my fifty-year-old husband, I was wholly inspired.

The other remarkable event that took place in 2018, before our mission, was that the dream I'd had of sending the advanced obstetrical training course to Ghana literally came true. The Leyaata Ane Project welcomed a team from the Society of Obstetricians and Gynecologists of Canada (SOGC) who trained sixty Helping Babies Breathe nurses, midwives, and doctors in Advances in Labour and Risk Management (ALARM). The impact of the training was immediately measurable. In 2018, and in the three years to follow, there were zero maternal deaths in the districts where these trainees were from. Zero. I recalled the health official who shared with us in 2011 that ninety women had died during childbirth that year alone. He had then requested our help "until we can stand on our own."

Off to Ghana we went, and my youngest child Jessica (lovingly known as "my Jessie") was on the team.

Jessica and I call ourselves kindred spirits. We are drawn to similar things, moved by similar themes, and she and I definitely have the thinnest skins in the family. Jessica, even from a young age, has always been a caregiver and a peacemaker who exudes warm friendliness. Graham often jokes that she will most certainly be the one caring for us in our old age. At fourteen, and in her first year of high school, she was more than ready for Ghana.

When we arrived in Carpenter, the largest contingent of Ghanaian health professionals we had ever partnered with were ready to greet us. At that time, NEA was supporting thirty-one post-secondary scholars, and half of them were in health care: physicians, nurses, medical assistants, pharmacists, anesthesiologists, and hospital human resources. As a result, our collective expectations for serving, teaching, and transferring skills were at an all-time high.

Ernestina was excited to announce that she was now "retired," but she was quick to tell us, "I'm retired but not tired!" In fact, she was as busy as ever, serving as a Helping Babies Breathe Master Trainer with Leyaata and as a member of the Leyaata Hospital Board. She had been waiting her entire career to see a well-run hospital come to this part of Ghana, and she would become a big part of it.

Eric was back with us, too, having completed his Masters of Anaesthesia with honours. He was thrilled to have the opportunity to glean more knowledge and skills from our two anaesthetist teachers, Dr. Karen Leyden and Dr. David Cressey.

One of our HBB Master Trainers, Alexandria Gbiel, was quick to seek me out, as she wanted to greet Jessica. As she was walking away, she turned around and said to us, "Doctor, I feel so at home in this place."

I agreed with her. This sentiment was true for so many of us now. Our leaders were all back, and Carpenter was a second home to us too. It was a thrill to welcome first-time team members into our nexus. Martin and I were particularly excited to welcome our young optometrist Dr. Joshua Smith to the team. Josh should have been with us the year prior but unexpected tragedy struck his family, requiring him to withdraw at the last moment. His enthusiastic leadership skills, resilience, and fabulous refereeing skills (on the soccer field) were a wonderful addition to our team (in addition to his optometry skills, of course).

We wasted no time and set to work running our staff clinic on day one. Sadly, it was time for me to give up my translator and "son," Soale. His leadership skills were needed to help oversee our massive operation alongside Abraham, and so a young man named Daniel Mensah stepped in for him. Daniel was David's nephew and the big brother of Joshua, the baby who had almost died from pneumonia in Yaara, during our early years in Ghana. Daniel had grown up watching our team visit his village every year. He remembered us saving his brother's life and had been inspired to become a health care worker. After completing secondary school, NEA sponsored him to train to become a physician assistant. When finished, God willing, he will work at the NEA hospital.

That year our team brought two portable ultrasound machines with us. One of my former students and family friends, Dr. Kate Bacon, an ER physician in Calgary, secured and brought them to Ghana for our team to use. We were not long into our first clinic when I saw her passionately coaching NEA's recent physician graduate, Dr. David Aduwia, on how to use it. I was so proud of her. Those ultrasounds, used in our clinic and the operating theatres, allowed us to provide a higher level of diagnostic accuracy and perform more precise procedures on our patients. Lives were saved because of them.

Off to Nyamboi village we went the following day, and the heat was blistering. David Mensah announced to our amusement, "November isn't really the best month to come to Ghana."

All sectors of the clinic ran like a well-oiled machine, and the nurses put Jessica to work weighing babies, taking temperatures, and administering deworming medication. She was a natural, and I didn't see her until we climbed back on the bus at day's end. A delegation of health leaders, along with the District Director of Medical Services, toured our busy clinic. His concluding comment surprised me. As he shook Abraham's hand and then mine, he said, "This is more than mere friendship."

When we returned home for dinner, Dan (the man I had charged with bringing a piano to Ghana) was operating on his last case of the day. He was exhausted and suddenly, what should have been a very simple surgery, became complicated. Dr. Simon Atkinson, who had been with us in the village, didn't waste a moment and scrubbed in to assist his colleague. I was soon informed that Dan and Simon were medical school classmates and each had been the best man at the other's wedding. Although they both went into surgery, they lived and worked in different cities in England so they had never seen the other operate. It was touching to see these two best buddies operating together for the first time, saving a life in Ghana.

The following day was the paediatric surgical day. Our anaesthetist, Karen Leyden, who had special expertise in paediatric anaesthesia, created a new protocol to safely put our kids to sleep and reduce their fear when they woke up. A sip of Fanta orange pop laced with a sedative before going into the theatre expertly administered general anaesthesia, and a new soccer ball waiting to greet them on their bed when they awoke resulted in shorter operations and lower pain and anxiety scores. Unfortunately, one little boy had a severe anaphylactic reaction to his antibiotic (the first allergy we had ever encountered), but our teams acted swiftly to avert disaster. Eric was thrilled with all he was learning.

Week one ended with Kim announcing that 2,600 patients had received health care in Mo Land since our arrival. The best way to sum up that first week in 2018 is to tell a story about a Fulani boy who came to see me. One morning, a Fulani family was at my station, and one of the boys stood right beside my chair. His mom, the translator, and I were reviewing the children's histories when this boy started to speak in a loud, strong voice for about thirty seconds. He would stop talking, look at me, look at Dr. Mary Johnston (my study mate from my brutal EM exam prep course who had made good on her off-hand comment about coming to Ghana one day) sitting at the other end of my table, and repeat this thirty-second speech. He did this three times.

Curious, I asked my translator what he kept repeating. This six-year-old boy was saying, "You have such kind hearts. Had it not been for your help, most of us would die."

The weekend arrived, bringing promises of rest, relaxation, and rejuvenation. Our social convenor, Sue, added a book club and yoga classes with Bex to our recreation options for the day. Brenda arranged for an artisan to bring wares from Accra, and the gazebo was full of baskets, carvings, jewellery, and clothing. You would think we had not shopped for a year by the way everyone descended on the gazebo waving their Ghanaian Cedis.

In a discussion with me, the artisan explained that the income he made that day alone would feed his family for one year.

The year prior, some of the pre-teen boys on the compound had asked my daughter Amelia if she could send them a Monopoly board. I had no idea how they knew about this game. With Brenda's blessing, Amelia sent a deluxe Monopoly board that we presented to thirteen-year-old Emmanuel—who is now known as the President of the NEA Monopoly Club. After reading the instructions diligently, the boys played for seven hours on Saturday and another five hours on Sunday. A few days later, Emmanuel approached me to say he was having trouble reading the Monopoly cards. I gave him a VIP pass to the eye clinic, and Jessica accompanied the President straight to Martin's station, where he received his first pair of prescription eyeglasses. His Monopoly game and his grades at school took a drastic turn for the better.

Once again, our third annual Ghana's Got Talent was the highlight of our weekend. The surgical team outdid themselves with another brilliant parody to "Day Dream Believer":

Cheer up, knackered team
How hard can it be
To fix,
Three hundred hernias
and we're—livin' the dream!

My favourite act of the night was the "Dental Dating Game." The blind bachelorette was our young dentist Carolyn Eaton, and the three bachelors were the other three dentists: Kyle, Neil, and Francois. It was epic. Her last question of the game went unanswered since it caused the room to explode with laughter. She asked with a perfectly straight face, "If you could be a tooth… what tooth would you be?"

Abraham closed the night with a heartfelt original song entitled, "Thank You, My Friends." I wish I could insert the video here.

Our church service that year was held in the courtyard of the surgical centre under the big tree. During a time of testimonies, David's mother made her way to the front in a royal blue dress and headpiece. She was in her nineties, and she carried a purple floral walking cane that one of my patients in Uxbridge had given me to take to Ghana. She explained that both her father and her husband had died from a hernia. She also spoke of the hardships her family had faced as a result of their deaths. Purple cane in the air, she pointed to the three operating rooms, the ward of recovery rooms, and to all of us. Then, singing a song of thanks to God, she started to dance her way around the perimeter of the courtyard, waving a white handkerchief. Magdi got up and offered her an arm, and together they danced in celebration over all the lives saved in that place.

After church, she requested a meeting with my daughter Jessica. Her first question to Jess was, "Do you have a boyfriend yet?" She was a little concerned that none of my daughters were married and that I had not brought my husband and son to Ghana. I promised her I would get to work on that and Jessica expressed the hope that, at fourteen, there might still be time for her to meet someone.

During our second week of visiting the sick in Ghana, I began to realize something remarkable. I noticed that there was a marked improvement in the health of the populations that we served. I noticed that our emergency whistle no longer blasted multiple times a day to signal the arrival of a life-threatening case. I noticed more people had health insurance and were choosing to seek medical care instead of calling the witch doctor. I noticed more families were reporting that they slept under a mosquito net.

Interestingly, what stood out the most was that many of the women were carrying purses. Until that moment, I had rarely seen a purse in Northern Ghana, except perhaps on the compound. Women usually used the fold of their skirts or a little black plastic bag to carry their belongings. That year, they came with their purses. Those designer knock-off purses represented a seismic shift that was taking place as progress and development were lifting their families and their communities out of poverty.

NEA had everything to do with that. That year, NEA expanded its work to add seven more wells (providing clean water to 6,930 more people), upgrades to seven additional health facilities, and two more community fishponds. In addition, 250 chiefs had joined in a vibrant network that promoted peace and resolved conflict. Thirty-one more students received scholarships, and 120 youth in four communities were enrolled in NEA's "Growing a Future" program—teaching them to farm and save money towards their education. Over 10,000 adolescents were now participating in NEA's adolescent clubs.

As I was at my desk finishing up with my last patient of the 2018 mission, I saw the front door open. In walked a tall, beautiful woman wearing a hot pink stylish business suit and jewellery, carrying a purse under her arm. In her hands, she held a wrapped gift. She was intercepted by Ernestina, who hugged her vigorously, and then came bouncing towards me with this woman in tow.

"This is your woman!" she said to me. Then, when it didn't register for me, she said, "This is Sarah."

Sarah? It was Sarah—the young woman with the massive facial deformity who visited me every year. After our last mission, a visiting plastic surgeon on a humanitarian mission had successfully removed the tumour from her face. Since then, she explained, her business had skyrocketed as people were no longer afraid to buy food from her. She was so successful that she now employed other vulnerable women. Then, she presented me with a pink, yellow, and green Kente cloth—the most expensive fabric in Ghana.

While I was thanking her, Soale's wife Esther appeared out of nowhere with baby Timothy strapped to her back, and quickly measured my hips and bust (she was always happy if those numbers increased from the year prior). Before I could say a thing, she whisked my gift away, determined to turn it into the finest dress she could sew by the next day's party.

In Michelle Obama's inspiring book Becoming, she spoke about something that Nelson Mandela had taught her. Feeling frustrated by the slow pace of change after a year in the White House, he reminded her that real change happens slowly, taking decades and lifetimes, not weeks and months. These words expressed my experience in 2018.

As we gathered that night in the dining hall for dinner, the room was full of laughter. Abraham stepped to the front of the dining hall, clinked his glass, and announced that he would like to say grace before we enjoyed our dinner. Glancing around the room, he removed his hat, broke into a huge smile, and said "I believe that the ultimate success of this mission comes down to one thing—we are all brothers and sisters now. Let us pray..."

We agreed with him wholeheartedly. The unity and friendship between us had elevated our collective performance and our nexus of teamwork to the highest level. That same unity allowed us to accomplish what seemed impossible. With God's help, and the support of many friends, family, and colleagues in our home countries, we had achieved the objectives that NEA had given us and, in doing so, had gained much more than we had given.

The depth of our relationships was also reflected by a poem that Francois decided to read to the team that evening. It was entitled, "I Think I Can Wear a Visor." Apparently, for many years, "some" of my teammates had been teasing me (behind my back) about the fact that I love to wear a sun visor in Ghana. In his thick French accent, verse by verse, he mocked me. The ending was my favourite:

Royals have the fascinators.
Serena Williams a visor.
Why couldn't I be just like her?
I think I can wear a visor.

When he was done, everyone looked to me for a response.

Now, I am not known for my wit—that is my husband's department. But as I glanced around the room and noticed that those laughing the hardest at me were "follicly-challenged," I simply said, in a sweet voice, "At least I have the *option* of wearing a visor." The room fell silent. A number of my male colleagues turned crimson as they processed my response. Then the room erupted in laughter once again. It was a proud moment.

By mission's end, 4,909 medical patients were cared for, 1,057 patients received eye care, 362 received dental care, 343 surgeries were completed, and twenty health professionals were trained. Mission accomplished.

Our final day in Ghana in 2018 began with morning devotions

under the gazebo with all of the NEA staff. The pastors sang two beautiful songs as their gift to us, testimonies were given, and David gave yet another inspiring address.

He wanted us to know that our medical, surgical, dental, and eye care mission to Northern Ghana was making an impact impossible to overstate. David described an enormous ripple effect that had washed over Northern Ghana because we had been steadfast about our mission over the past decade. He concluded with Galatians 6:9, a verse that encouraged us all to not grow weary in doing good, for we would reap a harvest at the proper time.

We ended our mission with a feast under the stars. There were well over 200 of us. The children were incandescent with excitement—as was I, in my new pink, yellow, and green dress made from Sarah's gift. The NEA team gave each of us a fresh jar of NEA's organic peanut butter. David asked us to remind our families every time they ate it that they are loved by NEA. Then, the music and the dance-off began. The prize was given to Nana Tibalakala (Paramount Chief David Mensah) and his brother Nana Yaara Kooko (Yaara Chief Joseph Mensah). The interactive call and response dance of these two brothers, laden with symbolism, was riveting. The children's performance was runner-up. It was a perfect end to our mission.

As I turned out the light in our room that final night, I could hear Jessica crying underneath her mosquito net. I asked her, "What's wrong?"

"I don't think I want to go home," she said quietly.

I asked her to tell me more.

"I love how everyone lives their lives together as a big family here—how the older kids take care of younger kids as if they were their own siblings. I love how the elderly men and woman are treated with such honour and respect. And I love how Peter calls me his daughter." She paused for some time, and then she asked me "Mom, what will happen to the children who get sick tomorrow, the next day, and the day after that?"

We sat side by side on her bed, listening to the night air—alive with the hum of insects. She put her head on my shoulder, and we let the silence lengthen. She needed to feel these things, ask these questions, and find her own answers in her way and in her time. Ghana's people had deeply impacted "my Jessie" and I was certain that they would influence the choices she would soon be making.

For the first time in many years, Murphy didn't accompany us on our journey from Carpenter to Accra. There were no cancelled (or crashing) domestic flights, no missing or broken-down buses, and no flat tires. When we arrived at the hotel in Accra, I let out a massive sigh of relief—what could possibly go wrong now?

The team lounged by the pool and enjoyed a beautiful dinner while we passed some time until departing for the airport. I was walking out to the pool when one of our Canadian surgical nurses, Sue Phillips, began walking towards me.

Her face was white, her brow beaded with sweat, and she was clutching the left side of her abdomen.

Oh no.

She laid down on the restaurant bench and lifted her shirt, indicating where she was having pain. A small bulge, the size of a walnut, was visible just to the left side of her belly button. I put my hand on it, and it was excruciatingly tender.

"I think you have a hernia, Sue," I said with shock and dismay.

She started to laugh uncontrollably all the while wincing in pain—how on earth could a surgical nurse who had just looked after 343 hernia patients suddenly develop a hernia of her own in Africa as she is about to board a plane home?

I called for Magdi and Rob. Sue indeed had a rare form of hernia—a Spegelian hernia—and it was incarcerated. If we could not "reduce" it (untwist the bowel trapped inside and push it back in), she would need emergency surgery that could not wait until we returned to Canada. We took Sue up to an empty hotel room, and Rob and Magdi did their best, without their scalpels, to untwist and push the hernia back in. Sue was so brave, but that hernia would not budge. Arrangements would need to be made for her to remain in Accra and undergo surgery—she would not survive the flight home to Canada. They stepped into the hallway to discuss what to do.

I sat on the bed beside my dear friend and colleague who desperately wanted to get home despite the intense pain she was in.

A steely determination began to rise within me—this was not how this mission was going to end.

Without saying a word, I put my hands on this painful, bulging mass and began to gently rock my hands back and forth. Sue and I locked eyes, and as I breathed a prayer while she exhaled to relax her abdominal wall, I pushed. Suddenly, we both felt the indescribable sensation of her trapped bowels squishing back through the tiny defect in her abdominal wall. It reminded me of one of those moments when the strongest person in the room tries and tries to get the lid off of the jar of pickles to no avail, and then the weakest person in the room, to everyone's shock, picks it up and untwists it like it is nothing.

We looked at one another and began to cry, laugh, and scream with delight, causing Magdi and Rob to come running back into the room. They looked at me in disbelief.

What could I say? I shrugged my shoulders at these two marvelous surgeons—now two of my best friends—and winked. Sue's pain disappeared instantly, and that hernia behaved itself until one of her colleagues at home could repair it.

On our flight home, I listened to a song by James Taylor called "Shed a Little Light." It was sent to me in 2018, just before our mission. Even today, I cannot listen to the chorus without crying (no surprise to anyone who knows me). It has a beautiful melody and speaks of all men and women being bound together in sisterhood and brotherhood. Those lyrics gave expression to all that was in my heart, soul, and mind as 2018 came to a close.

Yes, this was more than mere friendship. We were bonded forever by our desire to see the world become a place where all our children—in Ghana and our home countries—could grow free and strong. A place where babies do not die. A place where adolescents, like "my Jessie" and Sarah could thrive. A place where lives were not cut short by a mere hernia. We were bound together by this task that stood before us—to rise up and build a model hospital in Ghana—and we were prepared to walk the road ahead, however long or difficult it might be.

May we never grow weary of doing good.

CHAPTER 26

Rise Up and Build

"Start by doing what is necessary, then do what is possible; and suddenly you are doing the impossible."
~ St. Francis of Assisi

When I accepted the call to partner with NEA in 2007, I had no idea what was possible. We simply began by doing what was necessary. Guided by the simple objectives given to us by David and Brenda Mensah, we threw our whole hearts, souls, and minds into our mission. Before long, possibilities began to emerge. Like small plants peeking up through the spring soil, opportunities began to miraculously pop up all around us, and we responded.

Is it possible to bring more health professionals to Ghana? Let's do it. Is it possible to build operating theatres and safely perform hernia surgeries in Carpenter? Let's do that, too. Is it possible to bring eye doctors to treat medical eye disease? Why not? Could we somehow get a laser to Africa to reduce blindness from glaucoma? Check. Is it possible to do dentistry under a mango tree? What about X-rays and restorative dental work? Yes, yes, and yes. Is it possible to create a mobile, automated pharmacy to safely dispense medication in rural villages without electricity? Most definitely. Is it possible to teach and train local health professionals? Indeed. Is it possible to reduce the number of babies and mothers needlessly dying in childbirth? Absolutely. Could we make a tangible and measurable difference in the health status of an entire region through these programs? By all means. Step by step, we followed NEA's lead from the necessary to the possible.

Then, in 2013, David shared his sustainable health care vision with us in the Mensahs' living room: Is it possible for you to help me build a full-service hospital on the NEA compound? Umm...

no. That is too ambitious. And we told a disappointed David Mensah exactly why we thought we knew better. As God would have it, our answer would soon change.

Six years later, on a scorching hot day in February, David and Brenda placed a shovel into the ground on the southern end of the NEA compound. With that act, the construction of the Leyaata "Rescue Us" Hospital began. Suddenly, the impossible had become possible.

As we prepared to depart for Ghana in 2019, GRID, NEA and our leadership decided that the time had finally come to bring our short-term mission work to an end. The official announcement was made—this would be our last mission. With the hospital campaign complete, we collectively felt that all efforts in Ghana and Canada should pivot to support the opening of the Leyaata Hospital. We were tempted to run one more mission in 2020, but it just didn't feel right.

While we felt sad to consider the end of the Ghana Health Team, we discerned it was the right decision at the right time. I reflected on the Bible verse that David gave us on our last day in Ghana in 2018: "Let us not become weary in doing good, for at the proper time we will reap a harvest if we do not give up."

As I thought back over our years of work in Ghana—the patients we cared for and the challenges we overcame—I reflected that everything had happened at just the right time. I had no reason to doubt that the end of our short-term work and the beginning of sustainable health care was also taking place at the proper time.

We threw ourselves into preparing to bring Ghana our very best for the Grand Finale. We wanted to finish well and finish strong. We were determined to fight for excellence in our leadership and in our service. My friend and our assistant dental lead Francois (who held that title with exceptional pride) once said, "We are bigger and better when we are in Carpenter." It was with that mindset that we wanted to complete our race—bigger and better. Before leaving home, I copied some of my favourite leadership pearls in the front of my final Moleskine journal. They seem rather "extra" as I look back on them now. Still, they truly reflected my desire to give my best leadership as we approached the finish line: "Be me bravely," "exude prodigious energy," "crisis = danger + opportunity," "accept failure with opportunity and insight," "so shall my courage be firm," and "push on with directional dedication." And for the final mission, my children gave their "extra" mom a brand new white Lululemon visor!

Graham and I celebrated our twenty-fifth wedding anniversary in 2019. With the kids becoming more independent, we decided that it was finally time for him to join me in Ghana. Graham had been so intimately involved with this project and so generous with his time and our family resources. Still, we had never felt it was responsible to leave five kids at home while their mom and dad went to Africa and had little communication with home. So much had taken place since the day I placed the keepsake necklaces around my children's necks back in 2007. Now in 2019, with Olivia and Claudia away at university and Amelia and Jessica old enough to stay home alone, the time was right for both Graham and the final Wilson offspring to join me. Graham and Joshua were coming to Ghana!

The Ghanaians were so excited to finally meet Graham. He was held in high esteem there, honoured as the husband whose wife came to serve in their villages year after year. Several years into our mission, Brenda wrote to Graham with a surprising story. She and David had been visiting some of the remotest villages in the tribe. When they arrived, many of the women who had been part of the Leyaata Project wanted to introduce them to their healthy babies. Brenda noticed a trend as she was introduced to a baby Graham in one village, then another baby Graham in another village, and another baby Graham in a third. Families were naming their sons after my husband! The Mo tribe was just as excited (if not more) to meet my son Joshua, and they were about to express that excitement in a very special way.

All of our leaders were back again except for one. Our dear nursing leader Joan was undergoing cancer treatments and couldn't make the journey. We were devastated that she would miss out on the Grand Finale after investing so much of her life in this work.

Joan had led our nursing team for twelve years, and once she retired, she moved to Uxbridge to run our Leyaata equipment depot. The depot, which would store used hospital equipment for shipment to Ghana for many years, was inside our barn. We couldn't conceive of being in Ghana without Joan, but she had been training others to step in for her long before cancer arrived. Her team of nurses was determined to do her proud, and Joan gave them directions and suggestions from her chemo chair until they boarded the plane.

One young nurse that Joan was coaching right up to departure was Cheryl Dove. Cheryl, a vibrant nurse practitioner and mother of two young girls, was supposed to join us in 2016 but had to withdraw also due to breast cancer. That year, Cheryl was strong enough to travel with us, and she became the second nurse practitioner to ever join our team.

The first day of our last mission will always be memorable for me. I was delighted to have "my two boys" by my side as we gathered under the gazebo for devotions and a final commissioning service before beginning our work. I thought our collective singing was very enthusiastic until David announced, "Your singing is weak!" That was all it took for the place to explode with clapping and dancing. Dr. David Aduwia, the young Ghanaian physician who worked with us for many years, described operating on his very first hernia under Magdi's instruction years ago. Before the surgery, the patient announced, "This hernia is older than you are, son." He thanked our surgeons for giving him the courage to repair it and for helping him to stand on his own today.

Eric, our Ghanaian anaesthetist, shared similar sentiments, explaining that his expertise from working with Tony, Perry, David, and Karen (our team anaesthetists) over the years had made him one of Northern Ghana's top anaesthetists and a regional expert in intraosseous needle insertion. In fact, he spoke about how he fought to save the life of Peter—Princess' dad—when he became critically ill from a snake bite. When his hospital ran out of anti-snake venom, Eric travelled across the entire region to find more.

Soale shared an inspiring message from the book of Mark in the Bible about how beauty and joy arrive after the storms of life. He challenged us never to give up during a storm because the impact of our efforts will be beautiful.

Then Dr. Mensah commissioned our Canadian, UK, German, and Ghanaian team with words from the book of Nehemiah. Just as Nehemiah challenged his people to rebuild the wall around their city, David challenged us to continue to rebuild the broken walls of ill-health, hernia, glaucoma, and infections that had degraded and destroyed the lives of his people. He reminded us that Nehemiah faced internal and external opposition, and so would we. He closed with Nehemiah's words: "Let us rise up and build!"

Up we arose, with a scraping of chairs and shouts of enthusiasm, and followed Abraham and David to the construction site of the Leyaata Hospital. So many of us had been intimately involved in the planning of this model hospital and raising funds for it, but today we finally saw with our own eyes this great symbol of hope. First, we passed the brick-making factory where NEA made 2,000 cement blocks a day for the walls of the hospital. Rob, Magdi, and I had the privilege of each making one block and inscribing our initials on it. Then, Carlye, Charlie, and I stood with our physician team in the future emergency room where lives would be saved every day. I could hardly contain myself.

Sandra, Val, and Leslie stood with the nursing team on the steps of the future medical ward, where men, women, and kids needing hospital stays would be compassionately cared for.

Linda, Sherry, and the pharmacy team stood in the future pharmacy, where quality, life-saving medications would be available to all.

Rob, Magdi, and the entire surgical team stood in the future surgery department, where four operating theatres would be functioning every day of the year.

Kyle, Francois, and Neil stood with their team in the dental clinic where treatment for oral health conditions would be available to all without individual financial hardship.

Martin, Marion, and their eye team stood in the future optometry clinic where sight would be restored, and blindness averted for generations to come.

It was a day we will never forget. As we walked back to the compound, Graham placed his arm around my shoulders and, with a slight crack in his voice, simply said, "I'm so proud of you, babe."

I thought back to the look on his face during the "double-diaper change" when I first announced I was going to Africa. That twin boy whose diaper he had been changing now walked ahead of us, engaged in an animated conversation with our surgeons.

When we returned to the project site, Graham decided to join the men who were setting up the canopies for our staff clinic. I'm not sure how many times I had warned Graham that the African sun is different from the Uxbridge sun under which he had planted and harvested since his feet could barely reach the tractor pedals. Sunscreen, hats, water bottles, and avoiding direct sunlight were essential pieces of advice that Graham had been given by many—and that he promptly chose to ignore.

About 11:00 a.m., Ernestina rushed towards me and could barely contain herself. All she could say was, "Oh, your husband! Oh, Graham!" and then she dissolved into fits of laughter while slapping her thighs over and over again.

Moments later, the door to the NEA training room opened, and Graham walked in. His soaking wet hair was plastered to his head, his face was a brilliant shade of red, and his bright yellow volunteer shirt was drenched in sweat. No hat, sunscreen, or water bottle were in sight. His hands were burnt from handling the canopies' hot metal poles. He refused to make eye contact with me as he borrowed my water bottle and disappeared to try and lower his body temperature. I heard Francois shout, "Did you just run the Carpenter marathon, Graham?" to which Graham responded something about work that "real men" do.

At the end of the day, I wanted to check in with Josh to see how Day One had gone for him. I found him playing soccer with the compound kids in the dark, which was no surprise. Josh has always loved playing games and sports of any kind, and I had spent many hours in the stands of hockey and lacrosse arenas throughout Ontario cheering him on throughout his childhood. Josh and I have always had a very special relationship.

My girls tease me all the time that Josh is "clearly" my favourite and I'm always quick to assure them that he is not. The fact that he is my only son, and that we came so close to losing him as a baby, might have something to do with our unique bond. We walked back to the residence together and he thanked me for bringing him to Ghana.

The next morning, we set off for Nyamboi. Soale was needed on the operations and logistics team, so Noah's daughter Naomi was assigned to be my translator. Noah was NEA's project manager who had so lovingly greeted us year after year, arms enthusiastically in the air, and who had presented me with my first Ghanaian dress after I "cured" the pain of his arthritic ankle. That year, Noah was in his last months of life, suffering from end-stage heart failure and this time, I had no cure to offer him. It was an honour that his daughter, who had grown up watching our team visit year after year, would be my final translator.

Our team cared well for the people of Nyamboi under the hot African sun. At one point in the middle of the day, I was working side by side with our team paediatrician, Anne. Suddenly, Graham popped in and said, "Dr. Anne, I have a girl with a growth on her neck that I think you should see." Anne and I gave each other a knowing look, then surveyed the long line of patients yet to be seen. It was Graham's first time in a village, and of course, the needs were overwhelming. With his kind and tender heart—especially towards kids—Graham was likely to bring in every child with a rash here and a bump there for a paediatric consult.

Anne was gracious, however, and responded, "Of course, Graham—bring her in."

He motioned to a mother standing in the doorway. In her arms was a little girl with a mass on her neck that was half the size of her head. Anne looked at the child, then proclaimed, "Well done, Graham!"

He smiled like a proud medical student who just made a difficult diagnosis.

My husband did not leave his great sense of humour at home when he came to Ghana. As teenagers, whenever anyone planned a party or event, they always wanted Graham in attendance. If Graham was there, you knew your guests would have a great time. Ghanaians are also fun-loving people, and often throughout the day I would hear David, Abraham, Soale, the pastors, and my husband laughing like a bunch of schoolboys. Graham brought his trademark lightheartedness and fun to our Grand Finale mission.

All day I was dreading saying goodbye to the village of Nyamboi, knowing this was the last time I might ever see them. When the clinic ended, I had my speech ready for the final ceremony, but I never gave it. The clinic was packed up and the buses loaded, but the chief and leaders were nowhere to be found. We set off, and I was saddened to not say goodbye to this special village whose precious gifts—my stool, my wooden spoon, and my beautiful dresses—adorned my home.

The following day, as we prepared to go to Yaara, Brenda wanted to tell us the story of her first trip to the village to meet her in-laws. She remembered it as one of the most challenging days of her life. The journey from Carpenter to Yaara took their young family six hours on treacherous paths and across rivers with no bridges. On her arrival there she met a very sick man who was burning up with fever. She knew there was no way he could survive the journey she had just completed to seek medical care.

The helplessness she felt prompted her to dream and pray that perhaps, someday, a doctor or nurse might partner with them to bring health care to places like Yaara. She then looked around the room at the health professionals filling every seat at every table and marvelled at how this Ghana Health Team Program and its ripple effects were more than a dream come true. That day was the twenty-ninth anniversary of the Mensahs' arrival to begin their work in Ghana.

We spent two beautiful days in Yaara. Chief Joseph and his brother Peter were thrilled to finally meet Graham and Joshua. They introduced "my boys" to Joshua Mensah—the now robust pre-teen who would have died of pneumonia as a baby years ago, had it not been for Joan's life-saving IV. We brought a bag of Josh's hand-me-down clothes and some of his childhood toys for his Ghanaian brother.

The village clinic started with intensity as our doctors and nurses simultaneously cared for a man with a poisonous snake bite (he brought the dead snake in his thermos), a young child near death due to diabetic ketoacidosis, and a critically ill young mother.

Josh and Elsa (Rob's and Jo's daughter) were put to work weighing babies, taking temperatures, and consoling sick children. They were a great team and an invaluable help to us all. At 3:00 p.m. each day, the two of them would hand-deliver an inspirational quote and sugary treat to every team member and volunteer. That day, a quote from Florence Nightingale was most fitting for NEA's twenty-ninth anniversary:

> *So never lose an opportunity of urging a practical beginning, however small, for it is wonderful how often in such matters the mustard seed germinates and roots itself.*

As the first day of the clinic drew to a close, an epic story emerged from the operating theatre. Simon had been operating on a complex case being done under local anaesthetic, which means the patient remains awake during surgery. The procedure became technically challenging and after finally completing it, Simon said under his breath, "Hallelujah!"

His patient surprised him by responding with a resounding "AMEN," to which the translator translated a second resounding, "AMEN!"

Apparently, this sort of thing doesn't happen in UK hospitals. Simon suggested that perhaps we should all start calling him "Pastor Simon." From that day forward, that was his new name. Whenever I receive an email from across the pond, he always signs off with, "Sincerely, Pastor Simon."

Our two days in Yaara passed quickly, and as we packed up for the last time, once again there was no closing ceremony or fanfare. It really didn't make sense. Some of my team members were rattled. Some were sad, others were worried that the villages were angry that our mission was ending. Unable to explain it, I relied on the training I had received from David and Brenda and suggested that we may not be looking at the situation through the proper lens. There was probably more to this upsetting reality than we understood. I encouraged them not to dwell on it or become distracted by it, but to remain focussed on our objectives and carry on.

As we loaded the buses for the last time, I handed each of my weary and disappointed teammates their final bus snack. This was a tradition I had started on our first mission. Each year I would pack a small snack bag of salty, crunchy snacks for each team member and volunteer to enjoy on every bus ride home from our remote village clinics. That year, I brought 600 snacks in my duffle bags. My teammates reminded me of kindergarten kids anxiously waiting to see what their little baggie would hold. Would it be pretzels or maybe plantain chips? Maybe it would be Cheetos or Bits & Bites. It didn't matter. Like those kindergarten kids, "tradesies" were always happening. On the final day, I handed out the best snack of all—a Snack Stack of twelve delightful original flavour Pringles chips into eagerly awaiting dehydrated hands. I was always amazed at the power of a little treat to revive spirits and inject energy into an utterly knackered group of people.

As our day off finally arrived, we were so excited it felt like Christmas Day. After breakfast, we gathered in the training room for our annual presentation by the Leyaata Ane team. Mumuni and his team continued to post incredible statistics about this program which was coming to a close. In the end, the results of Leyaata Ane would be celebrated by the entire country:

- 18,000 women were empowered to take charge of their own decision-making regarding the labour and delivery of their newborns;
- zero maternal deaths were recorded since 2018;
- the neonatal mortality rate dropped to 4.4 per 1,000 (down from 40 to 45 per 1,000 in 2011);
- eighty-seven per cent of mothers delivered at a health facility;
- 16,617 adolescents had been educated about reproductive health, family planning, and effects of teenage pregnancy;
- and, thanks to our army of Helping Babies Breathe providers, 2,858 babies from 162 communities had been successfully resuscitated over those five years.

The impossible had become possible.

Rob's and Jo's daughter, Elsa, made a presentation to the Leyaata Team. The kids at her school in the UK had made hundreds of gifts for the girls in the Leyaata Adolescent Clubs. She bravely gave her speech until the emotion of the moment overwhelmed her and she began to cry—along with the rest of us. She looked to me and her mother as we sat side by side, crying harder than she was.

Elsa's father had no choice but to stand up and help her carry on with her speech. She and her classmates wanted to ensure that teenage girls in Ghana had access to menstrual products so that they could manage their periods and not be forced to withdraw from livelihood activities. Elsa then presented hundreds of beautiful, washable, reusable, menstrual health products built to last. Within a couple of weeks, the Leyaata team had distributed them all through the schools, to the delight of hundreds of young girls.

Lots of activities had been planned for the rest of Saturday, but Mo Land had something else in mind. David Mensah very excitedly asked us to go and get into our best clothes and be ready to gather under the tents when the talking drums began to beat. Unbeknownst to us, the entire region was about to host a Durbar in our honour.

A Durbar is a rare event, held to commemorate someone of prominence, such as the President. Suddenly the entire compound was a buzz of activity, joyful anticipation, and excitement. I quickly put on the dress that Sarah, the woman with the facial tumour, had given me. As I was leaving my room, a group of NEA women who had been cleaning our residence shook their heads in disapproval. Conversing amongst themselves, they took the pink, yellow, and green sash that I had draped over my shoulder and began to twist it around my head, where it was transformed into a beautiful headpiece. They adjusted my skirt, played with my neckline, and then stood back smiling and clapping. Apparently, I was now ready for a Durbar. Graham wore a beautiful smock given to him by Ernestina, which featured a white symbol on the chest containing a long white arrow pointing to his groin. It was the symbol for fertility. Graham walked like a very proud peacock in that smock. I confess, I gave my proud peacock a pep-talk prior to the ceremony, reminding him that the Durbar was probably not the time for questionable jokes or self-deprecating humour if he was called to the microphone. Graham's sense of humour was famous for coming awfully close to "crossing the line" at times, and I knew a Durbar was probably not the time and place for any "line-crossing." To this day Graham still asks me why he got a lecture while Josh was told to "have fun and enjoy the moment."

When the drums started "talking," we gathered as instructed. Over the next three and a half hours under the blazing hot sun, our team was honoured for our "good work and goodwill" in augmenting the health care system over the past twelve years. Chiefs, Queens, Traditional Councils, Ministry of Health delegates, and political representatives from the whole area arrived in a colossal processional wearing their regalia to the beat of many drums. There were speeches, accolades, traditional cultural dances, and the presentation of many gifts. Our team and NEA were presented with over 400 tubers of yams, two cows, two sheep, five goats, and a citation that read:

> *In honour of Dr. Jennifer Wilson, Team Leader for the Northern Empowerment Association (NEA) Medical team for the meritorious services in health delivery within DEGA and Ghana in general. Given by Nyamboikoro-Nana Okoforban Sarfo-Kantanka II*
>
> *Dr. Jennifer, you have led NEA Medical Team in bringing health delivery to our doorsteps for the past ten years.*
>
> *Your interpersonal skills, coupled with your coordinating ability, has brought to bear the highest level of professionalism, and this is highly commendable.*
>
> *You have demonstrated explicitly in the eyes of all your clients that you are a real genius in your profession, not only in medicine but also in the humanities. More grease to your elbow. You have done a yeoman's job internationally.*
>
> *We hail you and pray for more higher awards in your future endeavours. AMEN.*
>
> *Written by Nyamboikoro on behalf of Mansie (Nyamboi), Asantekwa, and Yaara Communities.*

I was overwhelmed by the thought and detail that had gone into planning this event and by the incredible generosity that we were recipients of. We were all deeply moved by such a genuine display of gratitude.

Then my son, Joshua, was called to the centre of the gathering. He was honoured with 150 yams, a goat, and a smock that was placed overtop the smock Ernestina had already given him. He handled the pressure exceptionally well, and I was very proud of him. He had fun and enjoyed the moment! Unfortunately, he was also given a touch of heatstroke from wearing his two smocks in the forty-degree temperatures.

The Durbar was unlike anything we had ever seen and we finally understood why the villages hadn't said goodbye to us at the end of our clinics—they had planned something much bigger and better in Carpenter.

Naturally, Rob and I were expected to give a speech, after which we watched the chiefs interpret and dance to the talking drums. This was most interesting and very mysterious. Finally, the event concluded with an address from David Mensah, who was in his full chieftaincy regalia.

David told an animated hunting parable about a wolf and rabbit that made his Ghanaian audience roar with laughter. As he got to the end, he became very serious, and the crowd fell silent. The moral of the story was that David thought that poverty would be an "easy kill" when he first came to Mo Land after finishing his PhD. Poverty, he explained, turned out to be a much more complex and dangerous creature that would require more hunters—with unique skills and a variety of weapons—to defeat it. He thanked us for being those hunters.

The tribal Ted Talk was completely logical to an audience that relies on hunting for life and as I listened to his choice of words, I was suddenly enlightened that David had taken a big risk in bringing us to Ghana all those years ago. He and Brenda had no idea if the people of Mo Land would even accept Brenda's people or our Western medicine. His words, I realized, represented healing in more than just a physical sense, and spoke of the power of partnership and of forgiveness for the sins of our European ancestors.

The Durbar was a once-in-a-lifetime opportunity for us. It was an incredible celebration of all that we had accomplished together over the last twelve years through our shared global partnership. The ceremony was going perfectly until an unexpected noise caught my attention.

Graham and I were greeting the Chiefs and Queens when I heard the sacred talking drums begin to beat. However, I could tell that the drummers' hands were not the hands of the few men qualified to touch them. I realized with horror that I had forgotten to prep the team that no one was allowed to touch those drums. I turned around, knowing exactly what I would see.

Joshua was happily beating away on the drums, putting on display all that he had learned during his childhood drumming lessons. Beside him, Rob Hicks, our lead surgeon, was giggling away with him as the two of them proceeded to have a drum-off of sorts. I gasped, waiting for the tribe to respond—but the chiefs began to laugh and cheer them on. Grace and understanding prevailed. I held onto Graham's hand, preventing him from running over to join in.

Boys!

That night, Graham emceed the final Ghana's Got Talent show. Afterwards, he confessed to me that, for many years, he had secretly made fun of our talent show. He pictured a bunch of not-so-funny and extremely corny acts performed by type-A health professionals who tended to take life (and themselves) a little too seriously. He had no idea what he was in store for: Poetry by Martha, "The Twelve Days of Ghana" parody by our "Nightingale Nurses," a "Fawlty Towers" and a "Homeopathic ER" skit by the dentists, "Cold as Ice" song by the surgeons (since they had air conditioning in their bedrooms and theatres), "Ob-la-di, ob-la-da" pharmacy parody, and "Name That Tune" by the Spice Girls Eye Team, to name just a few. The talent show was truly amazing, and we had the time of our lives; Graham was very quick to admit he had been wrong.

Sunday was a beautiful day for our Grand Finale church service. Ernestina walked to the front during the time of testimony and told us a story about a boy named Benedict (known to us as Bernard) who was seven years old and had a massive umbilical hernia. The protrusion coming off his abdomen was as large as a soccer ball. He couldn't run and he couldn't go to school because the other kids bullied and beat him due to his deformity. His father died, and his mother needed to work all day on the farm, forcing her to leave him unattended while she worked.

Ernestina was visiting the Eastern Region of Ghana when she saw this young boy roaming the streets. She was concerned about his protruding abdomen and asked the women in the community about him.

They told her, "He is a bad boy. He runs with the bad boys."

Ernestina had the boy brought to see her, realized that this deformity was a massive hernia, and sent for his mother. The mother had taken Bernard to three hospitals, but the surgery to repair the child's hernia was unaffordable—more than a year's worth of her wages.

So, Ernestina and her husband paid to transport Bernard and his mom eight hours from Eastern Region to Carpenter to see our team. He had his hernia successfully repaired only four days before that church service.

As Ernestina finished her story, Bernard's mom walked to the front of our outdoor church service with her son trailing at her side. He was stooped over from the pain of the recent, large incision stretching across his abdomen.

With Ernestina translating, Bernard's mother gave an extraordinary testimony thanking God first, then Ernestina, then NEA, and then our surgical team for intervening in the life of her boy. She had lost hope to give her son a meaningful life, and now his life was changed forever.

On Sunday evening I wandered over to Ernestina's residence to visit with her. I knocked on her door and noticed that there was a mattress on the floor beside her bed. She explained that it belonged to Bernard and his mother. Every night, Ernestina moved the mattress into her tiny room so Bernard and his mother had a comfortable place to sleep under her watchful eye. Then she told me that she had made a decision to accompany Bernard and his mother back to Eastern Region. For the next two months, Ernestina would care for him during the day so that his mom could work on her farm in order to feed her family.

Reflecting on this woman's compassion and commitment to her patient I said, "Ernestina, I am so moved by all you have done and all that you plan to do for Bernard and his mother."

She responded, "He is a smart boy and will be a meaningful person. Maybe he will even be the President one day."

Bernard's story and Ernestina's role in it—just like the story of the incontinent little girl who now wears Ernestina's dress—speak to me in so many ways. They remind me of glaring global health disparities that we in the minority world can so easily forget. No seven-year-old child would be in Bernard's predicament in any of our home countries. They remind me that every person has great potential and deserves an opportunity to live a meaningful life. They remind me of the starfish story. They remind me of the incredible care and compassion that Ghanaian health professionals like Ernestina show towards their patients, and of their willingness to make personal sacrifices for the well-being of others—by all means.

I found myself thinking about this boy and Ernestina for the rest of the mission. Would their story change how I see the world? Would their suffering change how I live my life? Would it change how I practice medicine? Would the solidarity that continued to grow in our hearts towards the people of Ghana fade when we returned permanently to our busy lives at home?

A John Wesley quotation, delivered to us the next day by Josh and Elsa, settled my troubled heart. These words, like Sue's "Hey Jenn" parody, continue to encourage me when I feel paralyzed by the overwhelming wrongs in this world:

> *Do all the good you can. By all the means you can. In all the ways you can. In all the places you can. At all the times you can. To all the people you can. As long as ever you can.*

In the afternoon, Rob and I met with our leadership, and we unveiled the vision for the next phase of our involvement with NEA. Our organization would change from Ghana Health Team (GHT) to Ghana Health Partners (GHP). Our mission would foster collaborative consulting, teaching, and service partnerships with NEA's Leyaata Hospital in Ghana, West Africa. Our vision was that the Leyaata Hospital would become a fully-equipped and sustainable centre of excellence in Northern Ghana.

We also wanted to build an education centre for ongoing virtual and in-person teaching and training. Our values would remain the same: service, sensitivity, resilience, teamwork, professionalism, and (thanks to the good Dr. Martin McDowell shining a light on my leadership blind spot), "having fun along the way."

Every single one of our leaders was "in."

On the last day in Carpenter, Rob invited my son Josh into the operating room. He spent time watching Eric administer anaesthesia and Rob let him scrub in and "assist" him in the surgery. He was in awe of all that was taking place there. Josh loved and was most adept at math, science, and problem-solving, and the operating theatre with its machines, instruments, and technical devices fascinated him.

When our mission finally came to an end, Kim shared our statistics with me. Over the course of two weeks 5,735 patients had received medical care, 1,285 patients had received eye care, 175 patients had received glaucoma surgery, 375 patients had received dental care, and 290 hernia surgeries had been completed. Our goal was to finish strong, and we did. In fact, we finished the way we started—with excitement, teamwork, resilience, compassion, excellence, and a whole lot of laughter.

On our last morning in Ghana under the big gazebo, the pastors sang two beautiful songs in five or six harmonies to thank God and our team for all that had taken place in their midst. David spoke on Exodus 36:2-7 and asked my friend and experienced emergency room colleague, Dr. Shmuel Yablonsky, a star rookie on the team, to read the scripture in Hebrew.

It was a powerful moment as Hebrew was translated into Twi and then into English. This passage talked about how Moses asked his people to give their belongings to build the temple, but they gave so much that he eventually had to restrain them from giving more. Dr. Mensah used this story to thank the entire Ghanaian team and us for giving and giving and giving so much that now, he needed to restrain us. "You have given more than enough," he said over and over. We were grateful for his words, which provided important closure for us on that last day.

After devotions, we walked to the construction site of the Leyaata Hospital one last time. We took our final (and my very favourite) team picture on the doorsteps of the future emergency room. I wasn't sad, and I didn't shed a tear—my heart was racing with excitement at this moment, captured on film, which felt like the passing of a baton as the walls of the hospital rose up behind us.

After breakfast, my leaders shared their brief reports, and we said our final words to our beautiful team. Together, we had done precisely what Stephen Lewis had predicted when I received his challenge—we had brought solace and hope to so many.

I held it together pretty well until Kyle told us what his last patient, a little boy, said to him after his dental procedure. The boy looked at Kyle and quietly said, "We are friends now."

Indeed—those four words summed it all up. This work was built upon a foundation of precious relationships amongst NEA, our international team members, our supporters, our Ghanaian health care colleagues, and most importantly, our patients. Relationships of love and mutual respect had been the secret to the success of this work, and these same relationships would continue to be the foundation of our future together.

Our friends in Ghana changed us. They made us bigger and better, and we were all leading more meaningful lives because of them.

In 2007, a Ministry of Health official came to visit our first Ghana Health Team. He thanked us and asked for our ongoing support "until we can stand on our own." I have never forgotten those words that we metaphorically placed on the banner at our finish line—words that we had been working and running and serving towards since 2007.

Under the stars during our final party, Graham and I slipped away to say a final goodbye to Noah. I knew that it would be my last visit with him and I wanted him to know I loved him. His wife and son helped carry him out to the courtyard where we waited. I was wearing the dress he gave me in 2007. Between his gasps for breath, he quietly thanked me for relieving his pain year after year, for keeping him comfortable in his last days, and for our service to his people. Tears streamed down his smiling face. Words failed me—so we sat quietly together until I heard David Mensah calling me to the microphone to make my final speech. Graham stood supportively by my side as I said goodbye to Noah for the final time.

Rob and I stood before the great crowd gathered under the stars and asked all our leaders to come and stand with us. What a family we had become. We pledged to NEA our ongoing support as they prepared to open the doors of their hospital. They were now ready to stand on their own and deliver health care to their people and we vowed to cheer them on and be available to assist if and when they needed us. I looked down to see the smiling, supportive faces of my two boys, so proud of their wife and their mother whom they had sacrificially shared with Ghana for so many years.

Then, to the delight of our Ghanaian crowd, we led them in singing their song, the one that marked the end of every mission and would mark the end of the Grand Finale:

> *Unto the Lord be the glory, great things He has done.*
> *Unto the Lord be the glory, great things He has done.*
> *Great things he has done, greater things he will do.*
> *Unto the Lord be the glory, great things He has done.*

As we prepared to board the bus, Emmanuel, the President of the Monopoly Club, slipped me a one-page letter thanking me for the favour we had bestowed upon him and his friends. He spoke of his plans to become a medical doctor, and promised to study hard to achieve his aim. Only time would tell what impact our presence and our work would have on the children of Ghana—children like Emmanuel and his Monopoly Club buddies, the Leyaata babies, the baby Jennifers and Grahams, Joshua Mensah, Bernard, and the little girl in Ernestina's dress. Only God knows what the impact would be on our own children, like Josh and Elsa and their siblings.

I embraced Abraham, our young chef who was now the future of hospital leadership in Northern Ghana. "See you soon," we said simultaneously. Then, I embraced my sister Ernestina, who had taught me what it means to live and serve "by all means."

Soale was next—my translator who rose up the ranks of leadership and who now called himself my son. "Don't cry, Mum," was all he could say.

My last embrace, with David and Brenda, took a little longer. Our hearts overflowed with everything that had taken place since the day I turned around, with my hand on the doorknob and asked them, "Could I bring along a few medical friends if they're interested in joining me?" Since the year 2007, those "few medical friends" had cared for over 55,000 medical patients; 2,528 hernia patients; 6,335 eye patients; and 2,120 dental patients. On that final year in 2019, we only heard the dreaded sound—the three blasts of the whistle—once or twice (once it was due to a child happily blowing a toy whistle).

As our bus solemnly inched its way down the driveway, our Ghanaian family and the three flags of Ghana, Canada, and the UK, waved goodbye to their Ghana Health Team for the final time. Of course, we were sad to say goodbye to our brothers and sisters, sons and daughters in Ghana. Of course, we all shed tears. But our tears were tears of joy because we sensed that *greater things* were in store for us all—things that would be immeasurably more than all we could ask or imagine. After all, in one year, a new story would begin. Until then, we would count the days until our Ghana Health Partners could return to help cut the beautiful red ribbon on our Leyaata Hospital—a place of rescue for the people of Northern Ghana.

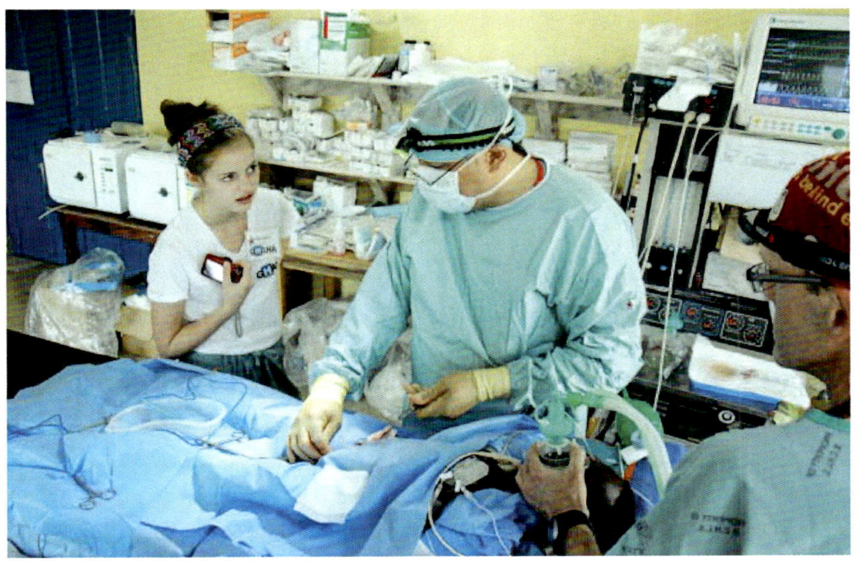

Olivia observing a hernia repair with Magdi

Claudia with Princess

Amelia helping in the oral rehydration station

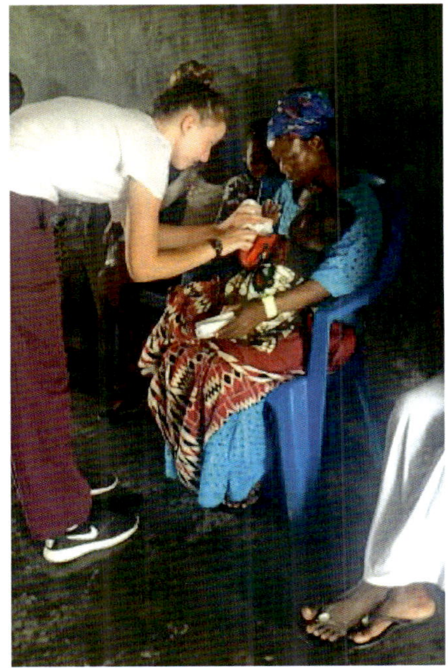

Jessica with the NEA staff kids

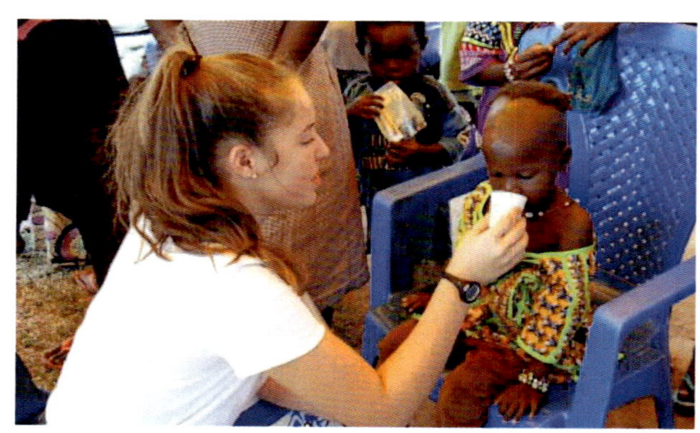

Jessica administering oral rehydration solution to a sick child

Joshua and Joshua—my two sons

Graham and "the boys"—Abraham, Soale, and Charles

"We are friends now."

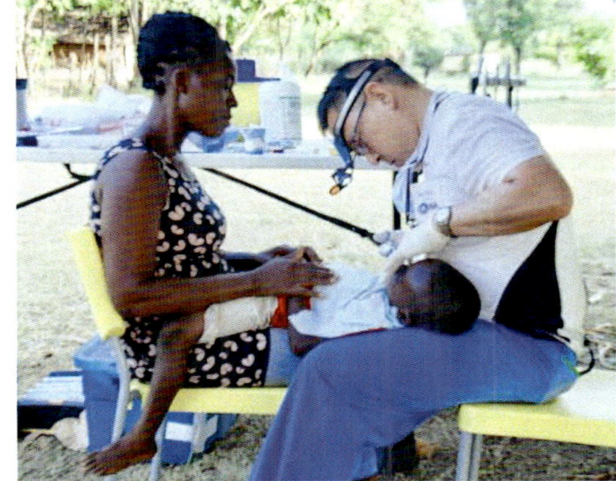

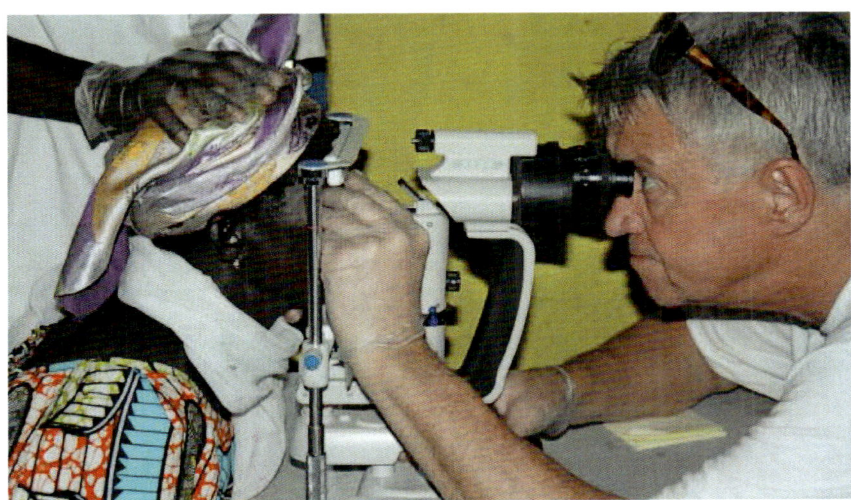

Martin treating a patient with glaucoma

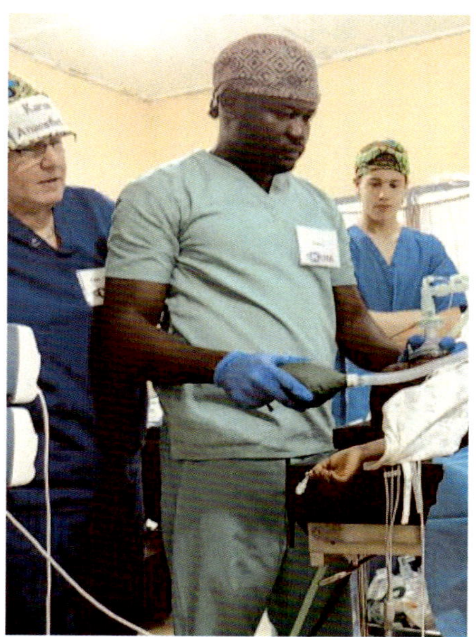

Anaesthesia team (with Joshua observing)

Rob and Brenda outside the "Brenda Theatre"

Elsa Hicks presenting menstrual supply kits to the Leyaata Team

Daniel and Eric, two Ghanaian health professionals who have been part of our team for many years

^ Dr. Nina

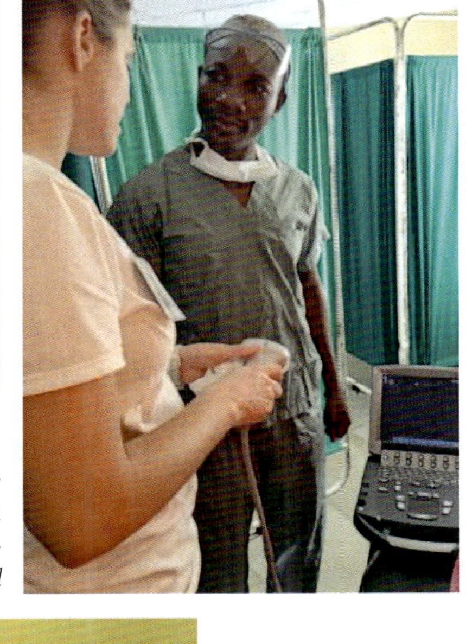

>
Dr. Kate Bacon and NEA scholar Dr. David discussing an ultrasound

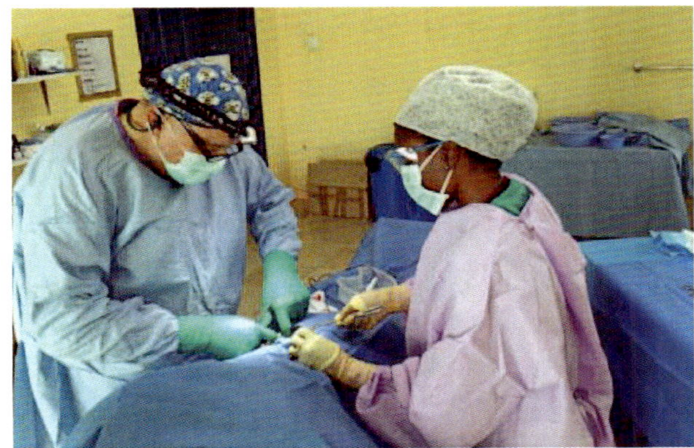

Magdi being assisted by a Ghancian nurse

Nurses Karen, Les, and Val broke into tears when our final clinic concluded

^
Surgical team camaraderie

>
The Eye team

Nursing station

^
Physician team with our translators

>
Pharmacy team after a very long day

2013 Ghana Health Team

2015 Ghana Health Team

2016 Ghana Health Team

2017 Ghana Health Team

2018 Ghana Health Team

The Leyaata Hospital

From vision to reality

<
Gene Paisley who travelled to Ghana with David Mensah in 1981. That trip fulfilled the dream of So-Naba Mahami Nantogmah's great, great grandfather, which resulted in the donation of 2,000 acres to NEA. The Leyaata Hospital will be built on that land. Gene is pictured here telling stories to the NEA staff (2015)

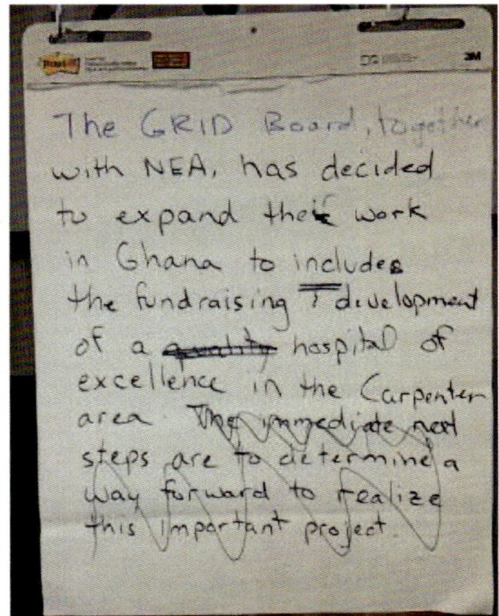

>
GRID Board's unanimous decision to proceed with a hospital at the 2013 AGM

GRID Board 2013 after the big vote!

Hospital Placement 2013:

The "stillborn cart" (that was later renamed the resuscitation cart)

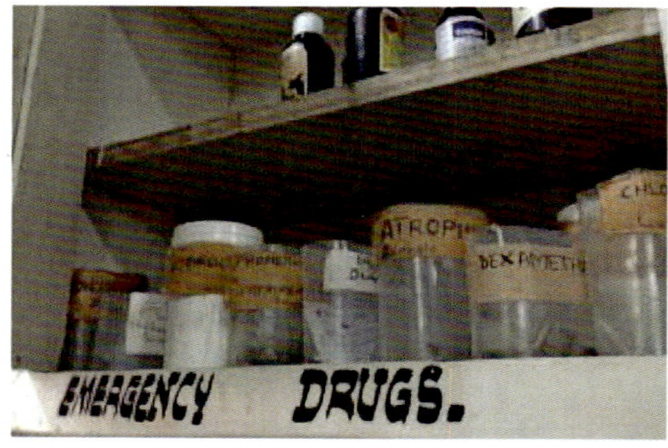

The empty emergency drug cupboard

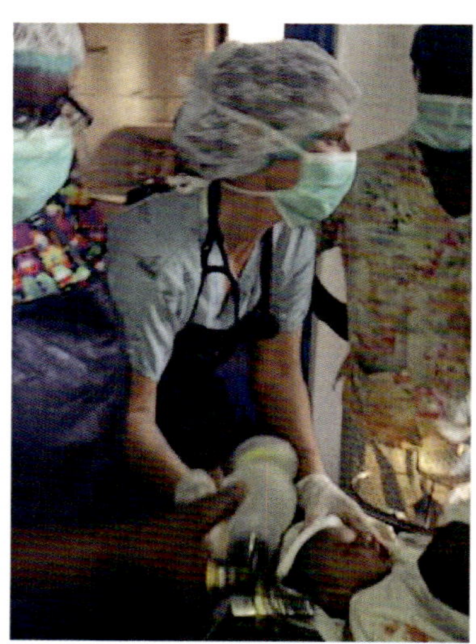

>
Teaching newborn resuscitation

<
Arriving to David and Brenda's home with Susan Fockler after my hospital placement

>
Eric and Dr. Ben joined us in Carpenter for the Helping Babies Breathe training, reuniting Dr. Ben and the Mensahs after many years

<
Carlye Jensen and I teaching the second HBB program (2016)

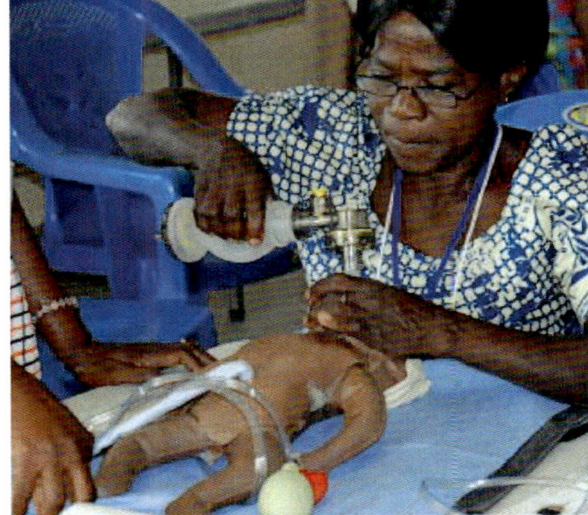

>
HBB trainer practicing her new skills

Training the trainers

The HBB trainers teaching the participants

<
Our first HBB graduation class (2013)

>
Engineering Ministries International Team (2014)

Campaign Champions speaking about why they were pledging to support the Leyaata Hospital: Dr. Rob Drury and Carol Smith Romeril (both GHT health team members and members of the hospital feasibility study); Paul Minshull (local business man and major donor for many years); Dr. Carlye Jensen (GHT physician leader and HBB instructor); Sandra Peniston (GHT nursing leader); Dr. Charles Peniston (GHT physician leader)

A hospital fundraising event in Stouffville, Ontario with my family, the Mensahs, and Lynnita Weber

My Arrow Leadership Group of girlfriends who planned the first Leyaata Hospital Fundraising Gala raising half a million dollars: Sharon Simmonds, Julie Fotheringham, Jenn Michel, and Lynnita Weber

Gala emcee Graham Wilson. I am wearing my "When a single tree receives a storm, it breaks" dress

David Mensah speaking at the Gala

The Mensah Family at the Gala

Magdi and Sue Hanafy travelled to Canada from the UK to be at the Gala. They lived with our family of 7 for a week

While Magdi and David were here, we conducted a site visit to Southlake Regional Health Centre in Newmarket, Ontario as part of our feasibility research. Pictured here with Dr. Charlie Peniston and the hospital and foundation leadership at Southlake (2014)

<
Construction begins!

>
Ground breaking ceremony (2019)

<
Volunteers from Uxbridge collected donated hospital equipment in our barn, filled multiple containers, and shipped it to Ghana

The Durbar in Mo Land that officially concluded our GHT short-term work (2019)

<
Jennifer, Rob, Magdi putting our initials into a fresh brick at the Leyaata Hospital Site (2019)

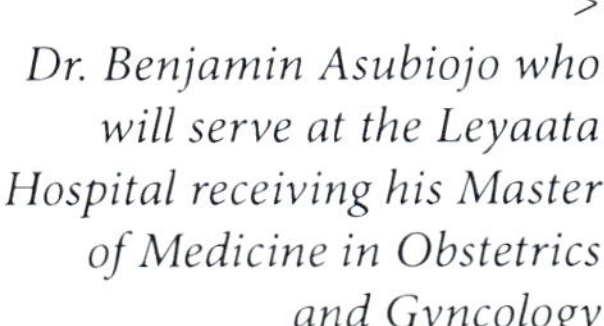

>
Dr. Benjamin Asubiojo who will serve at the Leyaata Hospital receiving his Master of Medicine in Obstetrics and Gyncology

Final GHT on the steps of the Leyaata Hospital, 2019 (my favourite team pic)

<
Construction

First truss going up on the hospital!

Hospital staff residences

Hospital construction panorama

Epilogue

Greater Things

"The idea that some lives matter less
is the root of all that is wrong with the world."
~ Dr. Paul Farmer

We didn't return to Ghana in one year.

One month after our return home from our 2019 mission, the first case of Coronavirus disease 2019 (COVID-19) was reported to the WHO. By March 11, 2020, a global pandemic was declared, and everything in society—including our ability to return to Ghana to open the Leyaata Hospital—was profoundly altered.

Carlye and I were in charge of our local COVID response. We often commented that we felt a simultaneous exhilaration and exhaustion that reminded us of our missions to Ghana. Every challenge we had learned to cope with in Ghana equipped us to deal with the pandemic—the uncertainty, loss, dwindling resources, and lack of control we had encountered there were unfamiliar and uncomfortable realities to our so-called "developed" health care systems. For me, the "I was born for this" lifelong mantra that occurs in times of crisis rang in my ear most days during the pandemic, providing a life-giving rhythm to my steps and my leadership. I was fiercely determined to defend my loved ones, patients, and community.

Today, I pray for all my colleagues around the world who were thrust onto the ever-changing front lines of this pandemic. I pray we will recover. I pray that we will find our strength once again so we can continue with our high calling—to care for the sick.

This unseen virus exposed our ignorance, weaknesses, vulnerabilities, and every crack in the system that society had neglected. Some might claim that COVID made visible the inequities and injustices in our world today, but I disagree—they have always been visible—we choose not to see them.

On June 19, 2020, our dear nursing leader, Joan, passed away from cancer in the home of a fellow Ghana Health Team nurse. A few short weeks before her death, our leaders gathered with her to reminisce about our work in Ghana, and she gave us our marching orders.

When it was time to say goodbye, we chose to say, "See you soon, dear sister and friend."

Joan may have missed our Grand Finale mission, but she planned one of her own. She established an NEA nursing scholarship fund which, after her death, collected $28,441 worth of memorial donations. Joan's legacy is now educating five young nurses who will serve in the Leyaata Hospital. And she has moved on to much greater things.

By God's grace, construction on the Leyaata Hospital proceeded full steam ahead. The Ghanaian team courageously carried the vision forward, despite pandemic related obstacles, while COVID grounded us. It was the ultimate test of an effective global health partnership—they continued the work on their own and we could not have been prouder of our partners.

God willing, the doors of NEA's Leyaata Hospital will open wide to the public on August 19, 2022. My leaders and I have received our invitation to return to help cut the red ribbon, and my visor is already packed.

A grand commissioning ceremony is planned and, as David says, "They will come in their numbers!" to see this 12,152.56 square metre (130,809.06 square foot) facility. Oh, how we will celebrate with the Mensahs, Abraham, Soale, Ernestina, Dr. Ben, the NEA staff, and all our health care colleagues! Many more tomorrows are about to be granted to Mo Land's men, women, and children by this sanctuary—this place of rescue. We will also be celebrating another remarkable achievement—Dr. David Mensah has been appointed Chairman of the Savannah Regional Medical Council.

After our very first mission in 2007, I asked David and Brenda if they could "debrief" our team and help us "process" what we had witnessed in Ghana before we re-entered our "ordinary lives." David, perfectly capable of providing such a debrief, was quick to respond, "By no means." Instead, he believed that each one needed to process what they saw, heard, and felt in Africa in their own time and in their own way.

In the same spirit, there will be no end-of-book lessons forced upon you, dear reader. I am not a theologian; I am not an expert in international development; I am not an expert in global health. I am still very much a student in all of these disciplines. In fact, in so many ways, I still feel like that sixteen-year-old lifeguard with a whistle around her neck and a first aid kit in her hand, just wanting to help someone.

Yet, as each day passes, this student feels increasingly persuaded that any moral to our story should not come from my mouth anyway. Instead, it should come from the mouths of my brothers and sisters in Ghana—the experts on their own lives—whose voices and lives fill the pages of this book. We, in the minority world, must finally create mechanisms for those with lived experiences of oppression and resilience to speak and to lead. We must remove the restraints that we have placed over their mouths, around their wrists, and upon their necks. Perhaps then, we might be invited to partner with them in finding sustainable solutions to the complex and interconnected challenges facing our globe today.

That is the tremendous story I want to keep telling. I pray that the strong voices of my global friends, brothers, sisters, sons, and daughters will ring out in this book—in their beautiful five-part harmony—as a reason for hope and a call to action.

What I would like to leave you with are my memorial stones. In the Bible, the laying down of memorial stones was a common practice to mark an occasion or commemorate a powerful vision. In Joshua chapter 4, Joshua told the Israelites to take up a stone "to serve as a sign among you. In the future, when your children ask you, 'What do these stones mean to you?' then you shall tell them… *'These stones are to be a memorial to the people of Israel forever.'*"

Today, with these chapters, I lift twenty-six memorial stones and lay them down. Twenty-six stones shall form my lasting monument of our Ghana Health Team—our friendships, successes, failures, and the lessons our African family taught us about life, death, faith, the practice of medicine, and global health.

I lay them down so that our children and our children's children will know what we were a part of and what we fought for. Generations to come need to know that their brothers and sisters, aunts and uncles, mothers and fathers, grandmothers and grandfathers made a difference in the individual lives of their global neighbours.

I lay down these stones on the altar of my thanksgiving to God for his guidance, provision, protection, and miracles along the way. It has been an honour to serve you in Ghana.

I lay down these stones to thank Graham, Olivia, Claudia, Amelia, Joshua, and Jessica for sharing me with the people of Ghana and embracing them as part of our global family.

I lay down these stones to thank David and Brenda Mensah, the staff at NEA, and my Ghanaian health care colleagues for inviting us to join them in their work—for trusting us, for teaching us, for forgiving our errors, and for loving us.

I lay down these stones to thank each member of my leadership team. We started as colleagues, became friends, and now we are family—forever. Thank you for adding to my courage and sharing the weight that my shoulders could not carry.

I lay down these stones to thank each of my teammates. You caught the vision, made sacrifice upon sacrifice, and then did the heavy lifting to make our collective dream come true. Words cannot express how each of you have enriched my life. Thank you for your friendship and for following me to Ghana.

Finally, I lay down these stones to thank all of our families, communities, and donors who supported us and cheered us on along the way. None of this would have been possible without you.

So shall these stones be a memorial to all of our children forever.

As for me, I press on to run my race "by all means." My boundary lines continue to fall in the most pleasant places, and my imposter syndrome doesn't rear its head as often anymore. I have found the answer to my question, "Who Am I?" and I am living each day, by God's grace, from that place.

Our new medical office building is complete. It is called The Oak Tree Medical Centre, and it is where Carlye and I and our wonderful team of friends at Uxbridge Health Centre care for over 30,000 patients each year. We are part of a growing hub of sustainable health care that will include a brand-new hospital that will soon be attached to our building. This health care campus, a unique partnership between upstream primary care and downstream hospital care, will become, like the great oak tree, an enduring presence in my incredible community of Uxbridge for generations to come. It reminds me so much of the river story that ushered me onto my path on my first day of medical school. I'm a "senior" doctor now—these buildings are full of young physicians and nurses taking on more and more leadership responsibilities and they will be the future of health care in my community. Someone asked me the other day what my plans were for retirement. I was utterly offended.

Now that my pandemic leadership duties have wrapped up, I've gone back to school. I am pursuing a Master's degree in Public Health with a specialization in Global Health at the Dalla Lana School of Public Health at the University of Toronto, where I am also a faculty member. What drove this decision was my desire to gain knowledge, frameworks, and skills in systems thinking that will allow me to become a more effective global health practitioner. I want to be better equipped to recognize and help redress the imbalances in global health. I want to better understand the structures and forces that are pushing people into the river in the first place. I want to be better prepared to help my communities at home and in Ghana to strengthen primary health care that is rooted in social justice, equity, solidarity, and participation. I want to spend the rest of my career using my unearned privilege to fight for the fundamental right to the highest attainable standard of health for every human being—every starfish on the beach.

I'm not the only person in our Ghana circle of friends who has pursued higher education. Abraham now holds his MBA in Hospital and Health Services. Dr. Ben graduated with a Master of Medicine in Obstetrics and Gynaecology, Dr. David Aduwia is completing his residency in General Surgery, and Soale has begun a Master of Strategic Management and Leadership. Deborah Mensah is now using her education in public health to lead a team across the African Region in providing technical support to Ministries of Health on Neglected Tropical Diseases like lymphatic filariasis, leprosy (also known as Hansen's Disease), Buruli ulcer, and Yaws. Our nurse practitioner Sandra is starting her PhD in Nursing Studies, and her thesis will be set in Ghana—creating nurse-led community clinics to manage hypertension and diabetes. One of our original pharmacists Alice Watt (who designed the software for our automated pharmacy) was accepted into a Master of Applied Science in Patient Safety and Healthcare Quality at the prestigious Johns Hopkins University.

A number of our young team volunteers have also ended up pursuing careers in the health profession; Justin Bowler (who married Elizabeth Mensah) is now completing his training as a Physician Assistant, Carole Mensah is now a practicing paediatrician, and Garrett Bent will soon be a fully-qualified dentist. My girlfriends from my leadership development group who planned our first fundraising gala have gone back to school, too: Julie now has her Master of Organizational Development & Leadership; Sharon, a Doctorate of Ministry in Leadership; and Lynnita is about to complete her PhD in Organizational Leadership. These friends of mine, along with all of the NEA scholars, are proving Nelson Mandela correct when he said, "Education is the most powerful weapon which you can use to change the world."

And that brings me to my beloved family.

Graham and I are now empty-nesters. Those five children who said goodbye to their mommy fourteen times in fourteen years are all adults who are pursuing their educational dreams and establishing their adult lives.

Olivia is halfway through medical school and just received her official white coat and entered her clinical training. She and Sandra published a research study, "Assessment of Cardiovascular Risk for Prevention and Control of Cardiovascular Disease in Ghana's Northern

Region—A Cross-sectional Study of 4 Rural Districts." This study will help inform programming at the Leyaata Hospital. It is a high honour for me to watch Olivia learn and grow on her journey to become a physician. She continues to be one of the most responsible people I know and her resolve to make the best of any challenge is as delightful to witness now as it was the day her Birkenstock sandal fell down the Yaara latrine. When she left for medical school, she gave me a necklace that has her GPS coordinates engraved on it. She wears a matching one bearing the GPS coordinates of our home. I hope that one day soon, I will have the honour to work alongside her—perhaps it will be in the halls of the Uxbridge Hospital or the Leyaata Hospital. *I love you, Liv.*

Claudia has graduated with honors from university with a Bachelor of Commerce in Management and a minor in Human Resources. She refused to let her dyslexia hold her back. We are so proud of her perseverance. Her clipboard and marching orders may now be electronic, but she continues to not let any grass grow under her feet and accomplishes whatever she sets her mind to. She isn't making citizen arrests over hard candies anymore, but you can count on her having a strong opinion on any current event, and she never shies away from a difficult conversation. Her interest in Ghana around team dynamics and organization is now bolstered by knowledge, theory, and maturity, which causes me to frequently turn to her for leadership or business-related advice. She has started her career as a Business Development Representative at a wonderful company—Lenbrook Canada Solutions. Claudia remains fiercely loyal to her family and her home, and it will be a true joy to see her apply all of these qualities to her own family one day. *I love you, Clauds.*

Amelia is midway through the Child Health Specialization of the Bachelor of Health Sciences degree at McMaster University. This path is not surprising to me after seeing how engaged she was with the children in Ghana and the issues facing adolescents there. Her adventurous spirit remains, and she hopes to spend part of her third year abroad pursuing further studies in child and global health. Like so many young adults who graduated high school and started university over the past two years, the pandemic impacted her mental health. I'm thankful to God that through the support of her doctor

(Carlye), counsellor, family, and amazing friend group, she has come through those dark days with even more insight, resilience, and determination to help others who are struggling. The "different lens" she has always looked through is maturing into a lens of equity and justice, and I can't wait to see how she will apply that to the rest of her beautiful life. God knows, and time will tell, what career path she will ultimately choose. *I love you Mels—you've got this.*

Joshua has decided to pursue post-secondary studies in Mechanical Engineering at the University of Waterloo. Throughout his applications and interviews he credited his time in Ghana—watching anaesthetic machines being fixed and the hospital being built—as the catalyzing event that steered him towards this career. I welled up when I read in his applications that he wants to use his engineering training to help contribute to a more just world. He survived growing up in a houseful of women and has become a kind and thoughtful young man. He always looks out for me and I continue to have a soft spot for him—which drives his sisters crazy. He still loves to play games. I'm going to miss playing cribbage and Dice Poker with him, and his dad will miss their endless, highly competitive ping pong matches. I can't wait to watch him learn and grow during this next season of his life. *I love you, Josh.*

Jessica will soon begin her nursing degree at McMaster University. In some ways, her career was launched early as she logged many hours as a resident attendant in our local retirement home during the pandemic. Due to pandemic-related staff shortages, she expanded her skillset quickly, applying the adaptability she saw modelled by our nurses in Ghana while providing care to our community's seniors. I can't quite imagine our home without "my Jessie." With her sisters away, the pandemic gifted us so much precious mother-daughter time together, and I'm going to miss her companionship. However, it is time for her to launch, and I know she will become one of the most skilled and compassionate nurses this world has ever seen. She is saving her pennies to return to Ghana at the first possible opportunity. Perhaps she will be able to do some of her training at the Leyaata Hospital alongside Ghanaian nursing students. *I love you, girl.*

I am so very grateful to our families, our community, and the people in this book who have been such a powerful and influential presence in my kids' lives. You have become a grove of trees that protected and helped mould the adults they are now becoming. Being a mother to these five has indeed been my most extraordinary mission, highest calling, and greatest joy. They so willingly shared me with Ghana, and their sacrifices allowed me to become an honorary mum to many more sons and daughters across the ocean. Their sacrifices also allowed us to fight for the right to life of countless other mothers just like me. I'm so glad that my mother—forced to drop out of school because of poverty—is alive to witness all of this.

My deepest gratitude, however, goes to my husband Graham. I heard it right—that day when he stood by the barn bridge with a calf slung around his neck: "This is the type of man I should marry. This is the type of man who will care for my children and me." He has done precisely that and more—every single day—with love and devotion for the past twenty-eight years of our marriage. I pray we are granted twenty-eight more. *I love you, Graham, for as long as we both shall live.*

While our home grows emptier, some days even more seats are being added to our dinner table (especially when Graham's outdoor pizza oven is fired up). We are growing extremely fond of the young men and women who fill those seats as we welcome them into our home and into our family. We love any opportunity to spend time with our kids and their significant others and can't wait to see how their families will make their marks on this world. With our arms raised high in the air, Graham and I will be praying and cheering them on in all things—life and faith and family.

What a privilege it has been for me to be part of this incredible story. I wholeheartedly believe that this tale is part of a much bigger meta-narrative that speaks of the day where "greater things" like justice, equality, abundant life, and health will become a global reality for all humankind. A new reality where every life matters.

The solutions to all the world's ills have yet to be found, but I am increasingly confident of the surpassing truth that we all have something to offer. Each of us has unique gifts that our families, communities, and world desperately need us to embrace and to use. Our gift doesn't have to be perfect—we don't need to be perfect—because, as Leonard Cohen reminded us, the cracks in our imperfect offerings are the way that light gets in. And when we combine our gifts and walk together in solidarity with others, transformation will occur—in our lives and in our world.

Eleanor Roosevelt, one of the most influential people of the 20th century, championed women's and civil rights and drafted the universal declaration of human rights. This was her nightly prayer. Through her words now, this imperfect mother, doctor, and global health student—whose heart is full to overflowing—shall set down my offering—these twenty-six living and lasting memorial stones:

> *Our Father, who has set a restlessness in our hearts and made us all seekers after that which we can never fully find, forbid us to be satisfied with what we make of life. Draw us from base content and set our eyes on far off goals. Keep us at tasks too hard for us that we may be drawn to thee for strength. Save us from ourselves and show us a vision of a world made new.*

And, with the words of the people I love, who taught us so much and who rescued us from ourselves, I end this story—for now…

"Korowii te ya kere"—May God grant us tomorrow.

The Wilson family

(from left to right:
Joshua, Olivia, Graham, Jennifer,
Jessica, Amelia, Claudia)

Afterword

In 1972 in Tamale, a small group of young high-school students, who had all been deeply impacted by the challenges of life in Northern Ghana, came together and began to dream—not just of how life could be better in their communities, but also of what they could do to make that "better life" happen. They knew from first-hand experience the realities of hunger and thirst. They had all seen family members die of preventable and treatable diseases—sometimes because they lacked the funds to pay for health services, sometimes because the health services were inaccessible.

So that's what they did, encouraging each other along the way, until the first trained member returned to the area to commence the Janga area integrated-development project in 1987. One by one they returned—some to work fulltime, some to offer their expertise when needed. We met and married while David was at university in Toronto, and arrived together in Tamale in 1990 to begin work in earnest. While much was accomplished over the following years in the sectors of food security, water and sanitation, health care for the community, education, gender equity, and peace-building, we kept dreaming of improved health care for the larger population that NEA's work had spread to.

We are grateful that "Dr. Jenn," as she is affectionately known in Ghana, took the time to record the details of that first meeting on the "three sacred chairs," a meeting that would be the springboard to seeing this dream come true. And we are grateful that she also faithfully took notes for each lifesaving and life-changing medical mission that was part of our journey together since 2007. It is important to tell the story of what may have just seemed like an insignificant meeting of three friends chatting over health care needs and possibilities in northern Ghana, which ended up evoking action and impacting thousands of lives over the course of many medical outreaches—an impact that will continue to be felt for generations to come.

We can't remember which of us said this to the other, but we do remember that about a kilometre before we reached Nyamboi, on the first outreach program in 2007, one of us had the courage to ask, "What if nobody comes to be treated?" Seeing the large crowds that had gathered as we rounded the corner into the village, we certainly never asked that question again.

We appreciate how this medical memoir has likened our partnership to a symphony with everyone playing their part. Our goal has always been to augment the efforts of the Ghana Health Service (GHS), and at all levels GHS has done all they could to help with necessary registrations and to release skilled Ghanaian health professionals to work on each outreach program. Dr. Jenn has mentioned a few of these very committed caregivers, who are often working or on call twenty-four hours a day, seven days a week.

As we look over the names of the international team lists, we are so grateful for each person who has given their time, resources, skills, and marathon-level energy to each mission. We are also grateful to their families who sacrificed time with them so they could compassionately serve the thousands who came to them in need. Many of these special partners (now friends) have returned numerous times to give and give again. We are grateful to Dr. Jenn and the leadership team that somehow managed to find new efficiencies with every mission—whether with colour-coded duct tape on the hundreds of hockey bags full of supplies, or colour-coded shirts for the various types of volunteers—in order to treat more patients. We are grateful to the NEA staff who wholeheartedly contributed in every way possible. We are grateful to those who gave generously year after year to equip the teams and supply the equipment and pharmaceuticals that were needed.

Numbers don't lie and as you have read this memoir, you have seen a lot of them, each representing a life that has been impacted for good. One year, at the registration area of one clinic we overheard one waiting patient say to another, "Thank God you have fallen sick when they are here!" We were glad for them to receive treatment, but the comment was a reminder of the other fifty weeks of the year. And while the Government of Ghana has made major strides in making health care more accessible (through interventions such as staffed community health compounds and the National Health Insurance Scheme), we knew that more needed to be done.

But the numbers—impressive as they are—don't capture the level of and great importance of compassion from all the health care providers over the years. The importance of compassion in a medical encounter resonates for us from two personal experiences.

The first happened in Halifax, Canada. One evening, about a week before our daughter was due to be born, our obstetrician called to ask how Brenda was doing and if there were any signs she was going into labour. He'd just had a call from *his* daughter who was in labour at the Halifax hospital (an hour away) and he and his wife wanted to go. But if Brenda thought her time was imminent, he would stay. In contrast, the obstetrician for our other daughter fumed into the examination room about a week before the delivery, exclaiming, "Three deliveries at the hospital today! That will really mess up my day!" Brenda looked down at her tummy and realized, *that's what he thinks of us.* At the end of the consult he said, "Oh, by the way, I only deliver Wednesdays and every fourth weekend, so it's unlikely I'll be delivering your baby." With that, the door closed. Brenda felt very concerned, particularly because of a near death experience with her first delivery, but there didn't seem to be any options. This was the nearest hospital. This was the specialist.

Our first encounter with profound medical compassion in Ghana was when our daughter Deborah, about seven, hit her head so badly on the terrazzo floor that she couldn't count fingers—a definite concussion. The doctor who treated her smoked all the time in the consultation room and got annoyed when she threw up. He never explained to us what was wrong, just said, "Take her to the second floor. She needs to be admitted," as he breezed out the door. We went there and found the admissions nurse asleep with her head on the table, a sheet draped around her.

We said, "Excuse us, but our daughter needs to be admitted."

She looked up. "We don't have any clean sheets."

We weren't sure what that meant. *Are we supposed to go and get sheets? Does this mean our child won't be admitted?*

Finally, she roused herself and Deborah was admitted. Unfortunately, they only had adult-sized IV needles, so at the least movement the needle would pop out, Deborah's arm would start to swell, and they would have to reinsert. They did this three times and it was painful to watch, yet we felt helpless to do anything about it when another nurse appeared. He'd recognized our car in the parking lot as he was leaving after his shift and searched the hospital until he found us. When he saw the problem with the IV, he sat all night holding Deborah's arm still so that the needle wouldn't pop out again. Finally, she was able to receive the medication she needed.

All that to say that whether in Canada, or Ghana, or any other medical encounter anywhere, it's the heart and compassion with which the skills are used that are so critically important and so greatly appreciated. And this is what has been so beautifully palpable through every mission from our international and Ghanaian health professionals.

Dr. Jenn has chronicled the initial response to NEA's bigger dream of a hospital in the area and all the thinking, processing, and planning that took place before it was approved to commence. Although a daunting project, the hospital was constantly on our minds and when we talked to the administrator of the nearest hospital south of Carpenter about this crazy dream of ours, he pulled out a book and soberly said, "It's not crazy. I've been compiling some statistics." He flipped through the book to the page he was looking for, scrolled down it with his finger and stopped. As he lifted his eyes to meet ours, he said, "Last year there were 576 people involved in serious traffic accidents between the nearest hospital north of Carpenter and this hospital. It's a good dream."

And miraculously, here we are, about to open a model hospital that will fill a big gap. Soon you will be able to read of more numbers—babies delivered safely, successful operations completed, lives saved in the emergency department, blindness averted, tooth pain treated, and illnesses accurately diagnosed, using the up-to-date diagnostic equipment. You will read of treatments dispensed through a well-stocked pharmaceutical department and of medical professionals further trained by our international friends and specialists who we know will return (again) to pass on their skills to others.

In a world where heartbreaking news is in front of us every day, it is our hope that this memoir inspires you to use your skills, energy, time, and resources to "love your neighbour as yourself."

Truly, we all can make a difference, one life at a time.

Dream BIG.

David & Brenda Mensah
Carpenter, Ghana

Teamwork

Surgical team v

^ *Don't Worry be Happy*

NRG for Life members ^

^ *Dental humour*

Pharmacy team ^

^ *This Little Light of Mine*

Ghana's Got Talent

Physician team ∨

^ "My, my, my—my hernia"

"Sing us a song, you're the Piano Man Dan ^

^ Mamma Mia

Musical interlude ^

^ Eye Team's Got Talent

Ghana Experiences

Monopoly club v

> Matching outfits

Our Durbar gifts v

"Listen to the man with the gun" ^ (Mole Game Park)

^ *A time to dance*

Storefront wisdom ^

^ *Wooden spoons*

Extracurricular and Sports

^ Hot yoga

Soccer >

v Running club

^ Volleyball

Baseball ^

Four-wheelin' >

^ *Kintampo Falls*

Fun at the Falls ^

More Medical

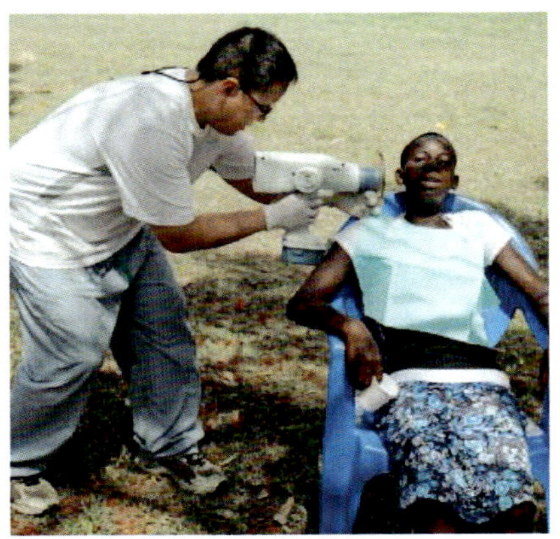

^ *Kyle's portable X-ray machine*

Tracey's lab ^

Charlie's dermatology book ^

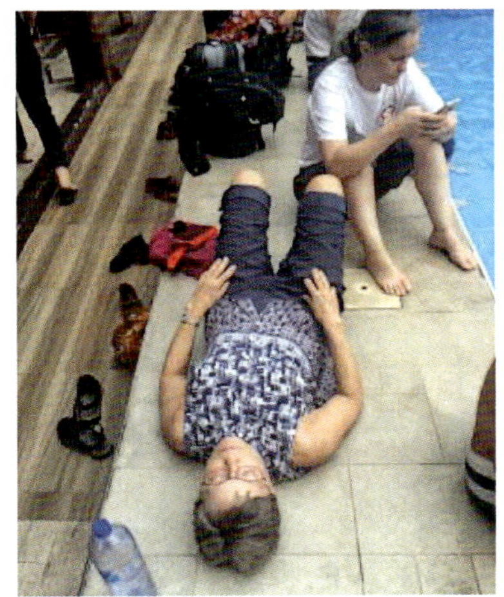

< *Sue, wishing away her strangulating hernia*

"We started as colleagues, became friends, and...

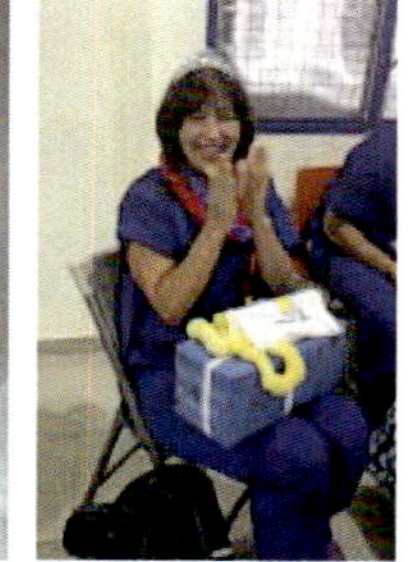

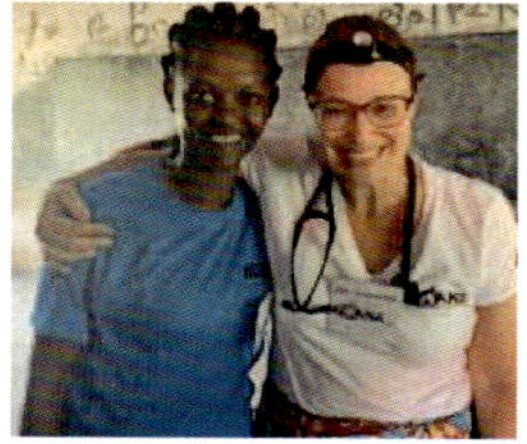

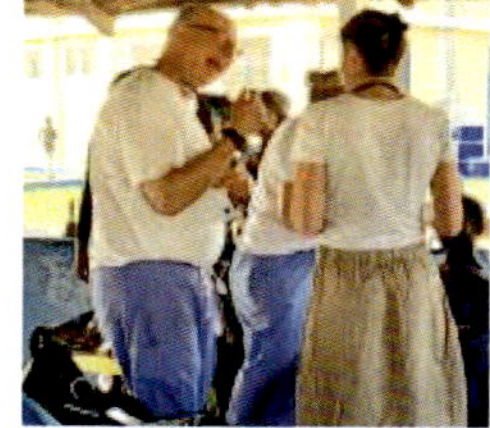

now we are family."

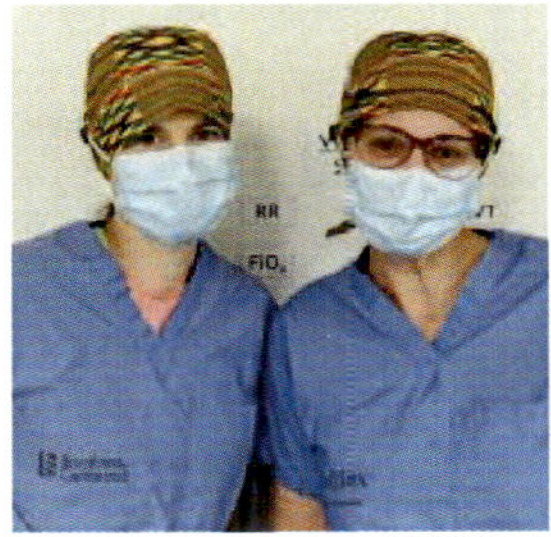

Travel

^ Arrival

Domestic flight ^

^ Logistics

^ On the bus

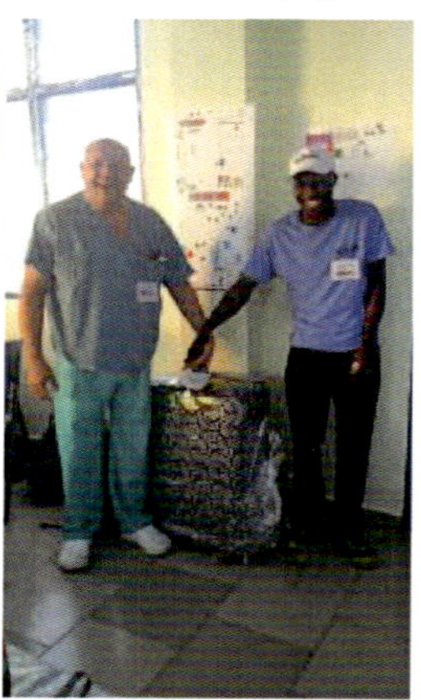

Magdi's lost bag ^

^ Broken bus

Water walk ^

v Stranded in Newfoundland

Acknowledgements

There are five people who were instrumental in bringing this book to life. Five people who were in my corner—cheering on this uncertain author—every step of the way:

Many years ago, knowing about my work in Ghana, one of my patients—educator and author Patricia Thompson-Boyko—told me to give her a call when I was ready to write my book. When I finally mustered the courage to make that call, Trish dove into this project with her entire heart, soul, and mind. For two years and endless emails, texts, and visits on her couch, she volunteered as my developmental and content editor. She knows and loves each chapter, theme, and character in this book so intimately that it was only fitting for her to be the one to write the Discussion Guide. Thank you, Trish, for your friendship and for your service to God and to the people of Ghana.

Many years ago, another one of my patients, Julie Fitz-Gerald, author, freelance journalist, and editor (https://www.juliefitz-gerald.com), told me to give her a call when I was ready to write my book. True to her word, she joined my team and became my line editor—pouring over every word, sentence, and paragraph for all three manuscripts. Thank you, Julie, for using your skills to make this book so professional, for placing every comma in the correct location, and for all of your kindness and encouragement along the way.

Brad Weber is one of our local English teachers and happens to be married to my girlfriend, Lynnita. I knew that Brad's love of literature and language would make him a perfect team member. I'll never forget what Brad said in our first meeting over Zoom: "You have a special voice. Our job is to make sure that voice is unaltered in the pages of this book." Thank you, Brad, for trusting my voice, empowering my voice, and for your endless patience with this doctor whose lowest mark in high school was in English!

How surprised I was when Sue Reynolds, an award-winning author, editor, and therapist (https://inkslingers.ca) was captured by this story and willing to join the team. Sue's incredible skill set not only helped elevate this book to the highest level but she designed the cover, contributed to the Discussion Guide, and helped me self-publish it so that more proceeds could get to Ghana. Her skills in therapy certainly came in handy on more than one occasion with her repeated use of three little words: "BEGONE IMPOSTER SYNDROME!"

I knew I wanted Brenda Mensah—the leading lady in this story—to read every sentence in this book for accuracy and consistency. She did just that. Right down to the fact that the lemon squares were baked by Brigitte, not by her! Brenda, you really are a Queen.

In Ghana, when you really want to thank someone, you thank them elephantly. To this team—this wonderful team of comrades who so selflessly used their time and skills to help me tell this story—I thank you elephantly for the unique and valuable contribution you have made.

Discussion Guide

1. You've been accepted to join a mission to Ghana. Based on the book, what do you pack?

2. What do you fear the most?

3. What is the biggest factor that would prevent you from participating on an overseas mission?

4. Who is your toughest goodbye?

5. The author describes feeling disoriented by her return to a more affluent lifestyle after witnessing the deprivation in Ghana. How might your life look/feel different on your return?

6. You are asked to organize one single mission. You will not return for any more. Capacity has no limits; money is no issue. Who is on the Dream Team you assemble, and why?

7. The author describes a number of physical discomforts, from pit latrines to wall spiders to extreme heat. Which ones would you find the most discouraging?

8. Who would you ask to provide support for the people you are leaving to go on mission? Are there circumstances which contra-indicate your going? In what other ways could you support the mission if you could not go?

9. The author is clear about her motivation for going to Ghana. What might motivate you to go? How might you motivate others to join you?

10. Do you believe that a desire for acknowledgement is inherent to good deeds? For you? For others?

11. Which of the patient stories were you most engaged by?

12. What would you identify as the main learnings the author acquired from working with her Ghanaian partners?

13. Which pictures resonated most with you? Did they correspond to the image you had in your mind's eye as you read?

14. The author describes some gut-wrenching moments which nearly made her give up on the missions. Which of the events described in the book would have been the one most likely to tempt you to return home early?

15. When families made decisions not to seek treatment, how did you react? What would your choice have been in their position?

16. What would your act be if you were on Ghana's Got Talent?

17. If the author wrote a sequel, which characters' stories would you be most interested in continuing to follow?

18. Where, in your life, have you felt an inner urge to step out of your familiar world and engage in a setting or a venture that would require courage?

19. The author had skills and abilities that were needed in this setting, that could improve the lives of others. What skills and abilities do you have that could make the conditions of life better for others—physically, mentally, spiritually, emotionally? How have you used your skills? How would you like to use them?

20. The author's faith was clearly a deeply motivating source of inspiration and strength for her in this work. What forces in your life do you draw on for strength and inspiration? What is that like for you?

21. The author was answering a call when she first began these missions. Where in your life have you felt a call to do something out of your comfort zone? How did that call come to you? In what ways have you answered the call? What would have supported you to answer it more fully?

22. The author continues to do courses and educate herself during the years of these missions. At the end of the book, it's noted that many of the participants in the missions are working on acquiring new skills, degrees, etc. If you could, what further education would you like to acquire? What new tools would you like for your toolbox?

Appendices

A Tribute To Joan Maguire

September 26, 1949 - June 19, 2020

Joan Maguire first set foot on Carpenter soil in Ghana, West Africa in 2009. Since that day, she dedicated her entire being to helping deliver health and hope to thousands of men, women, and children alongside the team at Northern Empowerment Association. Joan participated on eight international health missions as a nurse and was an integral part of the mission leadership team for a decade. She empowered and trained hundreds of nurses both in Canada and Ghana, whose impact will continue for years to come. Beyond the yearly mission, Joan spent her retirement committed to procuring, organizing, and shipping containers of used hospital equipment to NEA's Leyaata Hospital in Ghana. This work was so important to her that she moved to Uxbridge to live as close to her equipment depot as possible.

Joan was not just an exceptional and dedicated nurse—she was also a beautiful teacher, mentor, sister, friend, co-labourer, and team member. She lived and served with faith, hope, love, compassion, selflessness, and diligence—always giving credit to God for his guidance and strength. She was as skilled with an IV cannula as anyone we have ever met—saving many children's lives in Ghana with this unique skill. Joan could organize any amount of chaos and was a master list-maker who loved nothing more than ticking off her completed items—always in a red pen, of course! Joan's interpersonal, leadership and technical skills were such a big part of the success of the Ghana Health Team Missions.

Since 2009 Joan held the people of Ghana very close to her heart—from the African necklace that hung around her neck, to the pictures of Ghana that adorned her walls, to the daily actions she took to further the cause of GRID, NEA, and the Leyaata Hospital. While we will deeply miss Joan's presence at the grand opening of Leyaata Hospital in Ghana, her fingerprints and the ripple effects of her service will be present for generations to come in this state-of-the-art facility. Her legacy will live on in the lives of all she touched in Ghana and also in the memory of our organization here in Canada. The work that she has so joyfully and diligently been a part of will, with God's help, one day be fully realized for the people of Northern Ghana. She has been such a faithful servant.

We love this picture of Joan which seems to perfectly capture the essence of her life and service in Ghana—sweat on her brow, emergency nursing pack around her waist, a roll of tape handy, headlamp around her neck—always ready to serve with great joy and her whole heart. She will be missed dearly. As they say in Ghana, "We will not say goodbye; rather, we will say see you soon, our beloved sister and treasured friend."

We wish to extend our deepest condolences to Joan's cherished family: Meagan, Marcus, Noah, Finnley, Levi, Jeff, Robyn, and Emmett. We thank them from the bottom of our hearts for sharing their precious mother and grandmother with us and with the people of Ghana.

Ghana Health Teams, year by year

2007

Emmy Anastasiou
Robin Belanger
Shannon Brandon
Michael Caterer
Elizabeth Convery
Timothy Daly
Sara Daly
Michael Damus
Margaret Van Dyck
Luanne Evans
Susan Fockler
Catherine Grundy
Dale Heywood
Andrea Hoover
Marion Hurlburt
Lesley Joosten
Cindy Marsh
Kerry Mitchell
Laura Molyneaux
Ruth Ott
Gloria Ross
Carolyn Wilson
Heather Wilson
Jennifer Wilson
Doug Wu

2008

Lorna Adams
Sheila Arnston
Hosanna Au
Lila Bain
Robin Belanger
Michael Caterer
Elizabeth Convery
Dale Dawson
Michael Banh
Lorenzo Dimpel
Catherine Fockler
Susan Fockler
Julie Green
Brian Greenway
Jenny Greenway
Catherine Grundy
Sarah Hasted
Dale Heywood
David Hillebrandt
Sally Hillebrandt
Heather Holtby
Andrea Hoover
Marion Hurlburt
Lesley Joosten
Bertie Jukes
Andrew Kingsnorth
Jane Kingsnorth
Ardith Knechtel
Sue Mackenzie
Cindy Marsh
Chris Oppong
Chrissie Porter
Karen Prosser
Mary Reed
Dee Richards
Gloria Ross
Zena Saiphoo
Danielle Schier
John Simpson
Linda Stride
Margaret Van Dyck
Alice Watt
Jennifer Wilson
Wilson Woo
Jonathan Younis

2009

Lorna Adams
Michael Bahn
Martha Bailkowski
Lila Bain
Laura Banstra
Nancy Bent
Laila Bishara
Perry Board
Shannon Brandon
Craig Brown
Janet Burrows
Kyle Chin
Elizabeth Convery
Richard Dalton
Raj Dhumale

Catherine Fockler
Susan Fockler
Magdi Hanafy
Sarah Hasted
Cheryl Hatt
Marion Hurlburt
Robin John
John Kerslake
Andrew Kingsnorth
Jane Kingsnorth
Ardith Knechtel
Michelle Lee
Steven Lewis
Janice Li
Virginia Long

Sue Mackenzie
Joan Maguire
Cindy Marsh
Arlene McClure
Erin Moses
Chris Oppong
Charles Peniston
Karen Prosser
Dee Richard
Carol Smith Romeril
Margaret Salem-Matthew
Helen Simpson
Alison Stout
May Tracey
Jennifer Wilson

2010

Lorna Adams
Martha Bailkowski
Sam Balaji
Sarah Barclay
Amanda Bartodziej
Ira Bloom
Perry Board
Shannon Brandon
Kelly Bruce
Teresa Buckley
Janet Burrows
Giampiero Campanelli
Marta Cavalli
Kyle Chin
Elizabeth Convery
Tiina Derry

Sherry Doodchenko
Catherine Fockler
Susan Fockler
Cristina Frezzini
Karen Graham
Julie Green
Katy Griffiths
Magdi Hanafy
Sarah Hasted
Carol Hughes
Marion Hurlburt
Robin John
Brigitte Lapointe
Jacques Lapointe
Steven Lewis
Joan Maguire

Martin McDowell
Karen Monaghan
Chris Oppong
Charles Peniston
Dee Richards
Margaret Salem-Matthew
Danielle Schier
John Simpson
Sandra Skerratt
Carol Smith Romeril
Ali Stout
Robyn Synnott
Margaret Van Dyck
Sara Watson
Natalie Weeg
Jennifer Wilson

2011

Martha Bailkowski
Sarah Barclay
Amanda Bartodziej
Robin Belanger
Ira Bloom
Justin Bowler
Gillian Brakel
Shannon Brandon
Teresa Buckley
Jacqueline Burrow
Janet Burrows
Kyle Chin
Joe Chong
Glenda De Vries
Sherry Doodchenko
Linda Dresser
Elena Drury
Rob Drury
Julie Ellison
Susan Fockler
Sean Godfrey
Magdi Hanafy
Sarah Hasted
Antje Haupt
Rob Hicks
Morag Hogg
Carol Hughes
Marion Hurlburt
Sarah Jackman
Susan Johnson
Brigitte Lapointe
Jacques Lapointe
Lynda Lawton
Kirsten Lindner
Mary Lovatt
Joan Maguire
Cindy Marsh
Martin McDowell
Carole Mensah
Erin Moses
Danielle Schier
Paul Sutton
Laurence Turner
Sara Watson
Carolyn Wilson
Jennifer Wilson
Cathy Wright

2013

Karen Adamson
Charlie Alfano
Leslie Alfano
Jodi Barker
Jackie Barrow
Bhavani Sidhartha Mothe
Perry Board
Gillian Brakel
Sharon Broomer
Maureen Brown
Tony Brown
Kelly Bruce
Janet Burrows
Ed Chang
Kyle Chin
Joseph Chong
Dale Dawson
Tiina Derry
Linda Dresser
Elena Drury
Rob Drury
Julie Ellison
Susan Fockler
Nichola Goodwin
Magdi Hanafy
Sarah Hasted
Antje Haupt
Jerrod Hendry
Dale Heywood
Lauren Hubley
Carlye Jensen
Susan Johnson
Brigitte Lapointe
Jacques Lapointe
Brittany Lawson
Kim Lawson
Lynda Lawton
Joan Maguire
Chris Mann
Margaret Salem-Matthew
Gemma Mayo
Martin McDowell
Norma Peel
Charles Peniston
Rohith Rao
Sue Shepherd
Janet Skanes
Sandra Skerratt
Carol Smith Romeril
Balaji Swaminath
Margaret Van Dyck
Gerald Vanderpluym
Paula Vanderpluym
Sara Watson
Jennifer Wilson
Olivia Wilson
Cathy Wright
Randy Wright

2014

Hospital Feasibility Task Force

Rob Drury
Jacques Lapointe
David and Brenda Mensah
Carol Smith Romeril
Lynnita Weber
Jennifer Wilson

2015

Natacha Apentenchko
May Bakah
Tony Brown
Valerie Bruinse-Cheesman
Geraldine Burke
Kyle Chin
Susan Daly
Elena Damus
Michael Damus
Sheetal Desai
Sherry Doodchenko
Lorraine Dougan
Linda Dresser
Leslie Feddery
Tom Filosa
Susan Fockler
Helen Goodall Vickers
Magdi Hanafy
Sarah Hasted
Antje Haupt
Lisa Hurlburt
Marion Hurlburt
Jo Inchley
Kristel Jefferies
Carlye Jensen
Erika Jensen
Ambareen Kausar
Brigitte Lapointe
Jacques Lapointe
Kim Lawson
Lynda Lawton
Angela Mackie
Joan Maguire
Martin McDowell
Lois Mitchell
Karen Monaghan
Norman Musewe
Toylin Musewe
Kim Narduzzi
Bill Newton
Kathryn O'Shea
Ayoka Olabisi
Laurie Patry
Eni Rambi
Beth Romeril
Nicole Sabatine
Sue Shepherd
Jane Smith
Carol Smith Romeril
Anthony Soluri
Martin Stewart
Carly Van Kessel
Sara Watson
Jennifer Wilson
Doug Wu
Inessa Zenchenko

2016

Natacha Apentchenko
Tracey Barkey
Francois Bessay
Nichola Blunt
Perry Board
Tonja Bowman
Emma Brown
Tony Brown
Valerie Bruinse-Cheesman
Geraldine Burke
Kyle Chin
Colleen Cryan
Helen Dempster
Sherry Doodchenko
Linda Dresser
Diane Dugdale
Jessica Elliot
Leslie Feddery
Bryan Ferguson
Eric Fonberg
Nicole Giurio-Zorkin
Magdi Hanafy
Laurel Harris
Antje Haupt
Dale Heywood
Laura Heywood
Rob Hicks
Lisa Hurlburt
Marion Hurlburt

2016 *cont'd*

Paul Hurlburt
Lissa Ianuzzo
Carlye Jensen
Maimouna Koala
Ambareen Kuasar
Kim Lawson
Joan Maguire
Ramona Maria Fetita
Martin McDowell
Margie McGregor
Jennifer McLoughlin
Karen Monaghan
Dave Norton
Kathryn O'Shea
Laurie Patry
Charles Peniston
Susan Phillips
Elizabeth Russell
Steve Russell
Emily Scrivens
Larry Sheldon
Sue Shepherd
John Simpson
Janet Skanes
Sandra Skerratt
Jane Smith
Martin Stewart
Sara Watson
Mary Webster
Claudia Wilson
Jennifer Wilson
Stacey Wilson
Angela Yoon

2017

Martha Bailkowski
Tracey Barkey
Garrett Bent
Francois Bessay
Aaron Beyers
Nichola Blunt
Perry Board
Barb Brazier
Dan Brazier
Esther Brillinger
Valerie Bruinse-Cheesman
Emilia Burca
Kyle Chin
Stephen Craig-Paul
Elise de Francesco
Sherry Doodchenko
Linda Dresser
Elena Drury
Rob Drury
Diane Dugdale
Kaitlin Duncan
Leslie Feddery
Melissa Frost
Ashley Gayton
Stephen Greaves
Chris Grocock
Magdi Hanafy
Margaret Hart
Antje Haupt
Rob Hicks
Ted Hicks
Dan Higman
David Hunter
Marion Hurlburt
Paul Hurlburt
Jo Inchley
Carlye Jensen
Lisa Klassen
Steve Klassen
Kim Lawson
Joan Maguire
Neil Martin
Martin McDowell
Greg Meservia
Katie Mok
Amy Muir
Toylin Musewe
Bill Newton
David Norton
Andrew Patterson
Charles Peniston
Susan Phillips
Renee Rodger
Nicole Sabatine
Sue Shepherd
Kathleen Simmonds
Caitlin Skerratt
Sandra Skerratt
Anne Smith
Jane Smith
Karin Start
Judy Steele-Beckett
Elke von Haeften
Amelia Wilson
Jennifer Wilson
Angela Yoon

2018

Anna Alton
Simon Atkinson
Kate Bacon
Martha Bailkowski
Megan Baker
Francois Bessay
Alexa Blakney
Barb Brazier
Dan Brazier
Valerie Bruinse-Cheesman
Emilia Burca
Kyle Chin
David Cressey
Peter Cunningham
Sara Dalby
Helen Dempster
Sherry Doodchenko
Lisa Doubtfire
Linda Dresser
Carolyn Eaton
Anne Embleton
Leslie Feddery
Alisha Finnegan
Ashley Gayton
Deborah Green
Magdi Hanafy
Antje Haupt
Ruth Henderson
Toni Henry
Rob Hicks
Daniel Higman
Marion Hurlburt
Carlye Jensen
Mary Johnston
Rebecca Jones
Maimouna Koala
Kim Lawson
Karen Leyden
Rebecca Macdonald
Joan Maguire
Neil Martin
Martin McDowell
Jennifer McLoughlin
Gregory Meservia
Dave Norton
Andrew Patterson
Charles Peniston
Susan Phillips
Katie Rivett
Kirlis Sahib
Sue Shepherd
Duncan Simpson
Sandra Skerratt
Anne Smith
Jane Smith
Joshua Smith
Laura Starr
Martin Stewart
Jennifer Wilson
Jessica Wilson

2019

Simon Atkinson
Martha Bailkowski
Francois Bessay
Nichola Blunt
Barb Brazier
Dan Brazier
Valerie Bruinse-Cheesman
Lee-Anne Cairney
Kyle Chin
Stephen Craig-Paul
David Cressey
Peter Cunningham
Sherry Doodchenko
Gillian Doran
Lisa Doubtfire
Cheryl Dove
Linda Dresser
Jessica Elliot
Anne Embleton
Leslie Feddery
Alisha Finnegan
Magdi Hanafy
Antje Haupt
Daniel Hawkins
Toni Henry
Elsa Hicks
Rob Hicks
Dan Higman
Marion Hurlburt
Jo Inchley
Carlye Jensen
Rebecca Jones
Lisa Kemp
Maimouna Koala
Kim Lawson
Karen Leyden
Rebecca Macdonald
Neil Martin
Martin McDowell
Karen Monaghan
Susan O'Neill
Andrew Patterson
Charles Peniston
Susan Phillips
Karen Ryan
Kirlis Salib
Duncan Simpson

2019 *cont'd*

John Simpson
Sandra Skerratt
Anne Smith
Jane Smith
Joshua Smith
Laura Starr
Loretta Urbantas
Helen Warwick
Graham Wilson
Jennifer Wilson
Joshua Wilson
Shmuel Yablonsky
Charlotte York

2022

Leyaata Hospital Commissioning Team

Tracey Barkey
Valerie Bruinse-Cheesman
Eli Chin
Kyle Chin
Victoria Chin
Sherry Doodchenko
Cheryl Dove
Linda Dresser
Anne Embleton
Leslie Feddery
Magdi Hanafy
Rob Hicks
Marion Hurlburt
Karen Leyden
Martin McDowell
Jennifer McLoughlin
Daniel McLoughlin
Charles Peniston
Sandra Peniston
Margaret Salem-Matthew
John Simpson
Anne Smith
Carol Smith Romeril
Joshua Smith
Jennifer Wilson
Graham Wilson

Author Bio

Dr. Jennifer Wilson,

MD, CCFP(EM), DIMPH, FCFP

The phrase "think globally, act locally" proved too restrictive for Jennifer Wilson, a family physician in rural Uxbridge, Ontario. She decided to think and act both locally and globally. She founded the Ghana Health Team in 2007, led it until 2019 and has recently been appointed as the Canadian consultant of Family and Emergency Medicine and Director of International Partnerships at the Leyaata Hospital in Ghana, West Africa. Still a proud resident of her hometown, Uxbridge—where she and her husband have raised their five children—Jennifer continues to practice medicine there, as both a family and an emergency room physician.

She recently returned to school to complete a Master's Degree in Public Health with a Collaborative Specialization in Global Health at the Dalla Lana School of Public Health, University of Toronto where she is a Lecturer in the Department of Family and Community Medicine.

Find us online

www.grantustomorrow.ca

Stay up-to-date and join the community on Instagram

@grantustomorrow

Contact us

hello@grantustomorrow.ca